T0330264

A Research Agenda for Entrepreneurship Policy

Elgar Research Agendas outline the future of research in a given area. Leading scholars are given the space to explore their subject in provocative ways, and map out the potential directions of travel. They are relevant but also visionary.

Forward-looking and innovative, Elgar Research Agendas are an essential resource for PhD students, scholars and anybody who wants to be at the forefront of research.

Titles in the series include:

A Research Agenda for Global Crime
Edited by Tim Hall and Vincenzo Scalia

A Research Agenda for Transport Policy
Edited by John Stanley and David A. Hensher

A Research Agenda for Tourism and Development
Edited by Richard Sharpley and David Harrison

A Research Agenda for Housing
Edited by Markus Moos

A Research Agenda for Economic Anthropology
Edited by James G. Carrier

A Research Agenda for Sustainable Tourism
Edited by Stephen F. McCool and Keith Bosak

A Research Agenda for New Urbanism
Edited by Emily Talen

A Research Agenda for Creative Industries
Edited by Stuart Cunningham and Terry Flew

A Research Agenda for Military Geographies
Edited by Rachel Woodward

A Research Agenda for Sustainable Consumption Governance
Edited by Oksana Mont

A Research Agenda for Migration and Health
Edited by K. Bruce Newbold and Kathi Wilson

A Research Agenda for Climate Justice
Edited by Paul G. Harris

A Research Agenda for Federalism Studies
Edited by John Kincaid

A Research Agenda for Media Economics
Edited by Alan B. Albarran

A Research Agenda for Environmental Geopolitics
Edited by Shannon O'Lear

A Research Agenda for Studies of Corruption
Edited by Alina Mungiu-Pippidi and Paul M. Heywood

A Research Agenda for Digital Politics
Edited by William H. Dutton

A Research Agenda for Environmental Economics
Edited by Matthias Ruth

A Research Agenda for Academic Integrity
Edited by Tracey Bretag

A Research Agenda for Entrepreneurship Policy
Edited by David Smallbone and Friederike Welter

A Research Agenda for Entrepreneurship Policy

Edited by

DAVID SMALLBONE

Formerly Professor of Small Business and Entrepreneurship,
Small Business Research Centre, Kingston University, UK

FRIEDERIKE WELTER

President and Managing Director, Institut für
Mittelstandsforschung (IfM) Bonn and Professor, University of
Siegen, Germany

Elgar Research Agendas

Edward Elgar
PUBLISHING

Cheltenham, UK • Northampton, MA, USA

Published by
Edward Elgar Publishing Limited
The Lypiatts
15 Lansdown Road
Cheltenham
Glos GL50 2JA
UK

Edward Elgar Publishing, Inc.
William Pratt House
9 Dewey Court
Northampton
Massachusetts 01060
USA

A catalogue record for this book
is available from the British Library

Library of Congress Control Number: 2020933651

This book is available electronically in the **Elgar**online
Business subject collection
DOI 10.4337/9781786430946

ISBN 978 1 78643 093 9 (cased)
ISBN 978 1 78643 094 6 (eBook)

Printed and bound by CPI Group (UK) Ltd, Croydon CR0 4YY

To David – mentor, colleague and friend. You will be missed.

Contents

Figures

Tables

Contributors

Norin Arshed, University of Dundee, UK

Vera Barinova, Russian Presidential Academy of National Economy and Public Administration, Russia

Hang Do, University of Southampton, UK

Ian Drummond, Former member of the Department of Business Innovation and Skills, UK

Thami Mazwai, National Planning Commission, South Africa

Itsutomo Mitsui, Yokohama National University, Japan

Bitange Ndemo, University of Nairobi, Kenya

Bogdan Piasecki, University of Social Sciences, Poland

Jonathan Potter, Centre for Entrepreneurship, SMEs, Regions and Cities, OECD

Anna Rogut, University of Social Sciences, Poland

David Smallbone, Kingston University, UK

David Storey, University of Sussex Business School, UK

Friederike Welter, Institut für Mittelstandsforschung (IfM) Bonn and University of Siegen, Germany

Mirela Xheneti, University of Sussex Business School, UK

Li Xiao, Lancaster University Management School, UK

Jianbo Xu, Xuzhou University of Technology, China

Stepan Zemtsov, Russian Presidential Academy of National Economy and Public Administration, Russia

1 Introduction to *A Research Agenda for Entrepreneurship Policy*: why we need a different research agenda on entrepreneurship policy

David Smallbone and Friederike Welter

This chapter discusses why we need a changed research agenda on entrepreneurship policy. In recent years there has been a remarkable growth of interest in entrepreneurship and small and medium-sized enterprise (SME) development from policy makers, practitioners and academics. From a public policy perspective, entrepreneurship is seen as one of the driving forces behind a modern economy. That being the case, not surprisingly, policy makers and politicians have jumped on the bandwagon to take full advantage of this phenomenon. The widespread nature of entrepreneurship policy means that a review of where policy has reached will assist us in identifying an agenda for change.

Defining key terms

First of all, the terms 'SME', 'entrepreneurship' and 'public policy' need some definition. Entrepreneurship policy has, in practice, grown out of SME policy but with a different emphasis. Whereas SME policy is based on offering support to businesses that meet the size definition of SME, entrepreneurship policy is more sharply focused on those people starting a new business or projects within an existing business. Though some commentators use the term SME and entrepreneurship interchangeably, the two terms refer to rather different policy approaches. SME policy is solely based on the size of the firm, whereas entrepreneurship policy is more narrowly defined, focusing more on individuals.

1

Entrepreneurship policy refers specifically to attempts to stimulate the creation of new businesses as well as growth within existing organisations. In this case, the question of what constitutes entrepreneurship policy is answered through a list of the types of policy interventions that are likely to promote and support it. These include:

- The promotion of an entrepreneurship culture and more favourable attitudes towards entrepreneurship;
- The integration of entrepreneurship education in schools and at all levels of post-secondary education;
- A reduction in the barriers to entry and re-entry, combined with pro-active measures to make it easier for enterprises to enter the market;
- The provision of seed finance to facilitate business creation and subsequent development;
- The various types of start-up business support including mentoring programmes and business incubators, designed essentially to increase the number of new businesses and nurture their early development;
- Tailored effects to increase the participation in business ownership of under-represented groups, such as ethnic minorities, women and young people.

Although public policy might seem easier to define, what policy means and what processes need to be undertaken in order to apply that policy is not the same in all countries. In China, for example, recognition of the legal existence of small businesses began back in the 1970s with Deng Xiaoping announcing the willingness of the Communist Party to tolerate small businesses employing less than seven people. This was not the result of an explicit policy launch but rather was referred to in the speeches of leading members of the Communist Party, which were interpreted and implemented by local officials.

Even more difficult to define is the term 'policy maker'. In much academic writing the term is used rather too freely because there are relatively few genuine policy makers, for instance government ministers and senior civil servants. In practice, it is suggested that policy-related researchers need to distinguish more consistently between policy making and policy implementation. If making policy recommendations is an objective for a researcher, then it is important to distinguish between policy makers and practitioners.

Setting the agenda for public policy and policy-related research

Clearly, the agenda for public policy makers will, to a considerable extent, influence the focus of policy-related researchers. At the same time, the two do not completely overlap because there will always be some 'blue sky' research that may have a major impact on policy making. A good example is the work of David Birch, who drew attention to the fact that the vast majority of employment gains in the US economy came from enterprises employing fewer than 20 people.

The need to place more explicit attention on the role of context is a consistent theme throughout this chapter and research agenda. Indeed, the book itself was stimulated by the work of Welter and others in relation to context. Context refers to the historical, social, economic and, particularly, institutional environment and the interrelationship between them (Welter, 2011). Just as context is important for the study of entrepreneurship, it is also important for the study of entrepreneurship policy. This is because the needs, strengths and weaknesses with respect to opportunities facing countries, regions and/ or localities are variable, as are the possibilities of entrepreneurs to influence and change their contexts. As a consequence, the context in which entrepreneurship can take place varies considerably. For example, Xheneti's chapter demonstrates that context is a salient issue where policy transfer is involved.

To take another example, attempts to transfer policy from European countries to China have proven to be particularly difficult. This is not surprising because of the substantial differences between the cultures in terms of their institutional frames and historical legacies. The influence of contextualisation is well illustrated by an attempt to introduce an effective subsidised consultancy scheme at a local level in China. This is along the lines of a subsidised consultancy scheme managed by the European Bank for Reconstruction and Development (EBRD) in the former socialist countries in Central and Eastern Europe. The scheme is targeted at small businesses that had not previously used external consultants. The idea is that if the public sector subsidises the first round of consultancy use, and if the consultants delivering the advice and support are vetted and accredited, then there should be a double benefit. On the one hand, the market for consulting by small businesses is widened and, on the other, there is an increase in the number of consultants who have experience of working with small businesses.

Clearly, therefore, the percentage of the total consultancy costs subsidised is central to the question of the extent to which the measure incentivises business owners to make use of consultants. However, in China, the financial support from central government for a policy such as this is only forthcoming when there are some results. In other words, the financial support is retrospective. Clearly, this represents a very different philosophy and is problematic in the case of subsidised consultancy because, in the Chinese model, potential participating businesses do not know what the level of subsidy will be when they are expected to commit to the programme. This uncertainty makes it difficult to recruit small businesses for the programme. Clearly, in this example context matters because of a fundamental difference in the role and mode of operation of key institutions in China compared with countries where the subsidised consultancy model has been successfully applied. This includes a very different relationship between the Central Finance Ministry and the provinces and local cities. The method of dispersing funds in China is considered more of a reward than an incentive. This is an important point to keep in mind when making comparisons where transfer has been made between the two different contexts; and at the same time it opens up future avenues for comparative research on entrepreneurship policy.

A more process-orientated approach by researchers has already been started, with significant inputs from Arshed, some of which is referred to in her chapter with Drummond within this book. The study of public policy typically segregates the policy processes into a number of components. These have been described as, firstly, agenda setting, which refers to the awareness of the priority given to a particular issue; secondly, policy formulation, which refers to the methods used to develop policy options and strategies; thirdly, policy implementation, which refers to the forms and nature of public policy administration and the activities associated with it; and, fourthly, evaluation of policy. Arguably, research can have a role in each of these four stages. In addition, at the policy formulation stage there needs to be some attempt to canvas the views and experience of entrepreneurs and other stakeholders including researchers; to test potentially new policy measures in the way that market research would be used by a private company to assess the market potential of new products, and possibly to fine-tune the measure, including an attempt to identify any unforeseen consequences.

A third item to be added to the public policy agenda is policy monitoring and evaluation. This is not a new topic by any means, and it is true that a number of mature market economies have made a commitment to make more use of evaluation methods. However, still too often evaluation is simply equated with monitoring programme implementation in a very basic form; *ex ante* evaluations are lacking not least because of the efforts this requires to reach out to potential stakeholders and those affected by entrepreneurship policies. This needs to become more widespread, which would generate quite a lot of work with regard to training, for example, on evaluation methods as well as on the best ways to integrate feedback. However, this is what needs to be done because society will want to know what is being achieved with the money that is being spent.

Evaluations, both *ex ante* and *ex post*, will also help policy makers to recognise the unforeseen consequences that often occur in public policy. There are examples where policy measures trying to achieve what they set out to achieve are actually making the situation worse. In the example of maternity leave legislation for women, if one asks business owners who employ four or five people how they deal with this problem, nine times out of ten they will answer 'I do not employ women of childbearing age'. Clearly, this is discriminatory and not acceptable. Firm size is important here because if a business has a small number of staff, say three or four over a 12-month period, it would find it very difficult to cover their positions, specifically if the staff on maternity leave are specialised.

Despite the evaluation framework promoted by the Organisation for Economic Co-operation and Development (OECD) back in 2007 (OECD, 2007), the number of countries that have systematically applied this type of procedure has been very limited. By and large, policy evaluation is not given the attention that it warrants. This can be supported by the need for transparency in public policy terms and the need to justify the costs involved (the costs in relation to the benefits), but also because effective monitoring and evaluation can feed back into more successful policy development. The framework promoted by the OECD established certain principles justifying more robust policy evaluation, and contained guidance with respect to specific techniques that need to be employed.

A strong policy message which emerges from this review is that the absence of robust evaluation makes it impossible to know the real impact of a scheme in practice. This is a lesson one might suggest for all countries. Arguably, the key lesson emerging from Storey and Potter's chapter is that by not undertaking effective evaluation there could be an opportunity cost. The authors themselves pull out two key priorities. The first is for relevant government ministries charged with entrepreneurship policy to create an evaluation framework that can be applied across a range of policies. The second is to ensure access to data for evaluation, which is typically not included as part of programme requirements and therefore not always implemented, particularly in countries where the delivery of policy programmes is contracted out.

In recent years, there has been a growing tendency for policy makers to emphasise the role of evidence in policy formulation. In the UK at least, suitable evidence is limited despite the rhetoric that is often applied in this area. In addition, it may be argued that fundamentally this reflects the fact that enterprise policy is based more on a political rationale than an economic one. Hence, it may be suggested that one of the future policy priorities for both researchers and practitioners is that more explicit attention needs to be paid to the policy process. All we find is that economists working within the developing world have in many respects made more progress in this regard than those focused on domestic policy issues. For example, Young and Quinn's (2002) conceptualisation of the policy cycle demonstrates that research has the potential to influence the process at any stage, whilst the nature of the research may vary.

Another important issue which applies to both entrepreneurship policy and SME policy is that, whilst these terms imply interventions that are focused on the respective target group (whether this be entrepreneurs or SMEs), in practice SME and/or entrepreneurship policy may only affect a small number of people or businesses. In many ways a more useful concept could include the effects of all government policies and actions where they impact on entrepreneurship, although this is not necessarily the aim of the policy makers. The unintended consequences of policy constitutes an important theme for researchers to keep in mind for our future research agenda. Examples include the impact of government laws and regulation, particularly the unintended consequences for small businesses who, unlike a large firm, are unlikely to have specialists, for example in health and safety or for dealing with any kind of bureaucracy.

In other words, we want to put forward that we need to have a broad view on what constitutes policy, in particular entrepreneurship policy. Too frequently still, governments focus narrowly on supporting start-ups and SMEs and neglect the impact that other policy areas will have on entrepreneurship in general. A good example of this is provided by the draft industrial strategy presented by the German Federal Ministry of Economics and Energy in early 2019. This strategy underestimated the impact that the most commonly suggested measures it contained would have on Germany's manufacturing SMEs. The strategy focused on the promotion of large firms, whilst the recently passed Small Business Strategy from the same ministry clearly positioned SME and entrepreneurship policies as a priority policy area. The (initial – in the meantime the industrial strategy has been revised) contradiction between these two policies from the same ministry emphasises the need for a holistic approach based on a broad view of what constitutes policies to influence entrepreneurship and small business development.

The justification for taking a broad view is also illustrated in Ndemo's chapter, which focuses on the role of mobile communication technology in the development of entrepreneurship and small businesses in Sub Saharan Africa. Such a measure involving the diffusion of mobile innovation technology would not conventionally be included within the concept of entrepreneurship policy, but clearly the impact of this action, which represents a partnership between the public and private sectors, has had a considerable impact on the development of entrepreneurship in this region. This chapter, together with the chapter by Rogut and Piasecki, also demonstrates the close relationship between entrepreneurship policy and innovation policy in practice. The key point emphasised by Ndemo is the importance of an inclusive innovation policy, as far as both social inclusion and economic development are concerned.

Arguments against entrepreneurship policy have tended to focus on demonstrations of the inadequacies of entrepreneurship policy rather than necessarily the concept itself. These inadequacies highlight, but are not exclusive to, delivery issues. These include a common complaint that many small business owners do not know about, or do not understand, the variety of public policy support available to them, which is often very fragmented and sometimes introduced for short-term political reasons rather than economic argument. Whilst clearly these delivery issues are important since they can have a significant impact on the extent to which a policy is effective, other authors make a more fundamental critique of enterprise policy. The chapter by Arshed and Drummond, for example, makes a critique of enterprise policy in the UK, as does Robert Bennett (2008), who argues that even if market failure could have been demonstrated 20 years ago, most of those market failures have now been eliminated. Indeed, some have argued in this regard that enterprise policy is a waste of taxpayers' money, in that it generally encourages those who are already set on becoming entrepreneurs.

At the same time, implementing studies on the policy process presents a number of challenges. Arshed, for example, negotiated an internship within the ministry responsible for SMEs and entrepreneurship in the UK. Although Arshed was able to sit in on most of the key meetings, she was typically not able to join the meetings when a minister was present. As a result, the role of government ministers in the process is difficult to identify, and yet clearly in terms of the result the minister's influence is likely to be very important. Another point that needs to be recognised, once more, is the importance of context, which means that whilst the approach adopted by Arshed is potentially applicable elsewhere, the context may not be. Even within a single country, changes in government over time may well have some impact on the process, as well as, of course, the ruling party and their respective ideologies. Internationally, of course, one might suggest that differences in the background, knowledge and ability of government ministers is likely to show some variation.

At the same time, all the chapters in this volume contain lessons that are potentially of wider application outside of the country in which they have been developed. For example, Smallbone and Do's chapter on policy for internationalising SMEs demonstrates the political nature of entrepreneurship policy, which in this case involves the relationship between the European Union (EU) and national governments. This is reflected in the events leading up to the establishment of the EU's SME Centre in Beijing, and is also reflected in the failure of EU policies to help fill the gap in the case of smaller countries and those perhaps with much less experience of policies to support internationalisation. This chapter also demonstrates the need for rules and frameworks to lay down what is acceptable and not acceptable in terms of the role of internationalisation support programmes in supporting the competitiveness of national businesses.

Not surprisingly perhaps, the key theme emerging from the chapters is, yet again, the importance of placing entrepreneurship policy into context. This argument has been developed strongly with respect to entrepreneurship, but it can be argued that its role also applies very much to the policy arena. Clearly, a good example of this is townships in South Africa where, until 20 years ago, those living there were barred from business ownership. As a consequence, there are likely to be cultural barriers that will affect the current and future development of entrepreneurship. The main challenge for policy makers is to take steps to include social groups in a society based on independence and individualism in townships where a more collective approach is necessary. The main challenge for researchers is to recognise that contextualising entrepreneurship policy is not simply about studying entrepreneurship in townships, but it is about understanding the historical, political and societal contexts that possibly explain why entrepreneurship in townships may be different from what one would expect.

The book also contains cases of countries that only 25 years ago were operating under socialism and central planning, Poland being one example and Russia another. Although Poland and Russia share some common heritage, the two are quite different with respect to encouraging entrepreneurship development.

Another example emphasising that the nature of context for entrepreneurship and entrepreneurship policy needs to be considered is China, where individuals and institutional frames have changed enormously over the last decades. China shares some common characteristics with the former Soviet republics, but at the same time there are substantial differences, the main one being the ongoing control of society and the economy by the Chinese Communist Party. Whilst in both Russia and China bribery and corruption is rife, bribing the local officials in China to give permission for a particular development to take place may offer double benefits to the official, in that they will receive the bribe but they will also almost certainly be encouraged by local government to continue to implement the development.

Another issue emerging from a number of the chapters in the volume concerns the most appropriate level on which to focus public policy. Smallbone, Li and Xu's chapter on China, for example, demonstrates the importance of a strong policy presence at a sub-national level. The sheer size of China makes it necessary for policy to be sensitive to the spatial variations within the country. This is required because in a country as large as China, the nature and extent of SME support needs will almost certainly vary across territories. This aspect is taken care of by the current approaches of the Chinese government, which emphasises the need for interventions to be compatible with provincial- and city-level interventions. Within Russia, however, where the size of the country is also huge, the state has been very slow to recognise this aspect.

Another country example where the context is very specific for policy makers is Poland. The underlying issue here is the short-term nature of the opportunities for acquiring substantial development and restructuring funds from the EU, as well as the challenges involved in securing these funds. In the medium and longer term this is a danger because it is likely that the short-term emphasis on acquiring such resources has been to maximise the funds received from the EU, which may weaken some of the Central and Eastern European countries in the longer term. There is a danger that at the end of this funding period, when the money is either stopped or severely cut, public policy makers will not be in the position to identify what is required and design appropriate policy responses.

Future agenda on entrepreneurship policy for researchers and policy makers

We now turn to setting out a future agenda, differentiating between the research agenda for entrepreneurship policy researchers and that for policy makers.

Entrepreneurship policy researchers

- More attention needs to be paid to the definition of policy makers, with a clear distinction being made between policy making and policy implementation. This will enable recommendations to be more specifically targeted, distinguishing between policy makers and practitioners.
- Entrepreneurship policy researchers should stress the importance of contextualisation, which can vary between countries, of course, but also between regions.
- Entrepreneurship policy researchers should put more emphasis on the study of policy-making processes, which until recently has not been a major agenda item. This should involve, firstly, agenda setting; secondly, policy formulation; thirdly, policy implementation; and, fourthly, policy evaluation. Amongst other things this would help to narrow the gap between what public policy makers really need and what the universities and business schools are producing.
- Entrepreneurship policy researchers need to critically analyse the policy process, starting with the failure in most cases to undertake any kind of market research concerning the needs of businesses, the needs of regions and the needs of national economies.
- Entrepreneurship policy researchers should seek to address each of the four stages of the policy process. Absence of robust evaluation in many countries is a constraint on improving the quality and effectiveness of entrepreneurship policy. Policy measures focused on entrepreneurship are only likely to impact on a minority of a country's businesses. Researchers also must recognise that the effect of government policies on entrepreneurship and SME development goes beyond policy measures that are specifically targeted at these groups.
- Policy researchers have an important role in stressing the importance of context. When public policies are being designed or analysed, contextual differences, particularly with respect to the institutional framework, can have significant effects on the success of policy measures and programmes.
- Policy researchers have an opportunity to develop more robust concepts of entrepreneurship policy in order to increase their impact on policy making.

- If researchers are interested in strengthening their role in relation to public policy, they need to engage with policy makers in order to understand the policy process.

Entrepreneurship policy makers

- Policy makers should place more emphasis on context than is currently given, particularly where policy transfer is involved. Differences between regions and countries can affect the extent to which policies that are transferred are successful.
- Entrepreneurship policy makers and researchers need to take steps to narrow the gap between what public policy makers need and what the business schools and higher education institutions are producing in terms of research.
- Policy makers need to prioritise monitoring and evaluation, setting aside funding for the completion of this at the outset of new measures, and making sure that the appropriate data is collected in order to provide a baseline.
- If policy makers are genuinely interested in evidence-based policy, then research has a role in each of the four stages of policy making identified above.
- Policy makers should recognise the importance of monitoring and evaluation. This should involve including a budget for evaluation at the time a new measure is launched, as well as ensuring that baseline data is gathered during the life of the policy in order to provide a basis for robust evaluation. This may not be easy to achieve if the policy measure was inspired by political gain rather than wider social and economic benefits. Unfortunately, policy making is rarely a logical process, although researchers wish it were so.
- Policy makers interested in strengthening the evidence base for effective policy should be willing to engage with researchers as well as commissioning them to bid for research projects.
- Policy makers need to recognise the unforeseen consequences that often occur in public policy. The frequency of this could be reduced if policy makers made a more significant attempt to market test new policy measures before they are formally launched. In addition, researchers often have the knowledge and experience of SME support needs that policy makers might more systematically draw upon.

In terms of the future policy agenda, this chapter firstly seeks to identify what policy researchers need to take steps to address the needs of policy makers, communicated in the form that is likely to have the most impact. This is crucial if the role of academic research in policy making is to be increased. Alan Gibb (2000) identifies a number of what he calls 'myths' which are not helpful in policy making. Gibb's main argument is that many academics and business schools have not served the broadly defined business community well. On the other hand, Perren and Jennings (2005) question the lack of critical perspectives on public policy. This is a position which Xheneti, in her chapter within this volume, addresses in the context of a more critical approach to policy development. On the basis that the future policy agenda and future research in this field needs to be based on a critical view of entrepreneurship policy as it stands, the key arguments presented by Gibb justify further attention. Choosing one of Gibb's hobby horses as an example, we focus on the so-called myth that growth companies are the major job generators. In this regard, Gibb is not alone in his criticism, one aspect of which is the fact that the growth path of an individual firm may look very different depending on the precise years taken for comparison, on the basis that the future agenda for entrepreneurship policy will inevitably be shaped by the strengths and weaknesses that may be identified in contemporary approaches. In this regard, researchers have responded to some of Gibb's key concerns by placing more emphasis on the process of policy development. The work of Arshed is illustrative of this approach. Essentially, this work was initiated by Arshed in her PhD thesis, although clearly this has developed much more since then.

The rest of the book

The rest of the book is divided into two parts. The first part contains four thematic chapters. The first is by Arshed and Drummond and discusses the shortcomings of enterprise policy in the UK, which in a wider international context has often been seen to incorporate good practice. The chapter focuses on the policy process, which is particularly insightful since one of the authors is a former policy maker. This is followed by a critical piece by Xheneti, who applies some of the findings from her previous work on policy transfer to the wider enterprise policy agenda.

One of the most consistent criticisms of entrepreneurship policy is the lack of attention paid to robust evaluation, and it is fair to say that Storey and Potter have done as much as anyone to promote policy evaluation, as well as undertaking it. The chapter describes how policy evaluation is slowly attracting more serious attention. At the same time, the authors stress that to be effective public policy evaluation needs to be based on appropriate data access and use robust methods, which in their case means econometrics methods. The authors also point out that effective policy evaluation needs to be based on appropriate data and undertaken independently. Key problems identified include failure by policy designers to make provision for the data to be generated from day one. Another issue is the tendency for policy objectives to be insufficiently and unclearly specified, which almost certainly reflects a situation where policy objectives are more about politics than they are about economy. The final chapter in this part, authored by Smallbone and Do, takes a critical look at policies to support internationalisation. The focus in this chapter is on Europe, and both national- and EU-level policies are included.

The second part of the book contains country-specific perspectives on different aspects of a future research agenda on entrepreneurship policy. In the first chapter in this part, authored by Smallbone, Xiao and Xu, the relationship between national and sub-national policies is examined, which in China, the country that is the focus of this chapter, means the provincial and city level. This chapter utilises new material to demonstrate regional variations in entrepreneurship in China.

This is followed by a chapter on the Russian Federation, written by Barinova, Zemtsov and Smallbone, which has been one of the slowest of the transition economies to develop its SME sector. This is associated with the fact that large enterprises still dominate the Russian economy, but it also reflects the lack of an entrepreneurial spirit, which may be explained by the fact that Russia essentially moved from a feudal structure to a socialist one with no private enterprise experience in between. At the same time, the chapter adopts an upbeat stance, although only time will tell whether the current programme of support for SMEs will be successful.

The next chapter is also on a country, Poland, that for many years operated an essentially planned economy under socialism. However, unlike Russia, entrepreneurship took off very quickly once the reform process was underway. The chapter by Rogut and Piasecki discusses two interrelated issues, the first concerned with how to stimulate more innovation in Poland's SMEs and the second related to the EU as a source of funding for structural change.

The SME sector in Japan is something of a black box for many Western researchers because many of the researchers looking into entrepreneurship in Japan do not have a sufficient command of the English language. In this context, the chapter by Mitsui provides some valuable insights into the reasons for declining entrepreneurship, which clearly is a different message from that which Western researchers are used to hearing. Although very different to the preceding chapter on Poland, there is a shared interest in encouraging entrepreneurship that is innovative in nature.

The next chapter on Sub Saharan Africa, written by Ndemo, is particularly interesting for two reasons: firstly, because it demonstrates how entrepreneurship can be affected by a wide range of government policies and actions that are not necessarily targeted at entrepreneurs; and, secondly, because the author spent ten years in government himself, including a period as a government minister. The example in this chapter is the above-mentioned effect of mobile communications technology, which in Sub Saharan Africa is not just viewed as enabling self-employed and small businesses to widen their scope of operation.

The final chapter is concerned with South Africa, which some commentators view as an example of a transition economy with some similar features to those found in Central and Eastern Europe. Instead of a post-socialist context, the context in South Africa is post-apartheid, with a focus on the township. In this chapter Mazwai argues that that the lack of entrepreneurship in the black population has been a very difficult nut to crack, with a series of policy interventions which do not appear to have contributed very much to addressing the needs of entrepreneurs and SMEs. Thus, this chapter is concerned with increasing social inclusion on a very large scale.

References

Bennett, R. (2008), 'SME policy support in Britain since the 1990s: What have we learnt?', *Environment and Planning C: Government and Policy*, **26** (2), 375–97.

Gibb, A. (2000), 'SME policy, academic research and the growth of ignorance, mythical concepts, myths, assumptions, rituals and confusions', *International Small Business Journal*, **18** (3), 13–35.

OECD (2007), *OECD Framework for the Evaluation of SME and Entrepreneurship Policies and Programmes*, Paris: OECD Publishing.

Perren, L. and P. L. Jennings (2005), 'Government discourses on entrepreneurship: Issues of legitimization, subjugation and power', *Entrepreneurship Theory and Practice*, **29** (2), 173–84.

Welter, F. (2011), 'Contextualizing entrepreneurship – Conceptual challenges and ways forward', *Entrepreneurship Theory and Practice*, **35** (1), 165–84.

Young, E. and L. Quinn (2002), *Writing Effective Public Policy Papers: A Guide to Policy Advisers in Central and Eastern Europe*, Budapest: LGI.

PART I

Key themes in entrepreneurship policy

2 Reviewing and revising the rhetoric of enterprise policy: going back to basics

Norin Arshed and Ian Drummond

Introduction

Since the publication of the Bolton report on small firms in 1971, successive UK governments have asserted a commitment to support entrepreneurship and small businesses (Bolton, 1971). A raft of policies have been developed with the aim of encouraging and enabling dynamism, productivity gains and growth in the sector (Autio and Rannikko, 2016; Blackburn and Smallbone, 2011). Moreover, there is evidence that, in some respects at least, these policy goals have been achieved. The UK small and medium-sized enterprise (SME) population has grown markedly in recent years. For example, there were a record 5.5-million private sector businesses at the start of 2016, an increase of more than a million compared with the start of 2010 (BEIS, 2017). Publications from the Global Entrepreneurship Monitor (2018) and the World Bank (2018) consistently show that entrepreneurship levels and the business environment in the UK are amongst the best in the world. Similarly, EU Small Business Act UK Factsheets provide testament to the relative quality of UK enterprise policy (European Commission, 2016). However, this positive outlook on the state of the UK small business sector and its enterprise policy has been widely challenged over the years (Wapshott and Mallett, 2018).

This chapter unpicks the focus on headline figures and highlights the experiences and observations of a former civil servant and an academic who have worked on and researched enterprise policy. The aim of the chapter is not to dispute or challenge the UK government's goals of promoting and supporting economic growth, competition and innovation in the SME sector through enterprise policy. Rather, we hope to better understand why the policy development process, as it works in practice, tends to be ineffective. To this end, we identify a broader set of factors that shape policy development and constrain the impacts achieved than have been considered to date. Our analysis suggests that whilst many of these factors may well be influential, the unsystematic and eclectic use of evidence, and within this a narrow conception of what constitutes relevant evidence, are fundamental concerns.

Reviewing enterprise policy in the UK

Enterprise policy was traditionally 'centred on business start-ups and support for small business growth' (Huggins and Williams, 2009, p. 21), but over the years UK policy has focused increasingly on SME performance and growth (HM Government, 2017). In this chapter, we consider both entrepreneurship and SME policy under the broader umbrella of enterprise policy, because there is considerable overlap in their aims (Arshed et al., 2014; Audretsch and Beckmann, 2007). Although there is evidence indicating the relatively healthy state of the SME sector in the UK, these headline data belie a series of, often intransigent, concerns about the performance of the sector. These continuing concerns raise profound questions about the nature and effectiveness of enterprise policy in the UK (Acs et al., 2016; Beresford, 2015). For example, two key concerns are highlighted in the recent Industrial Strategy White Paper (HM Government, 2017). First, the productivity levels in the UK, not least in the SME sector, remain low in both absolute and relative terms as 'we have businesses, people and places whose level of productivity is well below what can be achieved' (HM Government, 2017, p. 6). Second, the White Paper highlights that innovation rates are also relatively low in the UK, as 'fewer of our small and medium-sized enterprises introduce new products and processes than their European competitors' (HM Government, 2017, p. 61).

Moreover, there are further causes for concern. These include persistent spatial disparities in entrepreneurship in the UK (HM Government, 2017); widespread deficiencies in management and leadership skills in the SME sector (Hayton, 2015); modest levels of ambition that are frequently not realised in practice (TBR, 2016); comparatively low proportion of SMEs that are women-led (BIS, 2015); the numbers of SMEs achieving high growth remains modest (Nesta, 2016); demand for finance to fund growth remains suppressed (BDRC, 2017); use of business support is falling and the number of SMEs exporting has been, at best, flat in recent years (BEIS, 2017). Indeed, some have argued that, in practice, enterprise policy is a waste of taxpayers' money, in that it generally encourages those already intent on becoming entrepreneurs, and mostly generates one-employee businesses with low-growth intentions and a lack of interest in innovation (Acs et al., 2016). However, government and many academics agree that there is a convincing rationale for intervention; there are well-documented market failures and issues where there is a valid role for government (Bennett, 2014; Storey and Frankish, 2016). If this is indeed the case, the problem is not enterprise policy per se, but rather the apparently ineffective way in which it is formulated and delivered (Arshed et al., 2014; Arshed et al., 2016).

Interestingly, the core aim of the Industrial Strategy is to make the UK 'the best place to start and grow a business' (HM Government, 2017, p. 13). This tagline remains identical to that espoused over a decade ago by the Small Business Service (SBS, 2004). But more than this, few if any of the current concerns and associated policy objectives listed in the Industrial Strategy document are original; almost all of these aims were cited in the SBS Action Plan report (SBS, 2004) (see Table 2.1).

The key point here is not so much that these problems exist but rather that they are, for the most part, the same issues that UK enterprise policy has been seeking to address for the past ten years. It is this persistence that provides what is arguably the most telling commentary on the effectiveness of UK enterprise policy. In some respects, this conclusion is counterintuitive because good prac-tice in policy development is well understood. The Green Book describes the ROAMEF cycle, which sets out six stages of the UK policy process: Rationale, Objectives, Appraisal, Monitoring, Evaluation and Feedback (HM Treasury, 2005). Whilst this model has been widely criticised by entrepreneurship schol-ars (see, for example, Blackburn and Schaper, 2016), the approach which it sets is logical, well rehearsed and recognised as best practice throughout govern-ment. Certainly, basing policy development around the ROAMEF cycle must be preferable to an unstructured approach. Whilst there is clearly substance in Arshed et al.'s (2014) conclusions concerning the inherent shortcomings of the policy development process and the ways this is used in practice, we build on their work by identifying and assessing a number of additional factors that may serve to undermine the effectiveness of enterprise policy. These factors are outlined in the following sections.

Table 2.1 Comparisons in policy rhetoric 2004 and 2017

Key areas	2004 SBS Action Plan for Small Businesses	2017 Industrial Strategy White Paper
Productivity	The UK still faces a persistent productivity gap of at least 20 per cent with its major competitors.	We have businesses, people and places whose level of productivity is well below what can be achieved.
Innovation	UK-owned businesses appear to be less creative and less able to introduce workplace changes than those in some other advanced economies.	Fewer of our small and medium-sized enterprises introduce new products and processes than their European competitors.
Uneven development	Enterprise activity is particularly limited in the UK's least prosperous regions and communities.	Many places are not realising their full potential. The UK has greater disparities in regional productivity than other European countries.
Management-level skills	Skill deficiencies, particularly at the management level, impose a significant constraint on output.	Studies suggest that the average UK manager is less proficient than many overseas competitors.
Better regulation	Excessive, unnecessary or poorly implemented regulation can reduce the efficiency with which markets operate. This is a particular problem for small businesses.	Smaller businesses, without the clout of scale, can suffer disproportionately from heavy-handed regulation and bureaucratic excess.
Growth	Too few UK small businesses grow fast enough. The proportion of UK small businesses that want to grow is greater than the numbers currently growing in practice.	We could do better in the longer-term process of building up successful businesses to reach large scale.
Access to finance	There are failures in finance markets that mean the 'right' amount of finance is not always provided.	We need to make it easier for businesses of any size, in any location, to access finance.
Business support	There are weaknesses in the demand for and the provision of business support.	Key factors for improvement include the availability of advice and mentoring for growing businesses.

Sources: HM Government (2017) and SBS (2004).

A future agenda for SME policy makers

Recognising the inappropriateness of the ROAMEF cycle

Arshed et al.'s (2014) study identified the process in which enterprise policy is formulated through the actions of the individuals involved, at different levels of the policy process. The study drew on institutional theory and highlighted five key stages of the formulation of enterprise policy: the area of interest for policy; briefing; collecting evidence; announcements; and publication of a White Paper/government document. The study highlighted how policy development is shaped by the personal interests of powerful actors and showed that the approach to enterprise policy making at the early stages tends to be ad hoc and piecemeal. One of the key elements that the study sought to understand was how the ROAMEF cycle is used and how this functions in practice. It has been claimed that the ROAMEF cycle may not be appropriate to the development of enterprise policy: 'the assumption that the Green Book is a way to "right all wrongs" is too simplistic' (Arshed et al., 2014, p. 646).

There are issues with the Green Book. For example, it specifies that the rationale for intervention must be based primarily on identified market failures. This may be problematic because, for example, recent research has shown that the ambition and behaviours of many small business owners are shaped by their innate dispositions and their associated mindsets. Limited ambition and growth resistant mindsets are not a market failure. As Theodorakopoulos et al. (2015, p. 37) highlight, 'growth-resistant dispositions as identified in this research are not the outcome of information failure and are not market failures in the sense that these are conventionally understood. At face value this conclusion represents a clear challenge to the current orthodoxy for policy intervention.' It is also the case that some aspects of the defined process, such as calculating the net present value of policy options, can be a technically demanding and uncertain process. But government departments employ a large number of skilled economists and should be able to deal effectively with these challenges.

Beyond this there are very real issues associated with the evaluation step in the cycle. Not the least of these is that the intended impacts of many initiatives will necessarily be lagged for a significant amount of time. Consider, for example, a policy measure designed to enhance management and leadership skills in small businesses. The effective development of these skills may well benefit a business for many years, but many impacts would not be captured by an evaluation that followed immediately after the implementation of policy. Notwithstanding these points, there is little reason to believe that the

ROAMEF process, which is well proven in other areas, is not appropriate to the development of effective enterprise policy. Certainly, it must be preferable to any unstructured approach.

Recognising the intractability of challenges facing the SME sector

There are a number of challenges for enterprise policy which are inherently intractable. Consider, for example, the longstanding policy goal of promoting less and better regulation. Although there may well be a credible rationale for regulatory reform, in practice, policy is largely driven by populist pressures from business representative bodies which create a political imperative. As Kitching (2006, p. 799) argues, naïve conceptions of regulation and its impacts on small businesses can 'positively encourage superficial and misleading results. More sophisticated approaches, using qualitative data, demonstrate that regulations generate a variety of consequences and should not be conceptualised solely in terms of costs and constraints.' Whilst the available evidence suggests that only modest gains have been made in this area, this is not the key point. In practice, it is certainly the case that even successful policy would not be sufficient to stem naïve populist calls for ever-greater reductions in regulation (Kitching et al., 2015).

Recognising that some issues facing SMEs are beyond the scope of enterprise policy

A number of key areas of enterprise policy involve not just the Department for Business, Energy and Industrial Strategy (BEIS), but also other government departments and non-governmental bodies. For example, rural businesses are a key concern for the Department for Environment, Food and Rural Affairs but less so for BEIS; policy relating to social enterprises is led by the Department for Digital, Culture, Media and Sport and workplace pensions policy is led by the Department for Work and Pensions. The involvement of these different departments inevitably makes policy development and implementation particularly challenging. Horizontal policy of this sort requires the joining of networks and government departments, which often leads to difficulties in maintaining relationships due to the complexity of the process and the number of actors involved (Acs and Szerb, 2007; Arshed et al., 2016).

Whilst we might argue that government departments should be capable of joined-up working, there are areas of policy where government influence is necessarily limited. Access to finance is a good example of this. In recent years government has introduced policy in this area by establishing the British Business Bank and through creating initiatives such as the Enterprise Finance

Guarantee scheme. However, it is clear that government's influence over banks and other finance providers is, in many respects, limited.

Furthermore, macro-economic conditions routinely create challenges to enterprise policy development that are not amenable to policy fixes. In the last decade alone, an economic recession and associated austerity measures have created emergent challenges for the SME sector. These challenges have impacted on policy development not least because they have occurred at a time of reduced resources within government (HM Treasury, 2010). Subsequently, uncertainties over Brexit have created conditions in which both the government and businesses themselves have been reluctant to invest. It is clear that these unfavourable conditions have tended to constrain the scope and effectiveness of a range of enterprise policy initiatives (Brown et al., 2018).

Recognising that some policy options may be too expensive or untenable

Enterprise policy, as is all policy, is constrained by costs and available budgets. Whilst it is generally possible to formulate policy measures that could potentially effectively address particular constraints to SME performance and growth, these can be prohibitively expensive. Policy implementation depends on both the direct impacts and the value of the initiative, and its value compared to other, not necessarily related, policy options (Maor, 2017). Beyond this, some options are flawed because of the size of the SME population; in practice it is simply not possible to engage directly with over five million small businesses, making it very difficult to target support for SMEs in a way that matches the specific problems and needs of very different firms (Kaufmann and Tödtling, 2002).

Recognising that segmentation and the targeting of business support is problematic

The extent to which policy formulation and implementation is constrained by resources is compounded by the very real challenges involved in targeting support to what is, in practice, a highly heterogeneous population of SMEs (Wapshott and Mallett, 2018). It is generally recognised that it is simply not possible 'to pick winners' – businesses that will improve their performance and businesses that will grow. More than this, the appropriate target for most interventions is businesses with latent and unrealised potential, which are even more difficult to identify pre-emptively. These problems exacerbate the risk of deadweight because investment in entrepreneurship and enterprise does not always achieve additionality, as some supported businesses would have developed without the intervention (Michael and Pearce, 2009).

Recognising the difference between evidence and ideology

The civil servants who formulate enterprise policy are constrained to developing and implementing policy in line with the wishes of the current government. If we look at the Labour years, enterprise policy evolved greatly. There was a focus on disadvantaged groups, Regional Development Agencies were established, and the Small Business Service (a dedicated agency to build an enterprising society) was introduced (Greene and Patel, 2013). That said, it is less clear that politically mandated shifts in policy have always been evidence based, progressive or more effective than what they replaced. Whilst the 'black box' nature of the policy development process means that we have no direct evidence of this, there have been developments that appear, at least, to be ideologically rather than evidence driven (Arshed et al., 2014). Consider, for example, the dissolution of the Business Link network. This was scrapped by the incoming Conservative–Liberal government despite a raft of evidence of its effectiveness (see, for example, Mole et al., 2007). Beyond this, there is clear enough evidence of tensions between an essentially neo-liberal approach – to make the UK the best place in the world to grow a business – and the perceived need to address specific problems or obstacles to improved performance and growth.

Recognising the limitations of a piecemeal approach to policy making

A number of authors have been critical of the apparently ad hoc and piecemeal nature of enterprise policy development. Greene and Patel (2013) describe the aims of these policies as being 'a patchwork quilt, "chaos", a labyrinth of initiatives or simply in a muddle'. Storey (2000, p. 276) argued that enterprise policies are 'rarely specified and appear to reflect the need to do something or to be seen to be responding, rather than as part of a coherent agenda designed to achieve clear objectives'. He identified a failure to specify SMART (Specific, Measurable, Achievable, Realistic, Time-limited) objectives as required by the ROAMEF guidance, the apparently reactive nature of much policy formulation, and the focused, rather than strategic, nature of most initiatives.

Storey's (2000) point is crucial in understanding why enterprise policy has tended to be ineffective. It is clear that SME performance depends on numerous factors, and that policy development in one area may be necessary but in itself is unlikely to be sufficient. Amongst other things, both start-ups and dynamic, productive and successful growing businesses require a congruence of ambition, skills, access to finance and a supportive business environment. Accordingly, improvements in just one or two of these areas are unlikely to achieve significant impacts. For example, there is little virtue in securing access to finance for SMEs if they lack the management and leadership skills to invest capital wisely and effectively.

To some extent, the recent shift towards a 'softer' approach to enterprise policy in the form of advice, consultancy, information and training (Greene and Patel, 2013; Roper and Hart, 2013) may be consistent with the need to move beyond piecemeal and partial policies. However, in itself this hardly meets the need for a holistic, comprehensive approach. As Blackburn and Smallbone (2011, p. 575) argue, 'developing public policy for SMEs may appear straight-forward on an issue-by-issue basis. However, in practice, developing a policy landscape that is conducive to SMEs, as well as meeting the demands of other stakeholders in the economy and society, is not easy'.

Recognising that appropriate supporting evidence should be sought wherever possible

Well-conducted policy formulation needs to be evidence based. The alterna-tive is 'opinion-based' policy making, which is clearly both dangerous and inappropriate. As the Green Book highlights, both the rationale for interven-tion and the intended impacts should be based on evidence (HM Treasury, 2005). It seems reasonable to assume that evidence-based policy should be possible, given the very extensive body of literature that considers small business growth and the factors that shape this (see, for example, Gupta et al., 2013). However, in practice, our understanding of the factors that shape small business performance and growth remains partial and limited. This may be because small business growth is too complex to understand or that we cannot conduct extensive surveys that cover enough variables.

However, there is an increasingly widespread recognition that the problem is broader than this. As Karatas-Ozkan et al. (2014, p. 590) argue, 'posi-tivist approaches and associated quantitative studies have dominated the field although post-positivist approaches and associated qualitative research designs are demonstrably underrepresented in entrepreneurship research. This is in spite of the ability of non-positivistic approaches to address interest-ing, even fundamental entrepreneurship questions'. Similarly, Braidford et al. (2017) argue that there is a well-established preference for the use of quanti-tative, statistical and econometric data within the civil service and that this is particularly the case with respect to those research outputs which, in practice, have shaped policy development.

Quantitative data are necessary and informative; they show the associations between directly observable factors and business performance and highlight differences between growing and non-growing businesses. However, such approaches are inherently limited because they provide little understanding of causality – of how and why particular outcomes occur. Beyond this, they are necessarily partial in that they fail to deliver the kind of multi-layered explanatory models needed. Despite this, to date, entrepreneurship scholars and successive governments have largely failed to engage with alternative, complementary epistemologies such as critical realism that may well be better suited to providing the kind of multi-layered modes of explanation required if policy formation is to have a more holistic and powerful basis (Braidford et al., 2017). A key point here is that if Karatas-Ozkan et al. (2014) are correct, the limitations of the available evidence base will not be corrected by further quantitative research; more and bigger surveys can add only marginally to our understanding. Moving beyond this impasse requires new and different forms of evidence.

Revising enterprise policy in the UK

These observations do not undermine Arshed et al.'s (2014) conclusions that the shortcomings of UK enterprise policy are, in large part, a consequence of deficiencies in the policy formulation process. Rather, they serve to identify a somewhat richer set of factors that may also be influential, thereby making some contribution towards answering Mason's (2009) call, echoed by Arshed et al. (2014), for an increased research focus on the effects of government policy making in understanding why 'bad' enterprise policy exists (Shane, 2009) and how to address the critics' concerns about the ineffectiveness of such a policy. Understanding why enterprise policy has been less than effective is not an end in itself. The real value of work in this area lies in its potential to improve the enterprise policy formulation process.

Although the evidence is limited, it does seem to be the case that there are issues with the ROAMEF guidance not being used, or at least not being applied systematically and effectively. Certainly, there is little evidence to show that it is being used appropriately. Whilst we should recognise that policy makers are often under very real pressures to address emergent issues quickly and with limited resources, not adhering to the government's own best practice model seems perverse to external observers and is potentially a compounding factor influencing the outcomes achieved. As discussed, there are other factors at play which potentially serve to limit the effectiveness of enterprise policy:

policy is clearly constrained by the availability of resources, segmentation is challenging, and there are real pressures to achieve the unachievable. Perhaps the foremost amongst these factors relates to the evidence used in policy formulation, and underpinning this is the arguably limited scope of much extant academic research.

It is clearly inappropriate to believe that policy in this area can fully and effectively address all the issues involved. From this perspective, our argument relating to the persistence of a range of problems is perhaps a little unfair. Appropriate and realistically achievable policy goals, and the criteria against which policy is assessed, should perhaps be less ambitious and framed in terms of continuous improvement rather than outright resolution. Some issues are inherently intractable, some are dialectical, and others are beyond the scope and resources of the government department and policy goals. For example, we have argued that effective policy needs to be more strategic and holistic. This is a valid argument, but achieving this in practice is always going be methodologically challenging. That said, there is clearly room for improvement and there are realistic measures that could be taken; there are forms of research, currently largely unused by both academics and policy makers, that can provide more multi-layered, holistic modes of explanation. It is unclear why enterprise scholars have essentially failed to engage with non-positivistic epistemologies. Such engagement would be challenging, but surely it is both achievable and, in all probability, very worthwhile. Certainly, other disciplines have long since productively engaged with alternative, complementary epistemologies.

Although the evidence base is never going to be completely comprehensive, some of its current limitations reflect the prevailing values and practices of policy makers. Privileging quantitative evidence to the extent that other epistemologies, and other forms of non-positivistic evidence, are seldom (if ever) utilised clearly limits understanding, and typically means that policy is less than fully evidence based. But any fault here extends beyond the eclectic use of the evidence base by policy makers. As Karatas-Ozkan et al. (2014) argue, this narrow focus is, in large part, a reflection of the nature and scope of the available academic research, which remains almost entirely positivist.

However, we should acknowledge that in recent years government has made some small steps towards engaging with different forms of evidence. One example of this is a study of the 'sociology of enterprise', which uses social theory to consider how business behaviours are shaped by the dispositions and mindsets of business owners (Theodorakopoulos et al., 2015). However, whilst this study shows that approaches such as this are feasible and useful, non-positivist research remains very much the exception rather than the norm. More effective policy making requires both more routine use of best practice and more engagement with complementary, and potentially powerful, new forms of evidence.

Conclusion

The starting point for this chapter was the established view that best practice in policy formulation is not always well suited to formulating enterprise policy and is often not followed in practice. Our analysis has identified and begun to explore some hitherto unconsidered insights into the enterprise policy-making process. In doing so, it has identified a number of additional reasons as to why UK enterprise policy has tended to be less effective than it might have been. We have identified a range of factors that tend to complicate, and in some cases confound, enterprise policy development. Whilst some or all the factors may well be influential, we see a central, if not singular, significance in the clear failure to develop truly evidence-based policy. There can be little doubt that the use of evidence in policy formulation is limited in a number of respects. It seems that policy makers do not always engage systematically with the available evidence. Beyond this, and perhaps even more importantly, there is a clear failure to engage with the need for multi-layered, more holistic conceptions of the factors that influence business performance. In large part, this reflects Karatas-Ozkan et al.'s (2014) argument that positivist approaches have dominated this body of research despite the apparent potential of non-positivistic approaches to address interesting, even fundamental, entrepreneurship questions. If these conclusions are valid, they present clear challenges, not just for policy makers but also for academia.

References

Acs, Z., T. Astebro, D. Audretsch and D. T. Robinson (2016), 'Public policy to promote entrepreneurs: A call to arms', *Small Business Economics*, **47** (1), 35–51.

Acs, Z. J. and L. Szerb (2007), 'Entrepreneurship, economic growth and public policy', *Small Business Economics*, **28** (2–3), 109–22.

Arshed, N., S. Carter and C. Mason (2014), 'The ineffectiveness of entrepreneurship policy: Is policy formulation to blame?', *Small Business Economics*, **43** (3), 639–59.

Arshed, N., C. Mason and S. Carter (2016), 'Exploring the disconnect in policy implementation: A case of enterprise policy in England', *Environment and Planning C: Government and Policy*, **34** (8), 1582–611.

Audretsch, D. B. and I. A. M. Beckmann (2007), 'From small business to entrepreneurship policy'. In D. B. Audretsch, I. Grilo and A. R. Thurik (eds), *Handbook of Research on Entrepreneurship Policy* (pp. 36–53), Cheltenham, UK and Northampton, MA, USA: Edward Elgar Publishing.

Autio, E. and H. Rannikko (2016), 'Retaining winners: Can policy boost high-growth entrepreneurship?', *Research Policy*, **45** (1), 42–55.

BDRC (2017), *Small- and Medium-Sized Enterprise Finance Monitor 2011–2017*, https://discover.ukdataservice.ac.uk/catalogue/?sn=6888.

BEIS (2017), *Annual Business Population Estimates for the UK and Regions in 2017*, statistical release, https://www.gov.uk/government/uploads/system/uploads/attachment_data/file/663235/bpe_2017_statistical_release.pdf.

Bennett, R. (2014), *Entrepreneurship, Small Business and Public Policy: Evolution and Revolution*, Abingdon: Routledge.

Beresford, R. (2015), 'New Labour and enterprise policy: Continuity or change? Evidence from general election manifestos', *British Politics*, **10** (3), 335–55.

BIS (2015), *Contribution of Women-Led and MEG-Led Businesses to the UK Non-Financial Economy*, https://assets.publishing.service.gov.uk/government/uploads/system/uploads/attachment_data/file/461784/BIS-15-542-estimation_of_GVA_for_certain_businesses.pdf.

Blackburn, R. and M. Schaper (eds) (2016), *Government, SMEs and Entrepreneurship Development: Policy Practice and Challenges*, New York and London: Routledge.

Blackburn, R. and D. Smallbone (2011), 'Policy support for SMEs', *Environment and Planning C: Government and Policy*, **29** (4), 571–6.

Bolton, J. E. (1971), *Small Firms: Report of the Commission of Inquiry on Small Firms*, London: Her Majesty's Stationery Office.

Braidford, P., I. Drummond and I. Stone (2017), 'The impact of personal attitudes on the growth ambitions of small business owners', *Journal of Small Business and Enterprise Development*, **24** (4), 850–62.

Brown, R., J. M. Liñares-Zegarra and J. O. S. Wilson (2018), 'What happens if the rules change? The impact of Brexit on the future strategic intentions of UK SMEs', https://ssrn.com/abstract=3066614.

European Commission (2016), *SBA Fact Sheet: United Kingdom*, https://rio.jrc.ec.europa.eu/en/library/2016-sba-fact-sheet-united-kingdom.

Global Entrepreneurship Monitor (2018), *Global Entrepreneurship Monitor Report*, http://www.gemconsortium.org/report/49812.

Greene, F. J. and P. Patel (2013), 'Enterprise 2050: Getting UK enterprise policy right', FSB discussion paper, https://www.gov.uk/government/uploads/system/uploads/attachment_data/file/225966/19_ATTACHMENT_6.pdf.

Gupta, P., S. Guha and S. Krishnaswami (2013), 'Firm growth and its determinants', *Journal of Innovation and Entrepreneurship*, **2** (1), 1–14.

Hayton, J. (2015), 'Leadership and management skills in SMEs: Measuring associations with management practices and performance', BIS Research Paper Number 211.

HM Government (2017), *Industrial Strategy: Building a Britain Fit for the Future*, White Paper, https://www.gov.uk/government/uploads/system/uploads/attachment_data/file/664563/industrial-strategy-white-paper-web-ready-version.pdf.

HM Treasury (2005), *The Green Book: Appraisal and Evaluation in Central Government*, London: The Stationery Office.

HM Treasury (2010), *Spending Review 2010 (No. PU978)*, London: The Stationery Office.

Huggins, R. and N. Williams (2009), 'Enterprise and public policy: A review of Labour government intervention in the United Kingdom', *Environment and Planning C: Government and Policy*, **27** (1), 19–41.

Karatas-Ozkan, M., A. Anderson, A. Fayolle, J. Howells and R. Condor (2014), 'Understanding entrepreneurship: Challenging dominant perspectives and theorizing entrepreneurship through new postpositivist epistemologies', *Journal of Small Business Management*, **52** (4), 589–93.

Kaufmann, A. and F. Tödtling (2002), 'How effective is innovation support for SMEs? An analysis of the region of Upper Austria', *Technovation*, **22** (3), 147–59.

Kitching, J. (2006), 'A burden on business? Reviewing the evidence base on regulation and small-business performance', *Environment and Planning C: Government and Policy*, **24** (6), 799–814.

Kitching, J., M. Hart and N. Wilson (2015), 'Burden or benefit? Regulation as a dynamic influence on small business performance', *International Small Business Journal: Researching Entrepreneurship*, **33** (2), 130–47.

Maor, M. (2017), 'Disproportionate policy response', Oxford Research Encyclopedias, Online Publication, January 2017, DOI:10.1093/acrefore/9780190228637.013.168.

Mason, C. (2009), 'Policy as a focus for small business research', *Environment and Planning C: Government and Policy*, **27** (2), 191–4.

Michael, S. C. and J. A. Pearce (2009), 'The need for innovation as a rationale for government involvement in entrepreneurship', *Entrepreneurship and Regional Development*, **21** (3), 285–302.

Mole, K., S. Roper, M. Hart, D. Storey and D. Saal (2007), *Economic Impact Study of Business Link Local Service*, http://ec.europa.eu/regional_policy/sources/docgener/evaluation/library/united_kingdom/0611_uk_business_link_eval_en.pdf.

Nesta (2016), 'Firm growth dynamics across countries: Evidence from a new database', Nesta Working Paper 16/03.

Roper, S. and M. Hart (2013), 'Supporting sustained growth among SMES – Policy models and guidelines', ERC White Paper no. 7, http://www.enterpriseresearch.ac.uk/wp-content/uploads/2013/12/ERCWhite-Paper-No-7-Roper-Hart-Supporting-sustained-growth-2.pdf.

SBS (2004), *A Government Action Plan for Small Businesses: The Evidence Base*, http://webarchive.nationalarchives.gov.uk/+/http:/www.berr.gov.uk/files/file39768.pdf.

Shane, S. (2009), 'Why encouraging more people to become entrepreneurs is bad public policy', *Small Business Economics*, **33** (2), 141–9.

Storey, D. J. (2000), *Small Business: Critical Perspectives on Business and Management*, London: Routledge.

Storey, D. and J. Frankish (2016), 'The financing of new firms: What governments need to know?', *Small Enterprise Research*, **23** (3), 276–92.

TBR (2016), 'Business growth ambitions among small and medium sized enterprises', BEIS Research Paper BEIS/16/17, https://www.gov.uk/government/publications/business-growth-ambitions-among-small-and-medium-sized-enterprises-2016.

Theodorakopoulos, N., M. Hart, G. Burke, U. Stephan, P. Braidford, G. Allinson, M. Houston and S. Jones (2015), 'Sociology of Enterprise', Research Report, BEIS.

Wapshott, R. and O. Mallett (2018), 'Small and medium-sized enterprise policy: Designed to fail?', *Environment and Planning C: Politics and Space*, **36** (4), 750–72.

World Bank (2018), 'Ease of Doing Business Index 2018', in *Doing Business 2018*, p. 4, http://www.doingbusiness.org/~/media/WBG/DoingBusiness/Documents/Annual-Reports/English/DB2018-Full-Report.pdf.

3 Placing enterprise policy in context: a policy transfer approach

Mirela Xheneti

Introduction

The past 30 years have seen enterprise policies becoming important staples of government action in seeking to solve various economic, social and, more recently, environmental challenges. An extensive body of scholarship has investigated the rationales for different government policy foci in support of enterprise development (Lundström and Stevenson, 2005; Audretsch and Beckmann, 2007). Numerous policies account for established or start-up business needs, as well as country- and regional-level differences in economic development, competitiveness and constraints to entrepreneurship (Lundström and Stevenson, 2005; Van Stel et al., 2007; Dennis, 2011; Smallbone, 2016). Yet, research repeatedly suggests that the impact of enterprise policy on entrepreneurial activity has been limited, leading some to question the value and quality of such initiatives (Curran and Storey, 2002; Shane, 2009). Critics of enterprise policy point to the poor links between policy and its outcomes, the (wrong) policy focus on start-ups instead of high-growth firms (for instance, Shane, 2009; Mason and Brown, 2013; Nightingale and Coad, 2014), the lack of clear objectives and coherence (Storey, 2000), and poor policy evaluation techniques (Pons Rotger et al., 2012).

However, there is a growing consensus that the (in)effectiveness of enterprise policy might also be related to our poor understanding of the enterprise policy-making process (for example, Arshed et al., 2014; Xheneti, 2017). One consistent theme in this group of studies is the need to shift away from a pure focus on the outcomes of enterprise policy towards the policy formulation process (see also Dennis, 2011; Smallbone, 2016), as well as the role of ideas, discourses, normative assumptions and, most importantly, context. In addition to this, and as the author of this chapter has argued elsewhere (Xheneti, 2017), there is a need to recognise how the transnational level at which enterprise policy ideas are developed, through different policy exchanges, interact with the process of translating policy at the national and local levels. This would give an emphasis to the role that a diverse set of actors, other than policy makers at the national level, have in the policy process. It could be suggested that these issues taken together would give more visibility to the multiplicity of the contexts of policy making, and the rich institutional and socio-cultural arenas that affect how policy is designed and developed. The context turn (Welter, 2011; Welter and Gartner, 2016) experienced in entrepreneurship studies is still to find its way into accounts of the enterprise policy-making process (see also Smallbone, 2016).

This chapter will, therefore, aim to understand how engagement with the policy literature might support entrepreneurship scholars to understand context issues in policy making. One possible avenue proposed in this chapter is the policy transfer/translation literature. We can capture issues of context by trying to understand how policy transfers, which countries and localities engage in to emulate or learn from policy innovations elsewhere, often lead to a number of outcomes that were not originally conceived. In providing support for this line of research, this chapter will first provide a short critique of the current knowledge on enterprise policy followed by a review of the policy transfer/translation literature. Second, the chapter will use the theoretical insights of the policy transfer approach to interpret some areas of enterprise policy and to highlight how enterprise policy studies can engage with, and contribute to, the debates in the policy transfer literature, by giving visibility to the policy context. By doing so, the chapter aims to draw an agenda for research on enterprise policy making and context.

Enterprise policy studies

The contributions of enterprise have often been discussed in relation to employment generation, raising disposable incomes, external income generation, the development of supply chains, innovation and service provision, amongst others (Fritsch and Mueller, 2004; Audretsch and Keilbach, 2004). The association of enterprise promotion with this range of outcomes has led to a long tradition in enterprise policy research of focusing on evaluating individual policy programmes and their impact (Norrman and Bager-Sjogren, 2010; Niska and Vesala, 2013). The increasing critique of enterprise policy typically emphasises the over-reliance on functional assumptions, such as 'means–ends' cause and effect nature of relationships. In contrast, there tends to be less emphasis on questioning the fundamental assumptions of these policies, the process of policy making and the way it accounts for the decoupling between policies and their results (Xheneti, 2017). As a result, research has failed to unpack what lies behind the failure of many governments to ensure a good fit between policies and the actual entrepreneurial environment (Minniti, 2008; Heinonen et al., 2010; Lundström et al., 2014).

These critical accounts have exposed the different power relations underlying enterprise policy and challenged key entrepreneurship assumptions (Perren and Dannreuther, 2013; Perren and Jennings, 2005; Ahl and Nelson, 2015; Orge, 2013). Other scholars have questioned the role given to entrepreneurship as a cure for all the problems in the economy (Howorth et al., 2009) and have pointed to the absence of policy aims and objectives, or, where present, their only modest resemblance with what entrepreneurs themselves want to achieve (Perren and Jennings, 2005; Dannreuther, 2007; Niska and Vesala, 2013). In a recent review of the Enterprise Allowance Scheme in the UK, Smith et al. (2019) suggested the disengagement of target beneficiaries in policy development as a long-standing feature of this policy, also accompanied by a reluctance to generate clear objectives and subsequent meaningful measures to afford effective evaluation. On the other hand, Wapshott and Mallett (2018), in a study of political manifestos spanning from 1964 to 2015, claimed that the use of broad categories such as small and medium-sized enterprises (SMEs) to denote businesses that have growth potential, lack access to finance and have difficulties complying with regulation has been very problematic. Rather than simply pointing to 'ineffective development, delivery and co-ordination of policy initiatives' (Wapshott and Mallett, 2018, p. 766), this homogenisation clearly highlights the need to not overlook the assumptions underlying these policies.

A smaller but growing number of studies, however, point to the need for more in-depth research into the process of policy making itself. By doing so, we can understand how policy problems are framed, how they enter the policy agenda, and how social values and beliefs influence the way in which policies are formulated (Béland, 2009; Fischer and Forester, 1993). This group of scholars moves away from casual explanations and value-free assumptions of policy. Instead, argumentation, language and interpretation are considered to play a large part in policy making (Fischer and Forester, 1993), drawing attention to the role of ideas and discourse in policy making (Hay, 2011). Ideas mainly refer to norms, world views, frames and principled beliefs, which construct and frame political reality and, in turn, affect policy making (Campbell, 2002). For example, in their study of ethnic enterprise, Ram and Trehan (2010) pointed out the importance of policy framing and the role of argumentation and interpretation in selecting what counts as evidence in policy making. Arshed et al. (2014) emphasised the importance of policy formulation, highlighting the complexity of the policy-making process and the different set of actors that are involved in this process. For Arshed et al. (2014), institutional entrepreneurs are the ones pushing particular interests and agendas forward, in a process where considerable time and effort is spent in legitimising these agendas rather than focusing on achieving policy aims.

The author of this chapter argues elsewhere the need to unpack the institutional dynamics that affect both how enterprise discourses are used by institutional actors in shaping policy making, and also the 'lived experiences' of those engaged in the policy process and the meanings they attach to various ideas and policies (Xheneti, 2017). Taken together, these studies have allowed for exploring the interactive processes within enterprise policy making, extending the scope of enterprise policy research by providing novel approaches to understanding how enterprise policy is formulated, and understanding the role played by ideas and discourses, policy actors and the institutional context.

But how do policy ideas and solutions enter policy agendas? How can entrepreneurship researchers better engage with these policy processes? One widespread view, at least in the UK context, has been the reliance on research or evidence-based policy making for designing, developing and evaluating policy. Evidence-based policy was popularised in the UK during the Blair government and had a focus on 'what worked' (Ingold and Monaghan, 2016). This view of the policy-making process attracted a lot of criticism, for assuming rationality in the policy process and for ignoring how different groups of actors might influence what counts as evidence. Just as important is the fact that very often evidence is not gathered at home, but ideas and policy solutions are found at the transnational level. The UK, for example, is widely known for borrowing policy ideas and solutions from the US (Ingold and Monaghan, 2016). In the field of women enterprise policy, Marlow et al. (2008) noted that the UK's ambition to increase the rates of female entrepreneurship to similar levels as the US has underpinned most motivations towards the development of female enterprise policies, often not taking into account the economic and social viability of encouraging more women in the UK to enter self-employment.

With the increasing global links in communication, trade and politics (Evans, 2009), and the exchange of policy assumptions through international academic and policy communities (Klyver and Bager, 2012), many domestic policy actors draw on the wide academic and policy knowledge available when framing problems and finding policy solutions in their uncertain environments. Peck (2011) captured particularly well what the policy transfer processes involved in his description of the contemporary policy-making process, which seems

> to be accelerating, as measured by the shortening of policy development cycles and the intensity of cross-jurisdictional exchanges. Today's 'fast-policy' regimes are characterised by the pragmatic borrowing of 'policies that work', by compressed reform horizons, by iterative constructions of best practice, by enlarged roles for intermediaries as 'pushers' of policy routines and technologies, and by a growing reliance on prescriptively coded forms of front-loaded advice and evaluation science. On the face of it, policy ideas and techniques have become mobile in entirely new ways – exhibiting an extended reach as well as a diversity of registers. (pp. 773–4)

Evidence-based policy and the policy transfer literature share a common concern with the use of evidence (international or domestic) in the policy development process. However, the policy transfer/translation literature, through a focus on the agency of those who select/translate evidence, may have more to offer to enterprise policy studies in their quest to understand the influences on the policy process, the actors that are involved in the travel of ideas, and how these actors interact with the local context of policy making.

The next section reviews how the policy transfer/translation literature can be applied in practice, first by delineating its main ideas and concepts and second by highlighting how its practical uses in other areas of policy can inform enterprise policy studies.

Policy transfer

Policy transfer is an umbrella term for a wide range of concepts including 'lesson drawing' (Rose, 1993), 'policy diffusion' and 'policy convergence' (Stone, 2012). This body of literature highlights how ideas, knowledge and institutions move from one setting to another (Dolowitz and Marsh, 2000, 2012). Having its origin in the political science literature, it has become truly multidisciplinary with scholars in geography and sociology, amongst others, using their own terms – mutation and mobility – to explore the processes through which policy ideas move. Policy transfer can take various forms from copying another country or region's policy to inspiration to create a new policy (Dolowitz and Marsh, 2000). Looking at other countries' or regions' experiences for improving policy is common and lies in the assumption that successful policies in one context can lead to the same outcomes in another (Dolowitz and Marsh, 2000).

The policy transfer approach distinguishes between soft transfer (referring to the adoption of policy ideas, objectives, concepts and discourses) and hard transfer (referring to the implementation of policy programmes, actions and tools) (Dolowitz and Marsh, 1996; Evans and Davies, 1999). Most policy transfer has been considered 'touristic' in nature (Ingold and Monaghan, 2016), implying that policy makers decide to adopt something they like from another country or region. There is consensus in the literature that policy makers choose policy transfer for internal reasons related to the economic, political and social characteristics in their country, or for external reasons related to pressures that might come from International Organisations (IOs) and their powerful discourses or their conditionalities (Dolowitz and Marsh, 2000; Hoberg, 2001). For example, the transition studies literature talks about conditionality of European Union (EU) membership (Schimmelfennig and Sedelmeier, 2004). Giest (2017), on the other hand, showed how uncertainty and competition push many policy makers in the field of innovation policy to adopt Silicon Valley models, although often with unsatisfactory results.

Despite most of the policy transfer literature privileging governmental actors over other policy stakeholders (Peck, 2011; McCann and Ward, 2012; Stone, 2012), there is also a large emphasis on the diversity of actors, other than governmental actors alone, who engage in spreading and legitimising ideas and knowledge (Prince, 2012; Stone, 2017). Hameiri and Jones (2016) argued that leading global institutions significantly shape the process of policy making in countries across the globe. Stone (2017), on the other hand, drew attention to a much wider body of actors that are engaged in policy transfer, including non-governmental organisations (NGOs), philanthropic bodies, think tanks, consultancy companies and professional associations, and the role they play in 'providing the norms, evidence and (social) scientific understandings as to "why" it makes bureaucratic and political sense to transfer policy' (p. 62). It is also worth noting that policy transfer does not occur only at the transnational scale but is embedded in complex multi-site and multi-scalar networks, from the international to the regional and urban (Jones et al., 2014). Giest (2017), for example, showed how the Silicon Valley model emerged as one of the main archetypes of entrepreneurial ecosystems and was transferred not only to other US cities such as New Jersey and Texas but also EU countries and South Korea.

In addition, different criteria have been used to judge whether policy transfer has occurred or not, and if it has been successful or has failed. The reasons for policy failure, though difficult to identify in practice, have been conceptually attributed to three conditions: 'uninformed transfer', when the policy transfer is based on inaccurate or insufficient information about the original policy; 'incomplete transfer', when crucial features of what made the policy successful in the original country/region are not transferred; and 'inappropriate transfer', when there are essential contextual differences between the policy-originating country/region and the policy-transferring country/region (Dolowitz and Marsh, 2000; Dolowitz and Medearis, 2009).

However, as McCann and Ward (2012) suggested, by linking policy transfer to failure, the study of policy transfer 'becomes the object of debate rather than facilitating analyses of the social processes that constitute policy transfer' (p. 327). Not only do the meanings and interpretations of policies change when they move from one context to another, but the linear transmission of policy is complicated by the numerous policy actors (in a broad sense) involved at different stages (Mukhtarov, 2014) with regard to the social and spatial embedding of the policy into its target audience. Policies are not simply learned and adopted but, rather, translated, hybridised, mutated or adapted through interaction between policy makers and the wide range of stakeholders (or policy pushers), including civil servants, political parties and pressure groups, policy think tanks, supranational organisations and international financial institutions (Peck, 2011).

These processes lead to certain policy ideas gaining acceptance as means of tackling social, economic or environmental problems in countries or localities (Jones et al., 2014). Considering the complexity of the policy process as contingent on both politics and context (Mukhtarov, 2014), policy making can be conceptualised as a socially embedded translation process (Lendvai and Stubbs, 2009; Peck, 2011; Prince, 2010), reflecting both policy makers' intentional choices and stakeholder influence (intended and inadvertent), shaped by institutional and cultural contexts (Dolowitz and Medearis, 2009).

What would this process of translation look like in practice? How can researchers engage in studying the policy-making process? Ingold and Monaghan (2016) captured the ideas behind the utilisation and translation of knowledge by considering the policy process as a continuous process of designing and re-interpreting policy to respond to policy problems (See Figure 3.1). As with most policy-making frameworks, the starting point is the need to solve a problem. However, the framework allows for considering the different contexts where ideas, knowledge and evidence come from, as well as the ways in which they are interpreted and by whom. It is not surprising that the model places policy translators (people, organisations, networks) at its core, in order to capture not just their agency but also their embeddedness in context.

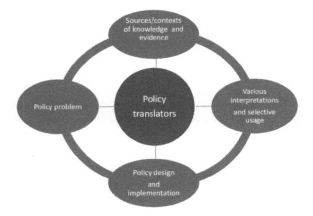

Source: Adapted from Ingold and Monaghan (2016).

Figure 3.1   Policy as translation

Finally, as a policy gets designed and implemented, it is subjected to a process of continuous interpretation. Insights from the literature reviewed show that knowledge exchange is highly dependent on the setting it occurs in, as well as on the actors involved in the process. As a result, there is a strong rationale for viewing policy transfer/translation as 'mediated action' or, in other words, as a process that is prone to different interpretations, localisations, as well as bricolage or assemblage (McCann and Ward, 2013; Stone, 2017). These insights are important in our understanding of the development of enterprise policies in their context.

Using the policy transfer literature in studying enterprise policy

Although we rarely talk about policy transfer in enterprise policy making, there are plenty of such examples. This is evidenced in the prominence across the globe of the enterprise discourse and the promotion of entrepreneurship as something good, to be encouraged in order to improve the competitiveness of our economies. Like other areas of policy, academic and expert knowledge on enterprise is continuously shared through international academic communities such as the Global Entrepreneurship Monitor (Klyver and Bager, 2012), think tanks (Arshed, 2017) and consultancy organisations, which legitimise the inclusion and priority role of enterprise policy in government agendas. Most importantly, a number of IOs – EU, World Bank, Organisation for Economic Co-operation and Development (OECD) – provide normative standards in relation to how enterprise policy should develop and the policy dimensions that countries need to have in place. The EU, for example, has had an Entrepreneurship Action Plan since 2003 and a Small Business Act since 2011 (former SME Charter established in 2000), each aiming to promote entrepreneurship and to support SMEs through an enabling regulatory and policy environment. Similarly, the World Bank runs its annual Doing Business Survey, which captures various dimensions of the business environment.

Very often these different frameworks rank countries' level of enterprise development and emphasise 'best practices' in doing business or in establishing an entrepreneurial environment, which countries should utilise and learn from in order to improve their global rankings. Another recent example of enterprise policy transfer comes from another area of enterprise policy – social inclusion policy. In the case of policies for minority and disadvantaged groups, the EU and OECD in particular have played an important role, not only in raising awareness of the benefits of entrepreneurship for this group but also through sharing ideas and knowledge about how these policies might look like in practice, by providing examples of various different countries in their Missing Entrepreneurs' series. Additionally, a Better Entrepreneurship Policy Tool was recently launched with the aim of providing various stakeholders with a tool to rate and reflect on inclusive entrepreneurship policies in their countries/ regions, as well as to learn from various national good practices.

While what has been captured in these short paragraphs are all forms of enterprise policy transfer in action, there is very little enterprise policy literature that engages with ideas from the policy transfer literature in understanding how each of these different actors, and the practices they use, are translated into national policy making and with what effects. As the author has argued in her work on policy transfer in the case of Albania (a former socialist country looking to access EU membership), policy making is a complex process influenced by different actors, most notably IOs. While these transnational organisations do have an influence on how most countries achieve the different global/EU objectives in relation to enterprise policy, their influence is much higher in the case of countries like Albania who are undergoing institutional change, because of their need to have a clear framework to follow and their lack of resources. IOs' use of particular language, focus, policies and sites to communicate enterprise narratives leads to particular interpretations of problems and policies independently of their context (Xheneti, 2011; Xheneti and Kitching, 2011; Xheneti, 2017). These particular institutional dynamics – the interaction of the transnational and national level of policy making – provide the needed contextualisation of policy making. By placing an emphasis on 'the changing configurations of knowledge, policy tools and resources, and actors involved in the process and their understandings' (Xheneti, 2017, p. 334) we might be able to pinpoint those characteristics of context that lead to a gap between the policy's intentions and its outcomes. Transition countries, like Albania, might appear to be the obvious focus for using policy transfer studies to understand the role of the institutional context, given the unequal power relations between them and the organisations that offer 'soft' or 'hard' forms of policy solutions.

It can be suggested, however, that enterprise policy studies more generally can engage in many ways with the policy transfer/translation literature. First, the literature reviewed provides a useful lens for understanding what types of policy ideas and evidence enter the policy-making process, who pushes them, how they are understood across time and space, and how the local context is incorporated in policy making. By studying the actual process of policy making rather than its outcomes (as is currently the case with most enterprise policy studies) we can also find out how local actors use their beliefs and practices in modifying policies from abroad or other regions, rather than being mere passive learners. Stone (2017), for example, referred to how China's approach to policy transfer has been one of putting together various ideas from different sources when making policy reflect its long tradition of institutional bricolage. Another example is that of business accelerators, which have received considerable attention in supporting start-ups. While starting off as organisations within Silicon Valley, these types of organisations have now mushroomed in different countries/regions, with their aim changing from a limited focus on funding to that of supporting economic development despite limited evidence to suggest their effectiveness in practice. Vanaelst et al. (2018), for example, suggested that the EU's promotion of accelerators is 'part of a broader macro-economic plan ... to support accelerators in creating flourishing entrepreneurial ecosystems' (p. 137). The prominence gained by the accelerators across regions/countries points to the role of knowledge exchange, highlighting the relevance of the policy transfer literature in explaining accelerators' use as policy tools.

Second, and following from the above, the policy transfer literature also provides a great opportunity for understanding the role of a diverse set of actors in influencing the policy process. Apart from the role of IOs discussed earlier, one other avenue would be to look at the role of the consultants who these organisations hire to provide policy support in different countries/regions and different areas of enterprise policy. Prince (2012) suggested that the global policy networks which consultants are a part of 'are networks that cut across international space, creating communities of actors that are situated in their national political contexts but also in these international networks where their practices are often shaped, even if not entirely directed' (p. 200).

Consultants are, therefore, widely engaged in agenda setting and policy formulation despite their practices not being well understood (Prince, 2012). Looking at consultants and their organisations, the nature of their contracts, the networks they are part of, and how they utilise knowledge to inform policy would add value to the study of enterprise policy.

Third, the policy transfer lens draws attention to the methods used in conducting policy research. Most critical entrepreneurship studies rely upon discourse analysis of policy documents to understand the policy assumptions in different contexts (see, for example, studies on women enterprise policies: Ahl and Marlow, 2019; Ahl and Nelson, 2015). These studies, however, failed to unpack how these different ideas and discourses enter the political agenda, and the way local policy actors interpret and mobilise them within the social and cultural contexts that affect them. Enterprise policy scholars should use a more diverse set of methods to include not just policy documents (despite their valuable use) but also interviews, observations and participation of researchers in the organisations that influence and make policy. These different methods can help to tease out the contextual elements that explain how policy is designed and developed, and to provide a better understanding of the different practices utilised by different actors.

Conclusion

The aim of this chapter is to propose the use of policy transfer/translation literature as a lens for studying the enterprise policy-making process. Building on the current discontent in the enterprise literature with the impact of enterprise policies, the chapter aims to emphasise the role that an understanding of the policy-making process plays in drawing relevant conclusions about policy effectiveness. By highlighting the complexity of the policy process and the multi-site and multi-scalar networks involved in it, the chapter draws attention to the need to study the processes through which enterprise policy ideas travel across different countries/regions and at different points in time. One of the main takeaways from the literature reviewed in this chapter is the idea of an ongoing policy-making process through which policies are translated, amended, hybridised or mutated as they try to fit various contexts and speak to different audiences. While the similar engagement of countries with enterprise policies is well documented and evidenced in various studies, there is a need for research to take the policy dimension as the unit of analysis.

A better engagement with the policy transfer/translation literature and its uses in different disciplines would open up new avenues for researching the types of policies and mechanisms through which they move from one country/region to another, and the conditions that facilitate such moves including policy communities and various policy artefacts. Through placing focus on the agency of those who drive policy – politicians, civil servants, consultants, organisations, networks – this literature captures how different interpretations of policy are a reflection of contextual embeddedness. Through sensitivity to context, this body of literature is best suited towards understanding how different interpretations and localisations of policies would lead to reimagined policies in those particular contexts. The framework proposed by Ingold and Monaghan (2016) provides a starting point in using this policy lens to understand, and conduct research in, various enterprise policy areas.

Finally, this chapter suggests that the current methods used in enterprise policy research might not be entirely suitable for understanding the interpretive nature of policy making. As a result, alternative methods such as interviews or ethnographic studies might provide more useful information in researching enterprise policy. Overall, the chapter contributes to calls for ensuring a good fit between enterprise policies and the actual entrepreneurial environment, and for taking into account contextual differences in explaining policy outcomes by providing a better understanding of the enterprise policy-making process. As such, the intention is to further suggest that opening up the 'black box' of policy design and development should provide some of the answers the enterprise policy field is looking for.

References

Ahl, H. and S. Marlow (2019), 'Exploring the false promise of entrepreneurship through a postfeminist critique of the enterprise policy discourse in Sweden and the UK', *Human Relations*, https://doi.org/10.1177/0018726719848480.

Ahl, H. and T. Nelson (2015), 'How policy positions women entrepreneurs: A comparative analysis of state discourse in Sweden and the United States', *Journal of Business Venturing*, **30** (2), 273–91.

Arshed, N. (2017), 'The origins of policy ideas: The importance of think tanks in the enterprise policy process in the UK', *Journal of Business Research*, **71**, 74–83.

Arshed, N., S. Carter and C. Mason (2014), 'The ineffectiveness of entrepreneurship policy: Is policy formulation to blame?', *Small Business Economics*, **43** (3), 639–59.

Audretsch, D. B. and I. A. M. Beckmann (2007), 'From small business to entrepreneurship policy', in D. B. Audretsch, I. Grilo and A. R. Thurik (eds), *Handbook of Research on Entrepreneurship Policy*, Cheltenham, UK and Northampton, MA, USA: Edward Elgar Publishing, pp. 36–53.

Audretsch, D. B. and M. Keilbach (2004), 'Entrepreneurship capital and economic performance', *Regional Studies*, **38** (8), 949–60.

Béland, D. (2009), 'Ideas, institutions, and policy change', *Journal of European Public Policy*, **16** (5), 701–18.

Campbell, J. L. (2002), 'Ideas, politics, and public policy', *Annual Review of Sociology*, **28** (1), 21–38.

Curran, J. and D. J. Storey (2002), 'Small business policy in the United Kingdom: The inheritance of the Small Business Service and implications for its future effectiveness', *Environment and Planning C: Government and Policy*, **20** (2), 163–77.

Dannreuther, C. (2007), 'A zeal for a zeal? SME policy and the political economy of the EU', *Comparative European Politics*, **5** (4), 377–99.

Dennis, W. J. (2011), 'Entrepreneurship, small business and public policy levers', *Journal of Small Business Management*, **49** (1), 92–106.

Dolowitz, D. and D. Marsh (1996), 'Who learns what from whom: A review of the policy transfer literature', *Political Studies*, **44** (2), 343–57.

Dolowitz, D. P. and D. Marsh (2000), 'Learning from abroad: The role of policy transfer in contemporary policy-making', *Governance: An International Journal of Policy and Administration*, **13** (1), 5–24.

Dolowitz, D. P. and D. Marsh (2012), 'The future of policy transfer research', *Political Studies Review*, **10** (3), 339–45.

Dolowitz, D. P. and D. Medearis (2009), 'Considerations of the obstacles and opportunities to formalizing cross-national policy transfer to the United States: A case study of the transfer of urban environmental and planning policies from Germany', *Environment and Planning C: Government and Policy*, **27** (4), 684–97.

Evans, M. (2009), 'Policy transfer in critical perspective', *Policy Studies*, **30** (3), 243–68.

Evans, M. and J. Davies (1999), 'Understanding policy transfer: A multi-level, multi-disciplinary perspective', *Public Administration*, **77** (2), 361–85.

Fischer, F. and R. Forester (eds) (1993), *The Argumentative Turn in Policy Analysis and Planning*, London: University College Press.

Fritsch, M. and P. Mueller (2004), 'Effects of new business formation on regional development over time', *Regional Studies*, **38** (8), 961–75.

Giest, S. (2017), 'Overcoming the failure of "Silicon somewheres": Learning in policy transfer processes', *Policy and Politics*, **45** (1), 39–54.

Hameiri, S. and L. Jones (2016), 'Global governance as state transformation', *Political Studies*, **64** (4), 793–810.

Hay, C. (2011), 'Interpreting interpretivism interpreting interpretations: The new hermeneutics of public administration', *Public Administration*, **89** (1), 167–82.

Heinonen, J., U. Hytti and T. M. Cooney (2010), 'The context matters: Understanding the evolution of Finnish and Irish entrepreneurship policies', *Management Research Review*, **33** (12), 1158–73.

Hoberg, G. (2001), 'Globalization and policy convergence: Symposium overview', *Journal of Comparative Policy Analysis: Research and Practice*, **3**, 127–32.

Howorth, C., C. Parkinson and A. Southern (2009), 'Does enterprise discourse have the power to enable or disable deprived communities?', in H. Landström, D. Smallbone and D. Jones-Evans (eds), *Entrepreneurship and Growth in Local, Regional and National Economies: Frontiers in European Entrepreneurship Research*, Cheltenham, UK and Northampton, MA, USA: Edward Elgar Publishing, pp. 281–311.

Ingold, J. and M. Monaghan (2016), 'Evidence translation: An exploration of policy makers' use of evidence', *Policy and Politics*, **44** (2), 171–90.

Jones, R., J. Pykett and M. Whitehead (2014), 'The geographies of policy translation: How nudge became the default policy option', *Environment and Planning C: Government and Policy*, **32** (1), 54–69.

Klyver, K. and T. E. Bager (2012), 'Entrepreneurship policy as institutionalised and powerful myths', *International Journal of Entrepreneurial Venturing*, **4** (4), 409–26.

Lendvai, N. and P. Stubbs (2009), 'Assemblages, translation, and intermediaries in South East Europe: Rethinking transnationalism and social policy', *European Societies*, **11** (5), 673–95.

Lundström, A. and L. Stevenson (2005), *Entrepreneurship Policy: Theory and Practice*, New York: Springer.

Lundström, A., P. Vikström, M. Fink, M. Meuleman, P. Głodek, D. J. Storey and A. Kroksgård (2014), 'Measuring the costs and coverage of SME and entrepreneurship policy: A pioneering study', *Entrepreneurship Theory and Practice*, **38** (4), 941–57.

Marlow, S., S. Carter and E. Shaw (2008), 'Constructing female entrepreneurship policy in the UK: Is the US a relevant benchmark?', *Environment and Planning C: Government and Policy*, **26** (2), 335–51.

Mason, C. and R. Brown (2013), 'Creating good public policy to support high-growth firms', *Small Business Economics*, **40** (2), 211–25.

McCann, E. and K. Ward (2012), 'Policy assemblages, mobilities and mutations: Toward a multidisciplinary conversation', *Political Studies Review*, **10** (3), 325–32.

McCann, E. and K. Ward (2013), 'A multi-disciplinary approach to policy transfer research: Geographies, assemblages, mobilities and mutations', *Policy Studies*, **34** (1), 2–18.

Minniti, M. (2008), 'The role of government policy on entrepreneurial activity: Productive, unproductive, or destructive?', *Entrepreneurship Theory and Practice*, **32** (5), 779–90.

Mukhtarov, F. (2014), 'Rethinking the travel of ideas: Policy translation in the water sector', *Policy and Politics*, **42** (1), 71–88.

Nightingale, P. and A. Coad (2014), 'Muppets and gazelles: Political and methodological biases in entrepreneurship research', *Industrial and Corporate Change*, **23** (1), 113–43.

Niska, M. and K. M. Vesala (2013), 'SME policy implementation as a relational challenge', *Entrepreneurship and Regional Development*, **25** (5–6), 521–40.

Norrman, C. and L. Bager-Sjogren (2010), 'Entrepreneurship policy to support new innovative ventures: Is it effective?', *International Small Business Journal*, **28** (6), 602–19.

Orge, O. (2013), 'Entrepreneurship policy as discourse: Appropriation of entrepreneurial agency', in F. Welter, R. A. Blackburn, E. Ljunggren and B. Willy Amo (eds), *Entrepreneurial Business and Society: Frontiers in European Entrepreneurship Research*, Cheltenham, UK and Northampton, MA, USA: Edward Elgar Publishing, pp. 37–57.

Peck, J. (2011), 'Geographies of policy: From transfer-diffusion to mobility-mutation', *Progress in Human Geography*, **35** (6), 773–97.

Perren, L. and C. Dannreuther (2013), 'Political signification of the entrepreneur: Temporal analysis of constructs, agency and reification', *International Small Business Journal*, **31** (6), 603–28.

Perren, L. and P. L. Jennings (2005), 'Government discourses on entrepreneurship: Issues of legitimization, subjugation, and power', *Entrepreneurship Theory and Practice*, **29** (2), 173–84.

Pons Rotger, G., M. Gørtz and D. Storey (2012), 'Assessing the effectiveness of guided preparation for new venture creation and performance: Theory and practice', *Journal of Business Venturing*, **27** (4), 506–21.

Prince, R. (2010), 'Policy transfer as policy assemblage: Making policy for the creative industries in New Zealand', *Environment and Planning A: Economy and Space*, **42** (1), 169–86.

Prince, R. (2012), 'Policy transfer, consultants and the geographies of governance', *Progress in Human Geography*, **36** (2), 188–203.

Ram, M. and K. Trehan (2010), 'Critical action learning, policy learning and small firms: An inquiry', *Management Learning*, **41** (4), 415–28.

Rose, R. (1993), *Lesson-Drawing in Public Policy: A Guide to Learning across Time and Space*, Cambridge: Cambridge University Press.

Schimmelfennig, F. and U. Sedelmeier (2004), 'Governance by conditionality: EU rule transfer to the candidate countries of Central and Eastern Europe', *Journal of European Public Policy*, **11** (4), 661–79.

Shane, S. (2009), 'Why encouraging more people to become entrepreneurs is bad public policy', *Small Business Economics*, **33** (2), 141–9.

Smallbone, D. (2016), 'Entrepreneurship policy: Issues and challenges', *Small Enterprise Research*, **23** (3), 201–18.

Smith, A. M., L. Galloway, L. Jackman, M. Danson and G. Whittam (2019), 'Poverty, social exclusion and enterprise policy: A study of UK policies' effectiveness over 40 years', *International Journal of Entrepreneurship and Innovation*, **20** (2), 107–18.

Stone, D. (2012), 'Transfer and translation of policy', *Policy Studies*, **33** (6), 483–99.

Stone, D. (2017), 'Understanding the transfer of policy failure: Bricolage, experimentalism and translation', *Policy and Politics*, **45** (1), 55–70.

Storey, D. J. (2000), *Small Business: Critical Perspectives on Business and Management*, London: Routledge.

Van Stel, A., D. J. Storey and R. Thurik (2007), 'The effect of business regulations on nascent and young business entrepreneurship', *Small Business Economics*, **28** (2–3), 171–86.

Vanaelst, I., J. Van Hove and M. Wright (2018), 'Revolutionizing entrepreneurial ecosystems through US and European accelerator policy', in M. Wright and I. Drori (eds), *Accelerators: Successful Venture Creation and Growth*, Cheltenham, UK and Northampton, MA, USA: Edward Elgar Publishing, pp. 123–41.

Wapshott, R. and O. Mallett (2018), 'Small and medium-sized enterprise policy: Designed to fail?', *Environment and Planning C: Politics and Space*, **36** (4), 750–72.

Welter, F. (2011), 'Contextualizing entrepreneurship – Conceptual challenges and ways forward', *Entrepreneurship Theory and Practice*, **35** (1), 165–84.

Welter, F. and W. B. Gartner (eds) (2016), *A Research Agenda for Entrepreneurship and Context*, Cheltenham, UK and Northampton, MA, USA: Edward Elgar Publishing.

Xheneti, M. (2011), 'Entrepreneurship policy transfer: The case of the SME policy framework in Albania', in D. Smallbone and F. Welter (eds), *Handbook of Entrepreneurship Policy in Central and Eastern Europe*, Cheltenham, UK and Northampton, MA, USA: Edward Elgar Publishing, pp. 169–89.

Xheneti, M. (2017), 'Contexts of enterprise policy-making: An institutional perspective', *Entrepreneurship and Regional Development*, **29** (3–4), 317–39.
Xheneti, M. and J. Kitching (2011), 'From discourse to implementation: Enterprise policy development in postcommunist Albania', *Environment and Planning C: Government and Policy*, **29** (6), 1018–36.

4 A research agenda for entrepreneurship policy

David Storey and Jonathan Potter[1]

Introduction

Public expenditure on support of entrepreneurship is rarely documented in full. In part this is because expenditure is incurred by a wide range of ministries and agencies, of both national and sub-national government, as well as by international organisations such as the European Union (EU). This makes tracking all items of expenditure very time-consuming and hence expensive. However, where estimates have been made, they show that this expenditure is considerable and broadly in line with expenditure on the police or universities (Lundström et al., 2014). Given the scale and opacity of public expenditures on entrepreneurship, evaluation has a critical role to play in establishing the benefits achieved and the extent to which different entrepreneurship policy interventions are justified by their impacts.

A number of groups and organisations have been making the case for more widespread and rigorous evaluation of entrepreneurship and small and medium-sized enterprise (SME) policies for more than two decades. These include academic economists and consultants, but particularly international organisations such as the European Commission, the World Bank and the United Nations. The Organisation for Economic Co-operation and Development (OECD) has been one of the leading bodies in this endeavour through its Working Party on SMEs and Entrepreneurship.

In its OECD Istanbul Ministerial Declaration of 2004, ministers and representatives of government recognised:

> The need to develop a strong evaluation culture in ministries and agencies responsible for SME policies and programmes: Evaluation provides a means of ensuring

that SME programmes remain cost-effective and adapt to changing conditions in a dynamic world. Ideally, evaluation would be mandated and budgeted for when programmes are designed, would be carried out by independent but informed evaluators, and would generate recommendations for improving and strengthening those programmes that should be retained. (OECD, 2004, p. 4)

The OECD followed up this call by publishing the OECD Framework for the Evaluation of SME and Entrepreneurship Policies and Programmes (OECD, 2007). The Framework provides policy makers with a guide to best practice evaluation methods for SME and entrepreneurship policies, drawing upon examples from a wide range of countries.

At the OECD ministerial conference on SME and entrepreneurship policy in Mexico City in 2018, ministers and representatives of government reaffirmed their commitment to spreading an evaluation culture in this field, recommitting to pursue their efforts in 'continuing the development, implementation and evaluation of effective policies for SMEs' (OECD, 2018a, p. 4).

However, despite the improvements in data and techniques of entrepreneurship policy evaluation over the last 20 years, there is still some way to go before rigorous evaluation is adopted as an integral part of entrepreneurship policy making. This is evident from various reviews of evaluation practice in this area in specific countries.

For example, the United States Government Accountability Office (GAO) report for 2012 reviewed 53 entrepreneurship programmes in four different agencies – with an aggregate budget of USD 2.6 billion –and found:

> for 39 of the 53 programs, the four agencies have either never conducted a performance evaluation or have conducted only one in the past decade. For example, while SBA [Small Business Administration] has conducted recent periodic reviews of 3 of its 10 programs that provide technical assistance, the agency has not reviewed its other 9 financial assistance and government contracting programs on any regular basis. (GAO, 2012, p. 56)

A very similar theme emerged in a review for the UK National Audit Office (NAO), which further points to entrepreneurship policy evaluation being both less frequent and technically weaker than evaluation in other policy domains. The NAO review examined 35 UK government evaluations in the policy areas of active labour markets, business support, education and spatial policy, and concluded:

> our overall assessment would be that none of the business support or spatial policy evaluations provided convincing evidence of policy impacts. In contrast, 6 out of

9 of the education reports and 6 (arguably 7) out of 10 labour market reports were of sufficient standard to have some confidence in the impacts attributed to policy. (NAO, 2006)

The lack of an embedded system of rigorous evaluation of entrepreneurship policy is also true in many other countries, despite a growing number of top-quality individual evaluations. Calls for better evaluation frameworks and practices are standard in OECD country reviews of SME and entrepreneurship policies. For example, the OECD review of SME and entrepreneurship policy in Mexico highlighted that, although monitoring of entrepreneurship policy expenditures was very strong, there was only one example of a robust estimation procedure for the impact of an individual entrepreneurship programme funded through the government's main SME Fund (OECD, 2013).

Taking a more international lens, Eurofound (2016) identified and reviewed 66 publicly funded youth entrepreneurship programmes in EU Member States and reported that the growing interest in youth entrepreneurship has not been matched by sound evaluations of the impact of the initiatives. Only 3 out of 66 programmes used advanced and robust statistical methods to assess impact.

This chapter acknowledges that entrepreneurship policy makers may, in the past, have been uneasy over both the reliability of evaluations in this area and the time taken to reach conclusions in a fast-moving policy world. Such unease was magnified when evaluations were unable to point clearly to policy success. However, during the last decade, analytical advances, data improvements, and a diversity of policy initiatives and country contexts means an increasingly clear picture is emerging of policy impact. This reinforces the case for governments to conduct, or commission others to conduct, rigorous evaluations. This then enables the impact of current policies to be validly benchmarked and the findings to be incorporated into policy making.

The case for entrepreneurship policy evaluation

Evaluation is a critical tool for policy making in any policy field. It offers accountability for public action by showing benefits and costs and establishing whether an initiative offers value for money. It is the key basis for an evidence-based approach to making decisions about which policy measures merit being retained or scaled-up on the one hand, or scaled-down or terminated on the other, thus driving up the effectiveness and efficiency of the policy portfolio as a whole. Where evaluations can examine the impact of different policy designs and implementation approaches, they can also help identify how policy measures may be improved.

The central issue evaluation must address is whether each initiative under scrutiny is relevant and effective in addressing a significant economic or social problem – a market failure, a poor equity outcome, or a government failure – and whether it brings benefits in a cost-efficient manner.

The key rationale for many aspects of entrepreneurship policy is to address market failure. Information imperfections and externalities are among the most cited market failures in the area of entrepreneurship policy. Information imperfections are the basis for interventions such as enhancing access to finance for some or all entrepreneurs or enterprises. A similar justification underpins the public funding of advice, information or management training. The presence of externalities is seen to justify policies to support innovative start-ups, on the grounds that they provide spillover benefits for the rest of the community in terms of job and wealth creation. In principle, where there are important market failures, an entrepreneurship policy should be able to increase economic efficiency. However, whether it does so in practice needs to be established by evaluation.

In recent years, particularly in OECD countries, policy makers have placed emphasis on the social, as well as the economic, dimensions of entrepreneurship policy. For example, many OECD countries operate programmes to support the entry into enterprise of under-represented groups in entrepreneurship or of disadvantaged groups in the labour market – for example, women, youth, migrants or the unemployed (see for example OECD/European Union, 2017 and OECD/European Union, 2016). Evaluation has a key role to play in establishing whether entrepreneurship policies meet the objective of increasing social inclusion in a cost-effective manner.

Evaluation should, therefore, be the bedrock of entrepreneurship policy, demonstrating that the initiatives pursued have objectives that are appropriate to the needs and are effective and efficient in meeting their objectives. Systematic evaluation evidence across the whole policy portfolio is at a premium because of the wide range of different objectives and policy measures in place and the wide heterogeneity of the enterprises and entrepreneurs targeted.

Evaluation is particularly needed in the specific case of entrepreneurship policy given the existential questions posed of entrepreneurship policy, particularly the provision of resources for entrepreneurs or start-ups (such as loans or consultancy), as opposed to addressing problems in government insti-tutions. The concerns include ideas such as – many people are not suited to entrepreneurship; large numbers of supported enterprises and entrepreneurs are likely to fail given low survival rates in general; supported enterprises may displace non-supported enterprises; and attempted *ex ante* targeting of enter-prises experiencing both a market failure problem and a capacity for growth and survival is difficult. The concerns were most recently re-voiced by Shane (2009),[2] who argued that a policy seeking to increase the number of start-ups is flawed because the typical start-up is not innovative, creates few jobs and gen-erates little wealth. Furthermore, influential recent reviews suggested that the evaluation evidence currently available does not offer a clear-cut justification for entrepreneurship policy. For example, Acs et al. (2016, p. 35) say:

> Reviewing established evidence we find that most Western world policies do not greatly reduce or solve any market failures but instead waste taxpayers' money, encourage those already intent on becoming entrepreneurs, and mostly generate one-employee businesses with low-growth intentions and a lack of interest in innovating.

The issue about whether and when entrepreneurship policy is effective is 'live' in part because, compared with many other government policy areas, it is relatively novel. With the notable exception of the US Small Business Administration, no country in the world had a suite of entrepreneurship pol-icies 40 years ago. Its 'newness' as a policy area may be part of the explanation for why it is not yet fully established in terms of its justifications and opera-tional methods.

In this context, the policy maker has to rely even more heavily on evaluation evidence. There is effectively a policy experimentation process in place in which entrepreneurship support measures will often be introduced on a 'trial and evaluate' basis, with the policy maker needing to be prepared to remove the intervention or modify it if the evaluation is not positive. In the long run, a large and reliable body of evaluation will help policy makers decide where interventions are most likely to be justified, based on evidence that shows that a particular type of entrepreneurship policy intervention has been effective in a particular type of situation. Such an evidence base can help pin down which parts of an entrepreneurship policy portfolio are really effective and which are not. For example, is equity finance for innovative companies effective where grants for enterprises in non-tradable sectors are not? Or are start-up grants effective where advice and training for potential entrepreneurs are not?

Principles for entrepreneurship policy evaluation

The OECD (2007, pp. 32–5) Framework for the Evaluation of SME and Entrepreneurship Policies and Programmes identified a number of key principles for evaluation practice:

- Evaluation should lead to policy change.
- Evaluation should be part of the policy debate.
- Evaluators should be 'in at the start', including the establishment of an evaluation budget for a policy and tangible objectives against which to evaluate.
- Evaluation techniques should always use the most appropriate methodology, including provision for appropriate control and treatment group data.
- Evaluation should apply to all policies and programmes.
- International comparisons should be made where necessary.

The Framework considered the issue of the choice of evaluation technique in some depth. This included a discussion of the strengths and weaknesses of quantitative and qualitative evaluation, concluding that whereas qualitative evaluations have key strengths in engaging stakeholders and providing rich insights on how policy works, quantitative evaluations are essential for providing reliable evidence on impact. For quantitative impact evaluation the Six Steps to Heaven guidance was provided. This recommended that evaluators seek to undertake, and policy makers seek to commission, Step VI evaluations that use control groups and take account of selection bias. The techniques themselves will be discussed later in more detail, but here it is stressed that there are three critical principles for entrepreneurship policy evaluation – setting policy objectives, using evaluation results, and getting data.

Set out the objectives for each intervention

To assess whether an entrepreneurship policy is effective, it is necessary to clearly identify the impacts the policy is intended to have. These objectives should be set out by policy makers at the outset of introducing the policy; if not, they will have to be inferred by evaluators when they start work. Most importantly, the objectives should include expected outcomes, such as numbers of surviving start-ups or levels of export activity generated, rather than just inputs and activities, such as the numbers of potential entrepreneurs who receive training or the number of start-ups that receive finance.

There is a wide diversity of entrepreneurship policy objectives with important implications for what needs to be evaluated. Three key types of entrepreneurship approaches can be distinguished in this respect:

1. The start-up approach: Here the policy objective is to increase the number of businesses in the economy, or to increase the number of new businesses established (by implication ignoring the number of businesses that close). These become the key yardstick measures for evaluation.
2. The growth approach: The policy objective here is to create and support 'better', rather than simply 'more', firms. Such policies include providing hard and soft[3] support for more productive, innovative or exporting firms. The central justification for this policy is that it has been widely shown that job creation in start-ups is heavily concentrated in a small proportion of enterprises (often known as gazelles) which are more productive, innovative and more likely to sell overseas.[4]
3. The social inclusion approach: Here the focus is on increasing the labour market attachment of disadvantaged population groups in the labour market and achieving equal opportunities in entrepreneurship. The yardstick measures will, therefore, focus on employment and entrepreneurship outcomes for people in different social groups.

The challenge for researchers and policy makers is to judge the objectives of a programme and to assess it against these objectives.

Unfortunately, a key step that is frequently omitted in policy development is setting out a theory of change, or logical framework, showing the process through which the policy intervention is expected to address a problem and with what expected benefits, as well as possible positive or negative side effects. A well-designed policy and evaluation are mutually supportive; the design stage helps identify the processes and outcomes an evaluation should seek to measure, while the evaluation helps establish whether the processes and outcomes were as expected.

Make use of evaluation results

Evaluation should be a critical input into an ongoing 'policy cycle' informing policy formulation, implementation and re-formulation. At the policy formulation stage it is important to anticipate the evaluation activities that will take place and to appraise policy alternatives by taking stock of any relevant, existing evaluation evidence. During the policy implementation stage data has to be collected on the take-up of programmes, including by different target groups (for example, male and female entrepreneurs), and first results. This helps to identify any implementation problems that may require correction. A final evaluation should then review the impact, in terms of the specified objectives, once a programme has been running long enough to achieve results. These results should be used in a policy re-formulation stage, based on judgements on the extent to which the intervention has been successful. The evaluation itself should seek to make clear, evidence-based recommendations for future developments concerning the intervention. Unfortunately, evaluations are still often seen as historic, technical exercises that are separate from current policy making. The outcome of this is that decisions about policy are frequently made without reference to evaluation findings.

Finally, for maximum effectiveness, evaluation should be applied systematically across all entrepreneurship policy interventions in a given territory. Reliable and comparable evaluation evidence is needed across all interventions with the same objectives, in order to assist policy makers to arrive at an appropriate intervention mix. Only in this way can the cost-effectiveness of, for example, 'hard' and 'soft' policies be validly compared.

Getting data

Reliable impact evaluation depends on the availability of data on policy inputs and outputs. The latter are required for both a treatment and a control group. Ideally, data would be consistently available in a time series covering the period before the start of treatment and the period after treatment, as well as during the treatment itself. Unfortunately, it is often the case that while evaluators can obtain good data on policy inputs (for example, number of firms receiving advice, number of hours of advice, or public funding provided), the data on policy outputs (for example, enterprise start-up, survival, and employment and turnover growth rates, potentially by type of entrepreneur) are less available. Relevant data on outputs frequently exist within government administrations, for example in tax, unemployment and social security records, but legal and administrative barriers and lack of incentives to the holders of the data to share them often make them inaccessible to researchers.

Assessing the impact of policy

For any given outcome, policy impact is defined as the difference between the observed outcome with the intervention and what would have happened without the intervention (the counterfactual), in other words, the 'additionality' of the intervention.

The significance of this definition is reflected in a simple example. Assume one is estimating the impact of a Science Park location on the survival and growth of small technology-based businesses.[5] The policy impact of the Park is not the aggregate jobs/sales/profits of the Park firms, because these firms might have achieved the same (or possibly better) performance had they been located elsewhere. Instead, policy impact is the performance of the Park firms minus what those same firms would have been expected to have achieved at their next most productive location. To ignore the latter is to make the unrealistic assumption that these firms would have achieved zero jobs, sales or profits.

A failure to adequately capture what would have happened to either the firm or to individuals is to unjustifiably inflate the apparent impact of the policy. A valid evaluation, therefore, has to use a methodology which is capable of reliably disentangling the effect of the policy from the counterfactual scenario (what would have happened in the absence of the policy) so as to enable the policy maker to be confident of validly identifying policy impact.

OECD (2007) set out a range of evaluation methodologies that had been used at that time to assess entrepreneurship policy across a range of countries. Some methods never considered the counterfactual whereas others, although aware of the issue, failed to address it in a satisfactory manner. The effect was, therefore, to unrealistically inflate the reported impact of the policy.

To classify these diverse methodologies, the OECD used the Six Steps to Heaven approach to assess the reliability of an evaluation (see Table 4.1). The approach draws a clear distinction between monitoring and evaluation. Monitoring is based entirely on the views of the policy makers and/or the recipients of the policy. In contrast, evaluation is based on comparing outcomes between a treatment group of entrepreneurs/enterprises and a control group of otherwise similar firms or individuals that did not benefit from the programme. Monitoring was deemed a less reliable tool for assessing policy impact than evaluation, partly because it relies exclusively on self-report data among the recipients and policy makers, but primarily because of the absence of any counterfactual or control group. In short, the inclusion of a counterfactual or control group is a necessary condition for evaluation.

The key technical challenge is therefore to identify a group of firms or individuals which did not benefit from the policy (the control group) but which are identical in all other respects to the firms or individuals who did benefit (the treatment group). Any observed differences in the performance of the two groups over time, for example in terms of firm growth or survival, are attributed to the policy.[6] Steps IV to Step VI constitute evaluation because

Table 4.1   Six Steps to Heaven: methods for assessing the impact of entrepreneurship policy

Monitoring	
STEP I	Take-up of a programme
STEP II	Recipients' opinions
STEP III	Recipients' views of the difference made by the assistance
Evaluation	
STEP IV	Comparison of the performance of 'assisted' with 'typical' firms
STEP V	Comparison with 'match' firms
STEP VI	Taking account of selection bias Use of Randomised Control Trials (RCTs)

Source: Adapted from OECD (2007).

they include a comparison with a control group, but they differ in terms of the sophistication (and hence reliability) with which they capture the characteristics of the treatment group.

In Step IV the recipient group is compared with all enterprises or entrepreneurs in the economy. This is an imperfect comparison since the recipients may differ from the 'average' in terms of, for example, age, sector, location, education and so on. To address this, Step V takes account of these 'observable' differences and so compares the recipients with a group of enterprises or entrepreneurs that do not differ in terms of these observable characteristics.

However, entrepreneurs and enterprises also differ in terms of 'unobservables'. The clearest examples of 'unobservable' factors, in this context, are awareness of a programme and motivation to participate. It would be misleading, for example in examining a programme intended to enhance business growth, to compare treated enterprises or entrepreneurs with observably similar ones and infer that all differences in growth over time were attributable to the programme. This is because firms seeking participation in the programme (the treated cases) are more likely to have been motivated to grow and to be more aware of options to support growth, such as the programme. In short, even in the absence of a programme the firms are more likely to have grown. This is known as self-selection bias and to ignore it would, once again, act to inflate the estimated impact of the programme.

A second selection bias issue occurs when not all eligible applicants for a programme are automatically selected and, instead, their suitability for the programme is judged by a panel. If the members of the panel are good judges then the accepted firms/individuals will perform well, but it then becomes difficult to assess the extent to which this reflects the judgement of the panel and how much it reflects the impact of the programme per se.[7]

OECD (2007) identified several Step VI studies that addressed the challenge of taking account of such 'unobservables' by using statistical adjustment methods, such as by comparing the performance of policy recipients with another comparably motivated or informed group. For example, it reported on the Wren and Storey (2002) evaluation of soft assistance, which, to address the self-selection bias, compared the subsequent performance of small firms that used different amounts of a public advice programme, but such studies were uncommon at the time.

Finally, OECD (2007) also emphasised that impact evaluation using control groups did not preclude additional qualitative assessments of programmes. Rich case studies based on stakeholder interviews were acknowledged as throwing important additional light on the functioning of programmes and how they affect decision making that can help improve policy design and implementation. For example, they can uniquely pick up issues connected with the satisfaction of beneficiaries and programme managers with different aspects of a programme, or help assess the potential scale of take-up of the programme and its different elements. Qualitative analysis can, therefore, help widen understanding, but it is not a perfect substitute for robust impact evaluation.

Recent improvements in evaluation data and techniques

Improvements in data

Governments have traditionally collected and held a vast amount of data on individuals and enterprises through their tax, social security and other records. However, despite governments holding these data, until recently little use was made of the data for entrepreneurship policy evaluation. This reflects two main problems: the absence of mechanisms to share data across ministries that hold the data and the entrepreneurship ministry responsible for the evaluation; and concerns about potential breaches of confidentiality by releasing data for evaluation. However, in the last ten years or so there has been significant improvement in confidentiality rules and data protection legislation in many countries, as well as in the development of better IT systems, which is leading to much more frequent use of official micro data for evaluation.

Not only are ministries more willing to share data with other government actors, and capable of doing so, but they are also often making arrangements to share such data with researchers as part of new 'open data' policies. For example, governments are developing central data portals, giving single entry points to a wide range of data, and developing guidelines and standards to ensure that data meet necessary quality standards for use, for example through arrangements for data cleaning, machine readability and provision of meta data (OECD, 2018b). Governments are also increasingly making efforts to link data from different sources, enabling information on various policy outputs to be linked with information on participation in government support programmes.

A key issue in being able to make use of official data for entrepreneurship policy evaluation is the challenge of attributing a firm or entrepreneur to a treatment or control group status. To facilitate this exercise, it is useful to assign each enterprise a unique business identifier. In Mexico, for example, every enterprise that is formally registered for tax purposes has a tax registration number (OECD, 2013). If this number is systematically recorded for each of the enterprise's interactions with government, then evaluators would be able to identify which government programmes the enterprise has used and for which programmes they have applied. Government would also be able to track their employment, sales and taxes paid over time, before and after receipt of the programme support. This would provide invaluable information for the establishment of treatment and control groups. Denmark is an example of a country that has succeeded in the challenge of developing the appropriate IT systems and shown the political will to share information, and hence holds excellent data for rigorous entrepreneurship policy evaluation (Hoffmann and Storey, 2017).[8]

In addition, 'Big Data', often held in the private sector and collected using digital technologies, may become an increasingly important resource for evaluation if, for example, it is possible to match participation and non-participation in an entrepreneurship support programme with data on the activities of entrepreneurs and enterprises.

Improvements in evaluation techniques

The key evaluation developments since OECD (2007) have been the appearance of formally designed policy experiments known as Randomised Control Trials (RCTs) and the creative use of a wide range of proxies seeking to fully capture the characteristics of a valid control group.

RCT-based evaluations are undertaken when policy is delivered to a group of eligible recipients and the performance of the recipients (the treatment group) is compared over time with eligible recipients who were randomly excluded (the control group). It is for this reason that Table 4.1 now specifically includes RCTs as a Step VI approach alongside the more extensive use of statistical methods that explicitly address selection bias. In general, RCTs can be seen as a preferable methodology, although they can have drawbacks.[9]

Table 4.2 provides examples of Step VI entrepreneurship policy evaluations that have emerged since the OECD (2007) Framework was published. The table is not intended to be a comprehensive list of all such studies. Instead, it is intended to show that rigorous evaluation can be applied to diverse policy areas such as the provision of training and advice, finance and social inclusion policies. As a group the studies demonstrate how the 'science of evaluation' is moving on in entrepreneurship policy, most clearly in the willingness and ability to identify the role of valid control groups, albeit with different degrees of reliability.

The different studies adopted different approaches to the control group issue. For example, Pons Rotger et al. (2012) examined the performance of a range of start-ups that used different quantities of advice, and argued this provided an estimate of the marginal impact of incremental advice. Autio and Rannikko (2016), more questionably, benchmarked their assisted firms against other agency clients and against those rejected for the programme. In other cases (for example, Yusuf, 2014), the Heckman two-stage selection approach was used. The first stage explains who engages/makes contact with the organisation providing the treatment; the second stage uses this to explain performance outcomes. Finally, there are also examples of RCTs used to assess policy. In some instances these are well-planned exercises where the World Bank particularly has played the dominant role (Banerjee et al., 2015), whereas in other instances the use of RCTs was more opportunistic (Georgiadis and Pitelis, 2016).

The final column of Table 4.2 provides a brief statement of the impact of the policies under investigation. There are instances of positive outcomes. For example, Yusuf (2014) found that those taking advice were more likely to start a business and Caliendo et al. (2016) found that unemployed participants in a major German entrepreneurship programme were more likely to be benefitting 2.5 years later. However, there were also instances where the impact was difficult to identify (Fairlie et al., 2015; Dvouletý et al., 2019) or even negative (Loersch, 2014). In other cases, the results generated were highly sensitive to the period of time over which the evaluation was undertaken (Drewes, 2015).

Overall, Table 4.2, which can be considered to reflect studies of the impact of entrepreneurship policies undertaken in the last decade and using valid data and advanced statistical techniques, points to the difficulties policy makers face in confidently linking individual programmes to clearly identified outcomes. As is argued below, this reinforces the case for more and better evaluations to confidently confirm what works and what does not work in this policy area. It certainly is not the basis for concluding that entrepreneurship policy should be given a 'clean bill of health'.

Conclusion and an agenda for research and policy

Expenditures on entrepreneurship policy, in developed countries at least, are very substantial. However, concerns can be raised about whether public support to entrepreneurs can be, or is, relevant, effective and efficient and, if so, in which circumstances. Reliable evaluation of entrepreneurship policy interventions is, therefore, at a premium. However, although evaluation has increased considerably during the last decade, it is undertaken relatively infrequently and the creation of an evaluation culture in the field of entrepreneurship policy, called for in OECD (2007), has yet to be widely established.

In principle, salvation is near. There have been considerable advances in both the 'science' of evaluation and in the availability of evaluation data for entrepreneurship policy. It is now well established how to apply control group studies that compare over time the performance of beneficiary firms with matched non-beneficiaries. This chapter has reported on several examples of robust control group-based evaluation studies and RCTs in entrepreneurship policy.

For governments, there are two key priorities. The first is for the relevant government ministry charged with leading and co-ordinating entrepreneurship policy to create an evaluation framework to be disseminated across entrepreneurship policy makers. This could potentially be supported by the creation of a dedicated evaluation unit in the government ministry to promote evaluation.

Table 4.2   Recent examples of Step VI entrepreneurship policy evaluations

Policy area	Authors	Programme description	Country	Number of cases	Methodology	Impact finding
Pre-start business advice	Pons Rotger et al. (2012)	Public funding of counselling and advice prior to start-up.	Denmark (North Jutland)	859	Propensity score matching of control and treatment groups	Short-term survival is enhanced. Positive but weaker effects on sales and employment.
Worker and management training in small firms	Georgiadis and Pitelis (2016)	Government training programme for accommodation and food sectors.	UK	430	RCT	Profit margins were not significantly linked to management or human resources management (HRM) training. Log sales per employee were weakly linked to management but not to HRM training.
Guided preparation to nascent entrepreneurs	Yusuf (2014)	Market opportunity definition, business plan development and/or financial statement development through a broad range of public assistance programmes.	USA	680 nascent entrepreneurs in total; 62 treated	Heckman two-stage sample selection model to allow for self-selection bias	Guided preparation contributes to a greater likelihood of achieving a positive start-up outcome.

Policy area	Authors	Programme description	Country	Number of cases	Methodology	Impact finding
Consultancy and networking for start-ups	Autio and Rannikko (2016)	The Tekes NIY Growth Programme facilitates the growth of new entrepreneurial firms. It provides financial support for commissioning experts and networking among its participants.	Finland	64–66 treated; 54–64 untreated	Heckman adjustment for selection bias	Sales growth rates of treated firms double.
Subsidised entry of the unemployed into new business creation	Caliendo et al. (2016)	Bridging allowance (BA) and the start-up subsidy (SUS).	Germany	3100	Propensity score matching to allow for self-selection effects	Increased probability of being in employment or self-employment and positive effects on incomes after 2.5 years.
Coaching to entrepreneurs	Loersch (2014)	Coaching for potential entrepreneurs (EBCG) and coaching for unemployed potential entrepreneurs (EBCG-UE).	Germany	2936	Propensity score matching	EBCG has a negative effect on business survival, income, number of employees and job satisfaction. EBCG-UE has a positive impact on survival and number of employees but not on income and satisfaction.

Policy area	Authors	Programme description	Country	Number of cases	Methodology	Impact finding
Micro credits	Banerjee et al. (2015)	Review of microcredit programmes in six low-income countries on four different continents.	Bosnia, Ethiopia, India, Mexico, Morocco and Mongolia	Varies from 995 in Bosnia to 16560 in Mexico	RCT	'We note a consistent pattern of modestly positive, but not transformative, effects'.
Entrepreneurship training	Fairlie et al. (2015)	Growing America through Entrepreneurship (GATE) project offering entrepreneurship training to individuals interested in starting or improving a business in 14 US locations.	USA	4197 with 2094 treated	RCT	No strong or lasting effects on those most likely to face credit or human capital constraints, or labour market discrimination. There is a short-run effect on business ownership for the unemployed, but it dissipates over time.
Credit guarantee schemes	Dvouletý et al. (2019)	EU-funded guarantee programme.	Czech Republic	Varies by estimations but 530 treated and tracked firms and 18499 controls is typical	Propensity score matching	The average treatment effect on the treated (ATET) for six financial outcome variables (total assets, tangible fixed assets, personnel costs, sales, price–cost margin and return on assets) was estimated. Two years after the programme, statistically conclusive results were observed only for the tangible fixed assets of programme participants.

Policy area	Authors	Programme description	Country	Number of cases	Methodology	Impact finding
Business advice	Drewes (2015)	Largest ever SME advice programme – Business Link.	UK	746 treated of which 425 intensively, 321 moderately and 298 controls	Data linking and matching with official records	Evaluations conducted over a short time period generate different results from those over a longer period. The two-year report found intensive assistance had a positive and significant impact on employment growth of 2.8 percentage points. The Drewes study over seven years found a small and only short-term impact on survival; for growth there is a spike two-three years after treatment but no longer-run effect.
Training	McKenzie and Woodruff (2014)	A review of government training programmes.	Low-income countries	Review	A range of methods	Studies point to relatively modest impacts of training on the survivorship of existing firms. However, there is stronger evidence that training programmes can help prospective owners launch new businesses more quickly. Most studies find that existing firm owners implement some of the practices taught in training, but the magnitudes of these improvements in practices are often relatively modest. Few studies find significant impacts on profits or sales, although a couple of the studies with more statistical power have done so.

The framework should set out clearly the entrepreneurship policy measures and their objectives to be evaluated (using output rather than input-based targets), the timetable and procedures to be used for the evaluation, the techniques to establish impact, the method of supplying evaluation data for each measure, and the resources that will be made available for the evaluations. Some countries have already established such frameworks and guidance; for example, the Department of Innovation, Science and Research in Australia has developed and issued a *Best Practice Evaluation Handbook* that is distributed among programme managers to increase understanding and use of evaluation (OECD, 2013).

The second priority is to ensure access to data for evaluation purposes, including making tax and social security data on entrepreneurs and enterprises available, and linking the data sets to information on programme participants and non-participants. There is great potential for governments to make better use of existing official data on company performance and company interactions through sharing information across departments and programmes, where possible tied to the use of a single business identifier and a single enterprise database.

For entrepreneurship researchers, the challenge is to support the entrepreneurship policy evaluation agenda by providing and applying evaluation expertise. The case has been made for entrepreneurship policy evaluation to be undertaken in a rigorous manner, so as to provide important material for academic research as well as for policy development. Researchers should be proactive in seeking out opportunities to evaluate entrepreneurship programmes as part of their academic research agendas, seeking to exploit large-scale micro data sets that may be under the radar. In undertaking this effort, it is critical that researchers use the best evaluation methods available, using Step VI approaches that apply RCTs or control groups with statistical techniques to allow for selection bias. As the evaluation field has moved on, the exclusive use of self-report data provided by the treatment group is no longer acceptable in entrepreneurship policy evaluation methodology.

Finally, left open is the observation that the very mixed results from Step VI evaluations of publicly funded training and advice programmes seem at odds with much current entrepreneurship theory, which places the knowledge base of the business owner at the core of explaining new venture performance (Ireland et al., 2003). It remains a puzzle that, if training and advice succeeds in supplementing the human capital new business owners need for growth and survival, this appears to be rarely reflected in the results of the reliable Step VI evaluations. This contradiction is certainly worthy of further theoretical and empirical attention.

Notes

1. Disclaimer: This paper is published under the responsibility of the authors. The contribution of Jonathan Potter is in his personal capacity and the opinions expressed and arguments employed herein do not necessarily reflect the official views of the Organisation for Economic Co-operation and Development or its member countries.
2. One of the current authors raised similar issues in 1993 (Storey, 1993).
3. Soft support is in the form of advice and guidance, whereas hard support is directly financial. Many programmes of course combine the two.
4. The downside of this policy is that such firms are (very) difficult to identify and in many cases their exceptional performance is transitory. These are the 'one hit wonders' identified by Daunfeldt and Halvarsson (2015).
5. A helpful recent review of Science Park evaluations is provided by Ramírez-Alesón and Fernández-Olmos (2018).
6. Note this leaves open the option of a negative impact if the policy-assisted group performs less well than the controls.
7. Of course, the panel may also be poor judges, which, if it were not taken into account, would depress the contribution of the programme.
8. Sweden and Norway are other exemplars in this respect.
9. A valid questioning of RCTs in the current context is provided by Dalziel (2018).

References

Acs, Z. J., T. Åstebro, D. Audretsch and D. T. Robinson (2016), 'Public policy to promote entrepreneurship: A call to arms', *Small Business Economics*, **47** (1), 35–51.

Autio, E. and H. Rannikko (2016), 'Retaining winners: Can policy boost high-growth entrepreneurship', *Research Policy*, **45** (1), 42–55.

Banerjee, A., D. Karlan and J. Zinman (2015), 'Six randomized evaluations of microcredit: Introduction and further steps', *American Economic Journal: Applied Economics*, **7** (1), 1–21.

Caliendo, M., S. Künn and M. Weißenberger (2016), 'Personality traits and the evaluation of start-up subsidies', *European Economic Review*, **86**, 87–108.

Dalziel, M. (2018), 'Why are there (almost) no randomized control-based evaluations of business support programmes?', *Palgrave Communications*, **4** (1), 1–9.

Daunfeldt, S. O. and D. Halvarsson (2015), 'Are high-growth firms one-hit wonders? Evidence from Sweden', *Small Business Economics*, **44** (2), 361–83.

Drewes, C. C. (2015), 'The long-term impact of business support? Exploring the role of evaluation timing using micro data', doctoral dissertation, University of Aston, UK.

Dvouletý, O., J. Čadil and K. Mirošník (2019), 'Do firms supported by credit guarantee schemes report better financial results 2 years after the end of intervention?', *BE Journal of Economic Analysis and Policy*, **19** (1), 20180057.

Eurofound (2016), *Start-Up Support for Young People in the EU: From Implementation to Evaluation*, Luxembourg: Publications Office of the European Union.

Fairlie, R. W., D. Karlan and J. Zinman (2015), 'Behind the GATE experiment: Evidence on effects of and rationales for subsidized entrepreneurship training', *American Economic Journal: Economic Policy*, **7** (2), 125–61.

GAO (2012), *Annual Report: Opportunities to Reduce Duplication, Overlap and Fragmentation, Achieve Savings, and Enhance Revenue*, report to congressional addressees, Washington, DC.

Georgiadis, A. and C. N. Pitelis (2016), 'The impact of employees' and managers' training on the performance of small- and medium-sized enterprises: Evidence from a randomized natural experiment in the UK service sector', *British Journal of Industrial Relations*, **54** (2), 409–42.

Hoffmann, A. and D. J. Storey (2017), 'Can governments promote gazelles?', in R. Blackburn, D. De Clerq and J. Heinonen (eds), *The Sage Handbook of Small Business and Entrepreneurship*, London: Sage Publications, pp. 373–90.

Ireland, R. D., M. A. Hitt and D. G. Sirmon (2003), 'A model of strategic entrepreneurship: The construct and its dimensions', *Journal of Management*, **29** (6), 963–89.

Loersch, C. (2014), 'Business start-ups and the effect of coaching programs', doctoral thesis, University of Potsdam.

Lundström, A., P. Vikström, M. Fink, M. Meuleman, P. Głodek, D. J. Storey and A. Kroksgård (2014), 'Measuring the costs and coverage of SME and entrepreneurship policy: A pioneering study', *Entrepreneurship Theory and Practice*, **38** (4), 941–57.

McKenzie, D. and C. Woodruff (2014), 'What are we learning from business training and entrepreneurship evaluations around the developing world?', *World Bank Research Observer*, **29** (1), 48–82.

NAO (2006), *Supporting Small Business*, HC 962 Session 2005–2006, London, 24 May 2006.

OECD (2004), *Istanbul Ministerial Declaration: Fostering the Growth of Innovative and Internationally Competitive SMEs*, Paris: OECD Publishing.

OECD (2007), *OECD Framework for the Evaluation of SME and Entrepreneurship Policies and Programmes*, Paris: OECD Publishing.

OECD (2013), *Mexico: Key Issues and Policies, OECD Studies on SMEs and Entrepreneurship*, Paris: OECD Publishing.

OECD (2018a), *Declaration on Strengthening SMEs and Entrepreneurship for Productivity and Inclusive Growth*, Paris: OECD Publishing.

OECD (2018b), *Open Government Data Report: Enhancing Policy Maturity for Sustainable Impact*, OECD Digital Government Studies, Paris: OECD Publishing .

OECD/European Union (2016), *Inclusive Business Creation: Good Practice Compendium*, Paris: OECD Publishing.

OECD/European Union (2017), *The Missing Entrepreneurs 2017: Policies for Inclusive Entrepreneurship*, Paris: OECD Publishing.

Pons Rotger, G., M. Gørtz and D. J. Storey (2012), 'Assessing the effectiveness of guided preparation for new venture creation and performance: Theory and practice', *Journal of Business Venturing*, **27** (4), 506–21.

Ramírez-Alesón, M. and M. Fernández-Olmos (2018), 'Unravelling the effects of science parks on the innovation performance of NTBFs', *Journal of Technology Transfer*, **43** (2), 482–505.

Shane, S. (2009), 'Why encouraging more people to become entrepreneurs is bad public policy', *Small Business Economics*, **33**, 141–9.

Storey, D. J. (1993), 'Should we abandon support to start-up businesses', in F. Chittenden and M. Robertson (eds), *Small Firms in Recession and Recovery*, London: Paul Chapman Publishing, pp. 1–26.

Wren, C. and D. J. Storey (2002), 'Evaluating the effect of soft business support upon small firm performance', *Oxford Economic Papers*, **54** (2), 334–65.

Yusuf, J.-E. Wie (2014), 'Impact of start-up support through guided preparation', *Journal of Entrepreneurship and Public Policy*, **3** (1), 72–95.

5 Policies to support internationalisation: who needs them and what do they need?

David Smallbone and Hang Do[1]

Introduction

The contribution of small and medium enterprises (SMEs) to the European economy is widely recognised. In this context, it is not surprising that the European Commission has identified internationalisation as one of the main foci of the European Union (EU) strategy. This has been reflected in the introduction of the Small Business Act[2] (SBA) since 2008 and the Europe 2020 Strategy,[3] based on a view of the economy emphasising smart, sustainable and inclusive growth. As a consequence, support for internationalisation has been prioritised and SMEs within that. In this context, the first question that arises is what are the barriers that SMEs face when internationalising? Secondly, what kind of support would help them best deal with these challenges? But perhaps the most basic question of all is what do we mean by internationalisation? It is not uncommon to find that, in many cases, internationalisation and exporting are considered to be interchangeable terms. However, the definition used in this chapter is not narrowly focused on exporting but also includes international sourcing of imports, overseas sub-contracting and so on.

Previous studies have shown that the main barriers that internationalising SMEs face include finance, a complexity of regulations and administrative burdens (in the target market particularly), differences in business culture and language barriers (OECD, 2013; European Parliament, 2016), exchange rate fluctuations, finding customers and partners abroad (European Commission, 2010), managing relationships with international partners, a lack of innovative resources, and the level of uncertainty and risk when becoming dependent upon international sales (particularly applying to finance, in the sense of fear of not getting paid, or at least of seriously delayed payment) (Sinkovics et al., 2018). Other barriers include the limited knowledge of SMEs about the target markets and available support, procedure barriers and exogenous barriers such as the level of competition, and financial market risks (Suarez-Ortega, 2003).

Although finance typically appears at the top of the list in more general SME surveys, the perceived barrier effects of limited access to finance contains some additional features in the case of internationalisation. Firstly, there is the need for working capital in order to cover the costs of a particular international activity, such as exporting. Secondly, there is the uncertainty attached to dealing with people at a distance from different cultures, and possibly different types of political systems. This acts as a barrier as far as many SME owners are concerned, and is an area where selective policy intervention can contribute. A third support need relates to information about topics which may not be readily available in the home country. This includes information about intellectual property rights and how these are (if they are) protected in the target country, information about how to assess the reliability of potential suppliers, and even information on basic topics like market trends and human resources practices, amongst others.

Adopting a wider definition of what constitutes internationalisation, technological cooperation in specific fields may, if it has a potential European benefit attached, be well supported. One problem from an SME perspective is that the preparation for internationalisation can itself be expensive, in time and money terms. In some countries, Ireland being one example, government makes small sums of money available to encourage SMEs to cooperate with local universities and other firms in order to prepare for internationalisation. EU–Japan access is particularly important for this because of the high quality of support for technological development and cooperation in Japan.

Although the emphasis may vary, together with the support available, all European countries offer some assistance to firms that are seeking to internationalise their operations. This is because of the potential importance of the revenues generated, contributing to economic development as a source of external income. At the same time, whilst firms of all sizes may be affected by internationalisation forces, it may be argued that SMEs are the most in need of assistance in order to secure foreign market entry and establish sustainable foreign market exploitation.

Within the EU, policy support for the internationalisation of Europe's SMEs is provided at both the European and national levels (Eurofound, 2018).

Moreover, in some cases policy measures may be provided at the national level whilst paid for with EU money made available through Structural Funds. This particularly applies to the new member states of the EU that were previously operating under central planning, where exporting was centrally organised and where developing and implementing policies to support internationalisation was not a priority.

Although support for internationalisation is clearly an important field for public policy intervention, it may be argued that, for a number of reasons, within the EU the time is right for a critical review. These reasons include a growing emphasis in Europe's mature market economies on the need to review SME policies as budgets tighten and doubts about the value for money offered increase. In the UK there is the added reason in the form of Brexit, resulting in unanticipated market volatility and increasing uncertainty for SMEs.

Most EU member states have some form of export credit guarantees to remove some of the risks that businesses can face when exporting. This is particularly important in the case of smaller companies, where the more limited internal resource base means that non-payment or seriously delayed payment can cause cashflow problems. At the same time, there is considerable variation between countries, not so much in terms of the context of these export credit systems but, more particularly, in terms of the way they operate. Whilst the risk reduction associated with export credits and export credit guarantees is often shaped around the specific export structure of individual countries, there is a fair degree of similarity in the way these systems operate.

The methodology employed in this chapter was mainly desk-based research, supplemented by telephone interviews with key informants who were involved in the process of developing internationalisation policies in a number of countries. The empirical part of the chapter is focused on Japan as a destination or target for European SMEs. The rest of the chapter is divided into the following sections. The first section describes and discusses policies at the national level to promote and support SME internationalisation, focusing on Germany, Ireland, the Czech Republic and the UK; the second section deals with EU-level policies; and the third section deals with support available in Japan as a destination country for Europe's internationalising firms.

National-level policies

Space does not permit a detailed discussion of all national-level policies across Europe; instead, our approach seeks to capture the heterogeneity that exists both in terms of policies and in terms of the way in which they are used. Those countries featured in this section include Germany, which has one of the most elaborate systems for supporting trade and exporting in Europe; Ireland, as an example of a small domestic economy; the Czech Republic, as an example of one of the EU's new member states; and the UK, because of a fundamental recent review.

Germany

The German government supports the activities of German companies abroad through its foreign trade and investment promotion scheme and, in so doing, contributes to maintaining competitiveness and job security. In this context, the promotion of exports is a potentially important growth stimulus. These promotion schemes are managed by a consortium which includes PricewaterhouseCoopers, appointed by the German government for this purpose. The government guarantee schemes provide protection for foreign trade and investment activities in order to reduce the inherent risks that are inevitably involved, and in doing so make foreign market penetration more predictable and manageable. The package includes export credit guarantees and investment guarantees (which protect foreign direct investments against political risk) and untied loan guarantees (to back suppliers who supply commodities to Germany and to contribute to economic development abroad). With respect to the application procedures for obtaining guarantees, exporters are advised to get in touch with the consortium as early as possible and before the export contract is signed.

Although virtually all EU countries have a system of export credit guarantees and related products, Germany's is perhaps the most comprehensive, and it has been used to boost export activity in the country. One of the reasons the German system appears complex is the variation in the level of public support available across the country. This reflects wider regional variations in economic development in different regions, as well as the country's federal structure which gives some policy responsibilities to the regional authorities.

Turning to financing, KfW is a development bank that supports companies with global investments, export projects and imports. However, it claims to offer more than just financing and the associated advisory services as it has considerable market-specific expertise as well as a global network of cooperation partners.

In the context of the EU, Germany has an elaborate system for supporting trade and exporting, ranging from consultancy, financing programmes and guarantees to support for participation in trade fairs. The website of the Förderdatenbank emphasises the wide range of options that companies face in financing projects that may include internationalisation. These include using retained earnings and primary liabilities in the form of bank loans or government development loans. In addition, there is a range of alternative sources of finance available, which are greater in some parts of Germany than in others.

One aspect of the German approach to export promotion that is of wider interest is the IHK Company Pool Programme, which has been identified in an Organisation for Economic Co-operation and Development (OECD) report as an internationally inspiring practice (OECD, 2014). The programme offers coaching, market intelligence and deal-brokering support to groups of SMEs aiming to export to selected target countries through local Chambers of Commerce and Industry in Germany. The OECD reports that there are currently 31 company pools operated by various local chambers, each of which focuses on market entry in a particular country or a set of countries. A company pool programme in Ukraine was established in 1994 and this has served as a model for company pools that have been established since then. A company pool usually consists of up to 15 German SMEs that do not normally directly compete against each other and that intend to enter the same target market. The companies within a pool benefit from comprehensive services provided by a joint representative office in the host country. This office is managed by an experienced business expert who is appointed by the Chamber of Commerce. A standard service package includes preparatory and accompanying services in Germany, such as assistance in developing a market entry strategy and the organisation of regular meetings by participating SMEs in order to exchange information and experiences. In the analysis by the OECD, key success factors of this scheme include:

- Permanent accessibility and presence in the target country;
- The use of an already existing business network in the target country;
- Staff of representative offices have a special sense for the market and business mentality of the target country; and
- Synergies exist through cooperation and exchange of experiences with other company pool members.

The cost of joining one of these company pools varies according to the specific target country and the scope of the services used, but, typically, it is in a range of between €5,000 and €15,000 per annum. Clearly, this can be quite a large sum of money for the smallest companies, so to address this problem the Foreign Trade Support Programme of several German federal states offers financial assistance to cover part of these costs. Participation in these company pools is used by the larger SME manufacturing firms to facilitate entry into the target country. SMEs typically participate for two or three years in a company pool, after which they are able to cope on their own and continue their business activities independently.

Ireland

With 4.7 million people (as of 2017), the domestic economy of Ireland is of modest size. Start-up businesses with high growth potential need to look to export and make a presence on the international stage almost from day one, in a way that perhaps in the UK there would not be such urgency because of the larger home market.

The main government agency providing support to SMEs in Ireland is Enterprise Ireland.[4] Enterprise Ireland is a government organisation which is responsible for the development and growth of Irish enterprises in world markets and works in partnership with Irish enterprises to help them to start to grow, innovate and win export sales in global markets. Enterprise Ireland is involved in both assisting entrepreneurs to be successful and contributing to the basic security of employment and regional development. Enterprise Ireland provides a wide variety of different services which are potentially relevant to Ireland's internationalising SMEs. For example, the agency offers a range of funding supports, such as for expansion or research and development. Each of these funding supports could contribute to increasing the potential for internationalisation.

The funding available includes money for high-potential start-ups, some of which may be used to help these start-ups to become 'investor ready', and an equity fund to support innovative high-potential start-ups. Established businesses employing more than 10 people may access support which is designed to help these businesses plan and implement company development projects, and there is also funding available for large companies employing more than 250.

Because of the importance of international markets to the long-term growth of Irish businesses, a high priority for Enterprise Ireland is the provision of support for business growth through international sales. Enterprise Ireland produces an 'Export Start Guide', which is a practical guide about how to do business successfully in overseas markets.

Alongside the funding that Enterprise Ireland makes available for Ireland's businesses at different stages of their development, they also offer funding to researchers in higher education institutes in relation to three main objectives:

- To help to fund the commercialisation of research.
- To fund collaboration with industry in Ireland – in other words, to try to bridge the gap between the business community and the universities in the area of applied research.
- To provide funding for international research projects.

One of the characteristics of the Enterprise Ireland approach is the mix of funding and advice and expertise. This can be illustrated with respect to the R&D innovation support which Enterprise Ireland offers to Irish businesses. Enterprise Ireland offers financial support starting from €5,000 in the form of innovation vouchers. This can be granted through collaborative research and industry-led R&D at the top of the innovation ladder. This support may not necessarily be targeted at internationalising SMEs or any particular countries that SMEs seek to enter, because the size of the home market in Ireland makes it necessary for firms to look for international market opportunities at the very early stages of the development of a new business. It potentially can help to stimulate export activity.

The Czech Republic

Comparison between the German and Czech export credit systems shows that in principle they are, not surprisingly, very similar. However, many decades of experience gained by German institutions, as well as the nature of the supporting government agencies in Germany, makes Germany's system a model type of public support (Picha, 2014). It is not so much that the devil is in the detail (as is often the case), but rather that the process of applying the export credit scheme in the Czech Republic tends to be painfully slow. In this regard, the inevitable conclusion is that the availability of credit insurance is much higher in Germany than it is in the Czech Republic. As a consequence, this contributes to the competitive advantage of German exporters.

As in other EU countries, the Czech Republic export credit policies are delivered through an export bank, which is a specialised state-owned banking institution through which state support for exporting is channelled. Although the system of export credits, export credit guarantees and related products is a familiar one that is found across Europe, closer examination shows that the behaviour of Czech institutions is not the same as in countries like Germany, for example. This reflects a greater conservatism on the part of the Czech banks, which contrasts with Germany where the accumulation of experience over a number of years has helped to make German banks a little more flexible.

Comparisons between the Czech Republic and more advanced mature market economies again shows similarities and differences. Whilst the business support structures may look very similar, their operation is not. In this regard, as a new member state of the EU, the Czech Republic suffers from a lack of resources, which affects its ability to fully implement some of the programmes.

Turning to the financing of R&D as part of a longer-term view of internationalisation processes, the Czech Republic's administration of R&D funding is in the hands of a number of agencies, including the grant agency for the Czech Republic, the technology agency and seven ministries. There have been two EU–Japan forums so far in preparation for Horizon 2020, but there is a perception in the Czech Republic that preparing the materials for such projects is very burdensome. As a consequence, Czech institutions have decided that they don't have the resources to chase these opportunities.

The UK

In the UK, public provision of export finance and insurance is provided through UK Export Finance (UKEF),[5] the government agency which works in parallel to the Department for International Trade. UKEF is willing to consider supporting exporters, both large and small, for services as well as goods exported. In addition, UKEF cover is available for most overseas markets, although the terms may not be the same for each market. In Japan, for example, UKEF is able to support credit insurance businesses with a horizon of more than 24 months, reflecting the restrictions of European law which prevents governments supporting credit insurance of less than 24 months in this case.

UKEF offers a range of products to UK businesses seeking to export. Some of their products during 2017–20 include:

- Credit insurance – which is designed to insure against the commercial and political risk of a firm not being paid under an export contract.
- Insurance protection to exporters against the unfair calling of the contract bonds.

- Bond or Export Working Capital scheme – the scheme helps UK exporters to gain access to working capital finance both before and after shipment in respect of specific export contracts. Under the scheme the government department provides partial guarantees to lenders to cover the risk associated with export working capital facilities, whereby it provides such a facility with respect to a UK export contract. A typical case study business is Green's Power, a Yorkshire-based energy company who benefited from this scheme. Green's Power is the supply chain firm of another UK-based firm who exports to Africa. Due to the lack of cashflow, Green's Power could not provide a performance guarantee to secure the contract. However, with UKEF's intervention, the value of 80 per cent of the firm's bonds was guaranteed by HSBC, which enabled the contract to proceed.

UKEF (2019) reported that it has supported 181 companies' exports to 72 countries, 79 per cent of these companies being SMEs. The value of the support was £6.8 billion. Approximately 60 per cent of UKEF's participating companies sought support via the Bond or Export Working Capital scheme, with the Insurance scheme (33 per cent) coming next.

EU-level policies

Since the competitiveness of Europe's SMEs affects the European economy, the EU adopts a strategic view with regard to competitiveness, the barriers to it, and how these might be addressed. An important role of the European Commission (EC) in this regard is information provision to try to ensure that Europe's businesses are fully aware of the opportunities they have to access funding and business support. Another role is the dissemination of good practice in business support across Europe.

Two financial instruments that became available in August 2014 are helpful in increasing access to finance for SMEs. One of these products, the Loan Guarantee Facility, is funded from the Competitiveness of Enterprises and Small and Medium-sized Enterprises (COSME) budget (€2.3 billion, from 2014 to 2020), to help financial intermediaries to provide more loan and lease finance to SMEs. It has been estimated that the impact of this measure will be substantial because of leverage effects (European Commission, 2015). With every euro invested in loan guarantees expected to release up to €30 of financing for SMEs, the EC expects as many as 330 000 SMEs will receive loans backed by COSME guarantees, in fact, mainly micro enterprises employing ten or less.

The second financial instrument, which is part of the COSME budget, is dedicated to investment enriched capital funds that provide venture capital and mezzanine finance for the expansion and growth phases of SMEs, particularly those that operate across borders. This programme is known as the Equity Facility for Growth (EFG).[6] It is anticipated that around 500 firms will receive equity financing through the programme. At the same time, whilst these measures may contribute to an increase in finance for exporting SMEs, they are not specifically focused on this purpose.

In terms of its role in disseminating information relevant to businesses seeking to internationalise, the most common way of the EC doing this is through websites. In this regard, five portals are used for this purpose: the Enterprise Europe Network,[7] the SME Internationalisation portal, the Internationalisation of Clusters, the Your Europe business portal and the European Small Business Portal.

In terms of business support, a key element in the EC's offer is the Enterprise Europe Network, which offers help and advice for small firms in all EU matters, including on accessing markets inside and outside the EU. In Japan, the EU–Japan Centre for Industrial Cooperation adopts this role, thereby representing an entry point for Japanese businesses interested in trading or doing business in Europe as well as providing some support for European SMEs that are entering the Japanese market.

The EU–Japan Centre[8] for Industrial Cooperation is co-financed by the EC and the Japanese Ministry of Economy, Trade and Industry. In EU terms, the Centre is part of the concept of a global platform to provide EU companies with relevant information about business with third countries. The EU–Japan Centre for Industrial Cooperation is long established, although its strategic priorities have recently been reassessed and, currently, the main strategic priority is to reinforce the support given to SMEs, with a particular focus on the internationalisation aspects. This is in addition to other activities such as policy analysis, technology transfer, business round tables and others.

Overall, the objectives of the Centre are to contribute to developing business support and knowledge access to business opportunities in each other's markets, combined with a more fundamental diplomatic function which has emerged over time. It is questionable as to whether this aspect will fit well with the business support function that the Centre is now actively developing. New measures that are being developed within the business support function in the Centre include a public procurement helpdesk for SMEs and a so-called 'Keys to Japan' service, which involves selected SMEs being sponsored for help in drafting a business plan for expansion into the Japanese market.

Whilst such an entry needs to be adequately researched and translated into business planning, it is questionable whether a model in which a third party develops the business plan to be distributed to participating businesses is the most effective approach. This is because the principles of business planning may be more important to the firm than the possession of a business plan. The latter may only be of value as a tool for accessing external money. When it is considered that the EU–Japan Centre offers training, policy analysis, seminars and business round tables, it is questionable as to whether grafting a business support function on to such a Centre is the most appropriate form of action.

There are a number of EU programmes which may contribute to increasing cooperation between European and Japanese businesses in the medium and longer term. However, SMEs inevitably need some help in identifying and exploiting these opportunities. Preparation for Horizon 2020 is a specific example of this. In this regard, the SME instruments include business innovation grants, for feasibility assessment purposes; business innovation grants, for innovation, development and demonstration; and business coaching, to support and enhance the firm's innovation capacity.

The EU–Japan Centre is one of a number of SME centres that the EU has established in target countries, particularly the BRICS (Brazil, Russia, India, China and South Africa), with varying degrees of success. In China, for example, there are two centres. Firstly, there is an Intellectual Property Rights (IPR) SME[9] helpdesk, which introduces European SMEs to the knowledge and tools they require to develop their IPR and to manage related risks. The helpdesk provides free information, first line advice and training support to European SMEs to protect their IPR in China. Its services are free and evaluations that have been undertaken suggest that the IPR helpdesk is successfully addressing a real need of European SMEs seeking to operate in China.

Secondly, there is the SME Centre in Beijing, which has been more controversial. Following an abortive attempt to establish the Centre through a competitive bidding process, the Centre is now run by a consortium of former bidders for the EU Contract. More fundamentally perhaps, one might ask why the SME Centre was established in Beijing where the density of European SME support agencies is the highest in China. One wonders why, given the Chinese government's emphasis on developing the western regions, the Centre was set up in Beijing rather than in a less developed region. Another issue which commonly recurs in SME support concerns how European SMEs find out about these services provided in China. The intention of the EC is that the Enterprise Europe Network is the main way that SMEs obtain this information. In some countries this is fine, but in others, such as the UK, the institutions that participate in the European Enterprise Network are not penetrating the full range of the countries' SMEs.

This investigation shows that finance and other resources required for internationalisation by SMEs can be obtained from EU sources as well as from national ones. The current basis of the EC approach is set out in the Small Business Act, which contains an advisory component delivered through the Enterprise Europe Network, and a financial component which is largely the same as that set out in the COSME programme. Without speaking to a significant number of businesses, it is difficult to judge, firstly, whether or not this is adequate and, secondly, the extent to which Europe's SMEs actually know about it.

Japan

One of the key policy objectives of the Japanese government in recent times has been to try to attract more foreign investment and business operations in Japan. The 'Invest Japan' promotion in JETRO (2018) indicates that inward investment in Japan stood at 5.2 per cent of GDP as of the end of 2017. Additionally, the government has prioritised its growth strategy with the aim of increasing its inward foreign direct investment (FDI) stock by 22 per cent by 2020 (JETRO, 2018). At the same time, it is necessary to note the change in composition of internationally mobile investment. This is because there are not only new sources of FDI, but also differences emerging in the characteristics of firms that are internationalising. No longer is the supply of FDI dominated by large US multinationals. Evidence shows that by the end of 2017, almost half of the inward FDI came from Europe (JETRO, 2018).

These days a growing number of medium-sized companies are interested in investing abroad as part of their expansion into some of the more developed economies, including the EU but also Japan. It may be argued that developing a strategy to attract this type of firm is likely to become increasingly essential. What this means is that coordination of the export effort of Japanese companies with market institutions is common.

In this context, it is likely that Japanese institutions responsible for attracting more foreign investment will need to take into account the implications of these changes, particularly with respect to the typical size of firm that may be attracted. To achieve this requires high-quality information made available in ways that SME owners and managers are able to clearly understand and are able to develop. The close relationship between FDI and SME policy stems from the fact that the backward linkages that may be developed from the incoming businesses themselves create business opportunities for local SMEs which, if they are flexible enough, can lead to strong local markets.

Looked at in this way, the current strategies used by the SME support agencies responsible for delivering the export programme need improving. It is one thing to state that the institution does not discriminate against foreign businesses; however, if there is a feeling that this is not the case it will need to be demonstrated. The absence of discrimination needs to be reflected in the marketing of these organisations. It would be good to seek to promote a diversity dimension, as this can be used to motivate staff. So, essentially, the challenge for policy makers in Japan is to convincingly deliver to the potential customer the claims that they are currently making, particularly with regard to the access of foreign SMEs to Japanese funds. Funds are available in Japan for joint alliances with foreign businesses; the most common of these can be used to support SME growth.

Japan is a potentially attractive market to many European SMEs, but, at the same time, it is also a difficult market, not least because of the cultural divide between Japan and Europe. This means that to be successful in doing business in Japan, European SMEs need to be fully briefed on the finer points of Japanese customs and etiquette. In this context, agencies such as JETRO and SMRJ need to be fully aware of the perceptions of many European business owners towards Japan, which need to be taken into account in the development of an attractive offer.

It is encouraging to see the metropolitan governments in Japan becoming more active in seeking to attract more foreign investment and business into their areas. The experience elsewhere in the world is that medium-sized companies, when looking to internationalise, are more interested in cooperating with a local business than simply trying to go it alone. This is because, in proportionate terms, the extra investment required for them to become established in foreign markets is considerably above what would be needed by a large enterprise.

There is very considerable competition for mobile investment, so Japanese metropolitan or remote areas are in competition with foreign destinations as well as with other cities in Japan. Experience elsewhere in the world, in

London for example, suggests that this type of medium-sized company is very interested in the extent to which there are local communities into which its own staff could easily fit. The larger cities tend to be favoured, where there are more likely to be a concentration of particular groups, such as Japanese people, to facilitate a foreign firm's capabilities when entering the Japanese market. Above all, the availability of competent professional staff or engineers who have enough English or other language skills is an important matter, and all the parties in Japan should make efforts in this regard. The issues of economic regulations and barriers, as well as those of social and institutional barriers and problems, must be recognised and reformed.

It would seem that the Japan Finance Corporation (JFC) is a potential source of funding for foreign SMEs interested in setting up in Japan, particularly those that are seeking to do this through cooperation with local companies, simply because this tends to increase the impact of what they are doing. However, at present, there is little evidence of foreign companies being amongst the client base of JFC, nor are foreign SMEs successful in local cooperation and collaboration projects. Regional banks may also be potential sources, particularly where they are located in depressed regions and are committed to participating in industrial collaboration projects. However, these developments are less known to European businesses, and information on these local projects, as well as the various opportunities and supporting measures, must be better diffused and utilised.

Conclusion and future policy agenda

Overall, the study investigated the sources of finance and business support for internationalising European SMEs – particularly those who invest in Japan – at both national and European policy level. By exemplifying several policy practices in Ireland, the Czech Republic, the UK, Germany and Japan, the research has analysed both good practices and the gaps that need to be addressed, and what can be learned across contexts.

It has become increasingly important to recognise that internationalisation is more than just export activity. It also includes imports, the effects of international migration, foreign sub-contracting and a wide variety of interdependencies between countries. In the case of imports, there is an argument for more support being given, particularly in relation to components, where price and quality can have a direct impact on competitiveness. Some governments recognise that internationalisation is more than exporting. Finland, for example, was one of the first to assist its companies in becoming established abroad, which some critics view as exporting jobs. Defenders of the approach would argue in favour of a comparative advantage in which Finland is focused on the higher value-added activities, with the overseas sites helping to reduce costs. More generally, a broad view of what constitutes internationalisation includes processes such as international sub-contracting and importing. From a policy perspective it is easy to understand why what are essentially supply-side processes attract much less attention than exporting. At the same time, it can be argued that these processes can have an important influence on the competitiveness of businesses, particularly in cases where the international supply of parts and components can have a significant impact on production costs and the competitiveness of a firm's final product. As a result, a strong case can be made for business support to be offered to importers and not just to exporters.

Surprisingly perhaps, the investigation suggests that there are increasing opportunities for firms seeking to enter the Japanese market to obtain finance from inside Japan. The claims that emerged from the research in this regard need to be fully verified, but a consistent theme emerging from the work undertaken in Japan pointed in this direction. The phenomenon represents the coming together of the policy objectives between Europe and Japan, which forms part of the context that makes Japanese finance more available to European firms. One of the roles of the European Commission is to disseminate information, particularly where there are cross-border issues, and most particularly with respect to the dissemination of good practice. However, the present strategies for information dissemination do not seem to be effective. In this regard, greater recognition needs to be given to the differences between countries with respect to where SME owners and managers turn to for business support. The important contribution that SMEs make to the European economy, particularly in terms of employment, means that policy makers are keen to ensure that the development opportunities for European SMEs are exploited. In this context, internationalisation represents an opportunity for SMEs to develop new markets, as well as to find new sources of components and other inputs.

In terms of the future agenda, this significant contribution of SMEs means that policy support that can be seen to add value and help internationalising SMEs to achieve their objectives is not going to go away. However, as is sometimes recognised, whilst support for internationalisation may largely be focused on the individual or firm level, this should not be exclusively so. It is also vitally important for markets to be kept open and governments to be challenged where this is demonstratively not the case. An example would be the high-speed rail system in China, which was protected by the government from foreign competition on the basis of its innovation policy. Based on the record so far, the EU has not been very successful in achieving change in this regard, at least not collectively. In other words, looking to the future it is important to ensure that Europe's SMEs with the potential to internationalise are not prevented from doing so by market failures or other barriers that may be eased, if not eliminated, as a result of policy intervention.

Notes

1. The authors would like to thank the EU Japan Office for funding the research on which this chapter is based. The authors would also like to acknowledge the contribution of Professor Itsutomo Mitsui, who undertook research in Japan and was responsible for drafting the Japan chapter in the project report. The work was conducted when Dr. Hang Do was working at Small Business Research Centre, Kingston University.
2. https://ec.europa.eu/growth/smes/business-friendly-environment/small-business -act_en.
3. https://ec.europa.eu/info/business-economy-euro/economic-and-fiscal-policy -coordination/eu-economic-governance-monitoring-prevention-correction/ european-semester/framework/europe-2020-strategy_en.
4. https://enterprise-ireland.com/en/.
5. https://www.gov.uk/government/organisations/uk-export-finance.
6. https://www.eif.org/what_we_do/equity/single_eu_equity_instrument/cosme _efg/index.htm.
7. https://een.ec.europa.eu/.
8. https://www.eu-japan.eu/.
9. http://www.iprhelpdesk.eu/china-helpdesk.

References

Eurofound (2018), *Born Globals and Their Value Chain*, Luxembourg: European Union Publications Office.

European Commission (2010), *Internationalisation of European SMEs: Final Report*, Brussels: European Commission, available at www.ec.europa.eu/enterprise/e_i/ index_en.htm.

European Commission (2015), 'COSME: Europe's programme for SMEs', available at https://ec.europa.eu/docsroom/documents/9783.

European Parliament (2016), 'Tailor-made support for SMEs towards effective implementation of the EU's trade and investment strategy', Workshop, available at http://www.europarl.europa.eu/thinktank/en/document.html?reference=EXPO _STU(2016)535025.

JETRO (2018), *Invest Japan Report*, available at https://www.jetro.go.jp/ext_images/ invest/ijre/report2018/pdf/jetro_invest_japan_report_2018en.pdf.

OECD (2013), *Fostering SMEs' Participation in Global Markets: Final Report*, Paris: OECD Publishing.

OECD (2014), *Italy: Key Issues and Policies*, OECD Studies on SMEs and Entrepreneurship, Paris: OECD Publishing.

Picha, J. (2014), 'Comparison of export financing programmes in Czech Republic and Germany', paper presented at the Construction Macroeconomics Conference 2014.

Sinkovics, R. R., Y. Kurt and N. Sinkovics (2018), 'The effect of matching on perceived export barriers and performance in an era of globalization discontents: Empirical evidence from UK SMEs', *International Business Review*, 27 (5), 1065–79.

Suarez-Ortega, S. (2003), 'Export barriers: Insights from small and medium sized firms', *International Small Business Journal*, 21 (4), 403–19.

UKEF (2019), *UK Export Finance Annual Report 2018- and Accounts 2018–2019*, available at https://www.gov.uk/government/publications/uk-export-finance-annual-report-and-accounts-2018-to-2019.

PART II

National case studies

6　China: a focus on local policy

David Smallbone, Li Xiao and Jianbo Xu

Introduction

It is widely acknowledged that entrepreneurship can act as a means to stimulate economic development in a region or country (Hart, 2003; Minniti, 2008; Autio and Rannikko, 2016). Moreover, in transition economies such as China, government has been a key factor influencing the extent to which the business environment has been transformed. In China, the institutional infrastructure and legal framework for small and medium-sized enterprise (SME) development and entrepreneurship has been improving over recent decades (Lundström and Stevenson, 2005; OECD, 2015). Furthermore, governments at the country, provincial, city and town level use entrepreneurship policy to address challenges related to economic growth and social development (in other words, job creation, unbalanced and inadequate development). At the same time, it is not always clear how local policies relate to national policies in seeking to foster entrepreneurship.

The story so far

Entrepreneurship policy is relatively new in China. Moreover, formal SME policy has only existed since 2002 when China amended the constitution to grant non-state-owned firms a legal status (Chen, 2006; Lundström and Stevenson, 2005; Zhu et al., 2012). A well-organised entrepreneurship policy did not exist until 2015. Of course, entrepreneurship policy is not the same as SME policy. Whereas SME policy is concerned with existing firms, entrepreneurship policy focuses on the creation of new firms and the growth of existing ones. Although SMEs and entrepreneurship have been responsible for much of China's rapid economic growth over the last four decades, there does not appear to be a strong relationship between the rapid growth of SMEs and public policies towards SMEs and entrepreneurship (Xiao and North, 2018; Atherton and Smallbone, 2013; Watkin-Mathys and Foster, 2006).

Nevertheless, government intervention has been a constant key in transforming the business environment over this period. The focus of public policies towards business has changed dramatically during the last 40 years. Initially, public policy at the central level emphasised supporting and reforming state-owned companies. In China's constitution, SMEs and the private sector were excluded from the mainstream of economic activity until the late 1990s. Town and village owned enterprises (TVEs) were created and grew rapidly, supported by town and village governments directly and indirectly during the 1980s and 1990s. However, from the early 2000s local governments were no longer allowed to own and operate TVEs and, more generally, government officials were no longer allowed to run their own private firms.

An entrepreneurship policy framework has formally emerged since 2015, aiming at creating a new growth engine for China's economy. A shift in public policy, from an emphasis on the existing stock of enterprises to a much broader focus on both nascent and existing entrepreneurs, has been made over a relatively short period of 11 years. Another change made to public policy included a greater focus on the entrepreneurial process in preparing, starting and fast-growing a venture. The attitudes of government officials and policy makers at different levels towards entrepreneurs and entrepreneurial activities has become more positive over time, helping to create a positive social image of entrepreneurs and promote an entrepreneurial culture. Entrepreneurship continues to develop across the nation, with the Eastern and Coastal regions having a higher level of entrepreneurial activities compared to other regions. At the same time, people's perception of cultural values and social norms relating to entrepreneurship overall has become more positive.

Entrepreneurship policies are more complex in China than in other contexts. The domain of entrepreneurial policy is larger in China than in countries like the USA and those in Europe. It not only encompasses activities at several levels of government and across different industry sectors (Hart, 2003), but it is also embedded in institutional transitions and social issues. One of the objectives in developing entrepreneurship policy initiatives at the national level in China is to use them as a means of enhancing the effects of institutional transitions on social and economic development.

Entrepreneurship policy initiatives introduced by provincial governments need to serve two purposes: firstly, implementing the principles introduced by the national government and, secondly, promoting regional entrepreneurial activities. City and town governments are responsible for implementing provincial policies to promote entrepreneurial activities and grow local economies. The more important the policy, the more government departments involved. For a relatively long time there has been a lack of explicit and consistent entrepreneurial policies because of the nature of institutional transitions. The contribution of SMEs and entrepreneurship to the rapid growth of China's regional economies has been far more than the support received over the last four decades.

Spatial variations in entrepreneurship

China is characterised by large geographical disparities in economic development (Xiao and Ritchie, 2009). As a consequence, public policy must at least be sensitive and flexible enough to accommodate these regional differences, and in some cases contribute to narrowing the gap. Specifically, the development of entrepreneurship in the Western and Central areas is much less than it is in the Eastern and Coastal regions (Lundström and Stevenson, 2005). Such large geographic disparities suggest that the challenges that subnational economies in China face vary enormously. Entrepreneurship framework conditions, entrepreneurship productivity and entrepreneurial culture reflect this variation. Thus, it might be expected that the kind of support that public policies give directly to new venture creation, innovative young ventures and specific industries differs according to the economic development of a host region.

One might also expect the kind of public support policies that give direct support to the intermediates (business incubators or technology business incubators) for the development and commercialisation of technology-based firms (incubated firms) to vary according to the level of economic development of a host region (Folta et al., 2006; Fritsch and Slavtchev, 2011). Regions with more advanced economies and more supportive infrastructure are likely to have an advantage over others lacking in these respects (Xiao and North, 2017 and 2018). However, little is known about how entrepreneurship policy incorporates the local, provincial and country level, and how public policies relevant to SME development and entrepreneurship actually operate and work in China.

Local policy and practice

In order to investigate the effects of spatial variations in entrepreneurship on public policy, a comparison of two contrasting provinces was undertaken. These were Guangdong and Sichuan – Guangdong to represent the Eastern and Coastal regions, which have more advanced economies compared to other regions in China, and Sichuan to represent the Western and Central regions (Table 6.1).

The data for this study came from both primary and secondary sources. Secondary data included documents relating to entrepreneurship policy initiatives (see Figure 6.1) and the results of the government's annual survey. This was supplemented by primary data consisting of results from face-to-face interviews with local officials. In order to provide a focus and facilitate a comparison, the empirical investigation concentrated on a policy called the Mass Entrepreneurship and Innovation Programme. This policy was initially introduced by the Central Party Committee and State Council in 2015, aiming to encourage both elite and grassroots entrepreneurship. The State Council requested that each province allocated a proportion of its budget to enabling start-ups and fostering the growth of early-stage ventures as a mechanism for further economic growth.

Public policies for the private sector were less restrictive in the Eastern and Coastal regions (that is, Guangdong) than in Western and Central regions (that is, Sichuan). Privately owned firms of entrepreneurs were seen to be seizing business opportunities and responding to market demands in an environment that was favourable to both state-owned companies and TVEs. These private ventures had grown rapidly in the Eastern and Coastal regions, as indicated by the job creation and wealth generation despite the fragile environment. Such ventures actually behaved differently from those in a more supported business environment, for instance focusing on short-term success and being reluctant to invest in long-term projects (Xiao and Ramsden, 2016). It would be logical, therefore, to expect that the level of entrepreneurship is higher in the Eastern and Coastal regions compared to Western and Central regions.

Not surprisingly perhaps, in terms of the socio-economic indicators, the gap between Guangdong and Sichuan provinces is reflected in the pattern of SME and entrepreneurship development. Table 6.2 shows geographical disparities in SME development and entrepreneurship between Guangdong and Sichuan, together with indicators that help to describe the gap in terms of the level of economic and social development in these two provinces. It firstly shows

Table 6.1 Differences in regional economic growth between Guangdong and Sichuan 2007–16

Region	2007				2016				2007–16 growth (%)		
	GDP per capita (Yuan)	Disposal income (Yuan)	Graduates No. (1000)	Proportion of province (%)	GDP per capita (Yuan)	Disposal income (Yuan)	Graduates No. (1000)	Proportion of province (%)	GDP per capita	Disposal income	Graduates
Guangdong	28902	17067	233.1	0.2476	69695	36837	489.4	0.4449	10.90	9.01	9.74
Sichuan	11290	10071	228.0	0.2805	37386	26382	362.1	0.4383	15.13	11.70	7.98
China	18050	13154	4478	0.3389	50876	32957	7042	0.5093	13.18	11.07	6.56

Note: Calculated according to survey data compiled from the China National Statistics Bureau Yearbooks for the years 2007 to 2016.

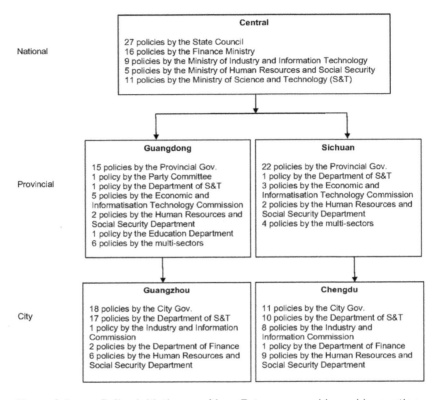

Figure 6.1   Policy initiatives on Mass Entrepreneurship and Innovation at the three government levels

a continued considerable gap in the level of employment in SMEs, with a total of 10.85 million jobs in Guangdong compared to a total of 1.95 million jobs in Sichuan in 2007. By 2016 this had increased to 2.17 million in Sichuan, but declined to 8.85 million in Guangdong. This is reflected in the average annual rate of decrease of 0.81 per cent in Guangdong compared with a rate of increase of 2.64 per cent in Sichuan. At the same time, it is evident that in terms of the number of people employed in SMEs employment, the significant gap between the two provinces is slowly narrowing.

Overall, the analysis suggests that a considerable gap exists in SME development and entrepreneurship between the two provinces, indicated by the number of employees, the share of SME employees of total employment, sales turnover and the SME sales turnover as a proportion of total GDP.

Table 6.2   Disparities in SME development and entrepreneurship in Guangdong and Sichuan 2007–16

Region	2007				2016				2007-16 growth (%)	
	Employees		Sales turnover		Employees		Sales turnover			
	No. (1000)	Proportion of province	Total (1 trillion Yuan)	Proportion of province	No. (1000)	Proportion of province	Total (1 trillion Yuan)	Proportion of province	Employees	Sales
Guangdong	10 850	0.8299	3558	0.6599	8858	0.6247	7096	0.5495	-0.81	9.92
Sichuan	1954	0.7590	710	0.6691	2173	0.6477	2730	0.6576	2.64	19.35
China	78 752	0.7685	39 971	0.6370	94 756	0.6625	72 255	0.6234	1.42	14.26

Note: Calculated according to survey data compiled from the Provincial Statistics Bureau Yearbooks Guangdong 2007 to 2016, the Provincial Statistics Bureau Yearbooks Sichuan 2007 to 2016, and the China National Statistics Bureau Yearbooks 2007 to 2016.

Interestingly, it was also found that such gaps either are narrowing or have been filled during the last decade.

Turning to the Mass Entrepreneurship and Innovation Programme, whilst it is a national programme it is up to provincial and local governments to design local policy initiatives whilst following the principles established by central government. This particularly applies where a city or province is seeking to obtain funding from central government. In this section, comparisons are drawn between the policy responses of the two provinces, paying attention to the target groups in terms of both people and sector, the methods used to deliver the policy and the resources available (Acs and Szerb, 2007).

Table 6.3 suggests that both Guangdong and Sichuan introduced relevant policy initiatives, targeting nascent and existing entrepreneurs. Guangdong focused on local, recent graduates and university students with the potential to set up an innovative business. Existing incubators are encouraged, through government grants and subsidies, to offer basic, free facilities (such as the use of office and lab space) to graduates and university students. By sharing the incubator building (such as the canteen and gym) as well as organising social events, graduates and university students can meet existing entrepreneurs of early-stage high-tech firms and exchange business ideas and information. The incubators also provide business assistance (such as business registration, government grant/loans application, amongst others) to help set up a business. In contrast, Sichuan paid particular attention to migrant worker returnees. Incentives given by local governments included rent subsidies, tax breaks and a range of advisory support.

Both Guangdong and Sichuan support existing entrepreneurs operating their businesses in a high-tech sector. In Guangdong, various government grants and subsidies are available to existing entrepreneurs capable of fast growing their ventures to become market leaders (measured by academic degree received, overseas experience, amounts of taxation paid, and patents granted).

Guangdong's policy initiatives have an industry focus. One priority is to facilitate the modernisation of traditional industries. In Foshan, for example, local government has focused on technological upgrading of its porcelain industry. Porcelain manufacturers have been experiencing problems with recruiting and maintaining skilled labour. The problem is that the number of younger people entering the sector is less than the number retiring. Many younger people see this work as unattractive due to concerns that their health may be damaged because of poor working conditions. One solution to the problem would be to use robots instead of skilled workers. However, these manufacturers have been

Table 6.3   Entrepreneurship policy priorities in Guangdong and Sichuan

	Guangdong	Sichuan
Target group	Local technological entrepreneurs with potential of growing fast Graduates University students Start-ups having employees	Technological entrepreneurs from overseas and the Eastern and Coastal regions Migrant worker returnees Graduates Small firms employing graduates
Industry focus	Local, traditional industries that are important to regional development Advanced materials Industry product design	Manufacturers from the Eastern and Coastal regions Agricultural product process and supply chains Industry product design
Delivery methods	Existing incubators University incubators Local financial market	Establishing new incubators University incubators Existing banks Local authorities
Resource available	A larger amount of public funds available to R&D and innovation Public budget available to innovative start-ups and early-stage firms	Sufficient amount of public funds available to unemployed graduates Public funds available to migrant worker returnees
Approach	Top-down approach and bottom-up approach	Top-down approach and bottom-up approach

reluctant to invest in upgrading their production lines, and do not know how to do so. Local government, working together with an elite university located in Guangzhou, introduced a range of policy instruments to facilitate the upgrading of the industry's technology. This included a specialised incubator, sponsored by the local government and the university, to encourage academics with the technological knowledge to start ventures, as well as providing technology upgrading services. Moreover, managers from the incubator brokered collaboration between technological entrepreneurs and manufacturers. High-tech start-ups that provided technology upgrading services to those manufacturing firms received government subsidies to cover the relevant expenses. In other words, manufacturers upgraded their production lines for free. Furthermore, managers from the incubator helped high-tech start-ups apply for innovation funding provided by the provincial policy initiatives.

In Sichuan, public policies towards migrant worker returnees paid particular attention to attracting these workers and encouraging them to set up businesses in their hometowns or the urban areas near their original neighbourhoods that do not have an industry focus. By offering incentives to migrant

worker returnees, local government might be able to address one of the province's major challenges, namely local job creation and financing for increased
demand for public services. In practice, the majority of the migrant worker
returnees started their businesses in non-agricultural sectors, including manufacturing, catering and accommodation. In addition, both provincial and city
governments are, to a certain degree, still working to remove institution-based
barriers to nascent and existing entrepreneurs of privately owned businesses
regardless of sector.

Both Guangdong and Sichuan rely on technology business incubators to
address the business support needs of pre-start-ups, start-ups and early-stage
ventures. Interestingly, but not surprisingly, Guangdong is keen on improving
the quality of support services offered by existing incubators, whilst Sichuan
has put more effort into establishing the kind of new-generation incubators
that serve start-ups and early-stage ventures operating in a specific industry.
This is because Guangdong has established more new-generation incubators,
whereas Sichuan is still catching up. In Guangdong, incubators provide business support to graduates and university students, including basic facilities,
training courses (for both nascent and existing entrepreneurs) and entrepreneurship competitions. Public money and resources are also available for
local organisations to build various platforms (for machinery testing, internet
finance, and others) from which a large number of nascent, start-ups and
early-stage firms benefit. Local government not only provides funding to the
selected firms but also encourages private investors to provide venture capital
to businesses by offering financial incentives.

Although the economic development needs of Sichuan appear substantially
greater than those of Guangdong, the resources available from the public
sector are significantly higher in Guangdong. This is reflected in the size of the
research and development (R&D) budget, as well as in the proportion of the
science and technology (S&T) budget allocated R&D and innovation. Table
6.4 shows that a much larger amount of the public budget was allocated to
R&D and innovation in Guangdong (RMB 74.30 billion in 2016) compared
to in Sichuan (RMB 10.11 billion in 2016). The proportion of the S&T budget
allocated to R&D and innovation over the last decade has also been greater in
Guangdong (3.8 per cent in 2008 and 5.5 per cent in 2016) than in Sichuan (1.2
per cent in 2008 and 1.3 per cent in 2016).

Table 6.4   Science and technology budget by province 2007–16

	Public budget (billion Yuan)		S&T budget (billion Yuan)		Ratio (%)		Growth rate 2007–16 (%)	
	2007	2016	2007	2016	2008	2016	Public budget	S&T budget
Guangdong	315.96	1344.61	11.93	74.30	3.8	5.5	17.9	20.6
Sichuan	175.91	800.89	2.08	10.11	1.2	1.3	19.4	19.5

Conclusion and future policy agenda

The analysis of entrepreneurship policy in China has demonstrated the role of both local and provincial policies alongside the interests of national policy makers. In this context, the Mass Entrepreneurship and Innovation Programme reflects the commitment of national government to the national policy objective. Alongside this, the size of China territorially and the inevitable diversity of policy priorities makes it very appropriate for local policy to reflect the particular support needs of firms in the locality.

It is evident that, up to now, central government has played a key role in designing a formal and systematic entrepreneurship policy to promote entrepreneurial activities in order to grow China's economy further. Central government also plays an essential role in implementing policy at provincial and local levels through each Ministry's network with the relevant regional and city government (for example, the Ministry of Science and Technology – provincial Department of Science and Technology – city Department of Science and Technology). Provincial and city governments follow the policy by the central government and design a broad spectrum of entrepreneurship policy initiatives accordingly, although local governments need to integrate the policy instruments into the economic structure and regional development.

The geographical variations in local SME and entrepreneurial policy initiatives between the Chinese provinces of Guangdong and Sichuan involve a number of key elements. Firstly, Guangdong's policy initiatives have paid more attention to technological entrepreneurs and innovative early-stage ventures with the potential of fast growth, whilst Sichuan's policy instruments emphasise migrant worker returnees who are interested in starting a business. Secondly, policy makers in Guangdong consider local traditional industries as a key element when designing local policy initiatives promoting entrepreneurship, whilst Sichuan is attracting manufacturing from the Eastern and Coastal regions (because of low wage rates and low-cost land use) which seems to play a key role in designing the policy instruments. Policy instruments in Guangdong place a greater emphasis on stimulating higher levels of entrepreneurship, which is still relatively new in China. At the same time, Sichuan places more emphasis on efforts to attract technological entrepreneurs from overseas and from the more developed Eastern and Coastal regions. These findings give strong support to the need for entrepreneurship policy to be sensitive to local conditions.

Entrepreneurship policy initiatives are characterised by selectivity, an emphasis on growth motivation, capacity building, hands-on support, networking, public–private collaboration, and the use of performance milestones (Hart, 2003; Autio and Rannikko, 2016). However, insufficient internal expertise has limited the capacity of some local governments in China to design and establish local policy initiatives to promote entrepreneurial activities. For instance, a significant number of the policy initiatives in Sichuan simply focus on allocating public funds to individual graduates who are experiencing difficulty finding a job. This kind of policy initiative aims to solve the unemployment of graduates rather than promoting entrepreneurial activities. In Guangdong, managers from local government and public agencies have more experience in designing entrepreneurial policy initiatives towards entrepreneurial activities and integrating them into local resources, and might be better able to operate the entrepreneurial policy initiatives. In this context, wage rates will need to rise if China is to remain competitive in the increasingly technological world.

Future priorities for entrepreneurship policies

There is a lack of evidence to measure the effectiveness of entrepreneurship policy initiatives in the two selected provinces and in China as a whole. It is challenging to examine the effectiveness of the local policies relevant to entrepreneurial activities, firstly because of the lack of data from the government services at all the levels, and secondly because of an emphasis on short-term policies (Autio and Rannikko, 2016). In China, rapid changes to local policy instruments make it even more difficult to measure the meaningful impact on economic growth that may take some years to appear. All levels of policy makers seem motivated to get the policy initiatives launched, but seemingly are yet to take the need for meaningful evaluation of impacts seriously. Perhaps only a handful of high-growth policies have a long enough track record for there to be a meaningful impact. Participation in such initiatives is subject to double selection; only some new ventures self-select to apply for such initiatives, and not all applicants qualify. The implication for all levels of policy making is that designing entrepreneurship policy initiatives should consider the evidence available of meaningful impact.

Policy initiatives aiming towards entrepreneurial activities might also create downside effects. For instance, policy instruments that aim to encourage graduates experiencing difficulty finding a job to start their own business does not seem to be a good basis for policy (Shane, 2009). It is clear that some policy instruments that are claimed to be part of the entrepreneurship agenda are in reality more about tackling the unemployment of graduates rather than promoting entrepreneurial activities. Meanwhile, nascent entrepreneurs with talent and motivation might not be qualified to obtain government grants or subsidies for starting a business. The complex institutional environment, which involves multiple institutions at both national and local levels of government, makes it difficult to identify key decision makers and, hence, for companies to anticipate important decisions. Entrepreneurship policies often lack detail, and are frequently incomplete, ambiguous and subject to unpredictable continuous revisions.

This research provides a comprehensive picture of the entrepreneurial policy efforts in China by identifying the marked differences in the entrepreneurship policy orientations of provincial and local governments. Overall, policy has a clear role to play in developing regional and local institutional infrastructures and the legal framework, which are needed to create a more favourable environment for SME development and entrepreneurship. Policy also has a role to play in developing regional and local physical and social infrastructures, which are needed to underpin and support entrepreneurial activities in the regions. In Sichuan, policy to promote entrepreneurship and SME development acts as a strategy mainly for creating employment, to absorb millions of new graduate entrants on an annual basis as well as rural migrant returnees; whilst in Guangdong, policy to promote entrepreneurship and SME development is a strategy mainly for building up the indigenous capacity for innovation and technology development. In order to achieve a high level of policy integration and synergy with other aspects of local development, local authorities should consider the specific contextual conditions when seeking to learn good practice from other regions as well as coordinating entrepreneurship policy. Ongoing research in this area could assess the meaningful impact of these policy initiatives on job creation and sustainable economic growth in the regions.

References

Acs, Z. J. and L. Szerb (2007), 'Entrepreneurship, economic growth and public policy', *Small Business Economics*, **28**, 109–22.

Atherton, A. and D. Smallbone (2013), 'Promoting private sector development in China: The challenge of building institutional capacity at the local level', *Environment and Planning C: Government and Policy*, **31**, 5–23.

Autio, E. and H. Rannikko (2016), 'Retaining winners: Can policy boost high-growth entrepreneurship?', *Research Policy*, **45**, 42–55.

Chen, J. (2006), 'Development of Chinese small and medium-size enterprises', *Journal of Small Business and Enterprise Development*, **13**, 140–47.

Folta, T., A. C. Cooper and Y. Baik (2006), 'Geographic cluster size and firm performance', *Journal of Business Venturing*, **21**, 217–42.

Fritsch, M. and V. Slavtchev (2011), 'Determinants of the efficiency of regional innovation systems', *Regional Studies*, **45**, 905–18.

Hart, D. M. (2003), 'Entrepreneurship policy: What it is and where it came from', in D. M. Hart (ed.), *The Emergence of Entrepreneurship Policy*, Cambridge: Cambridge University Press, pp. 3–19.

Lundström, A. and L. A. Stevenson (2005), 'Entrepreneurship policy in People's Republic of China', working paper.

Minniti, M. (2008), 'The role of government policy on entrepreneurial activity: Productive, unproductive, or destructive?', *Entrepreneurship Theory and Practice*, **32**, 779–90.

OECD (2015), *China in a Changing Global Environment*, Paris: OECD Publishing.

Shane, S. (2009), 'Why encouraging more people to become entrepreneurs is bad public policy', *Small Business Economics*, **33**, 141–9.

Watkin-Mathys, L. and M. J. Foster (2006), 'Entrepreneurship: The missing ingredient in China's STIPs?', *Entrepreneurship and Regional Development*, **18**, 249–74.

Xiao, L. and D. North (2017), 'The graduation performance of technology business incubators in China's three tier cities: The role of incubator funding, technical support, and entrepreneurial mentoring', *Journal of Technology Transfer*, **42**, 615–34.

Xiao, L. and D. North (2018), 'The role of technological business incubators in supporting business innovation in China: A case of regional adaptability?', *Entrepreneurship and Regional Development*, **30**, 29–57.

Xiao, L. and M. Ramsden (2016), 'Founder expertise, strategic choices, formation and survival of high-tech SMEs in China: A resource-substituted approach', *Journal of Small Business Management*, **54**, 892–911.

Xiao, L. and B. Ritchie (2009), 'Access to finance for high-tech SMEs: Regional differences in China', *Environment and Planning C: Government and Policy*, **27**, 246–62.

Zhu, Y., X. Wittmann and M. Peng (2012), 'Institution-based barriers to innovation in SMEs in China', *Asia Pacific Journal of Management*, **29**, 1132–42.

7 SMEs and entrepreneurship policy in Russia

Vera Barinova, Stepan Zemtsov and David Smallbone

Key characteristics of the SME sector in Russia

One of the most distinctive features of small and medium-sized enterprises (SMEs) in Russia is their relatively small contribution to the economy compared to many other countries, including other emerging economies. According to the Organisation for Economic Co-operation and Development (OECD, 2015), in 2010 there were just 3.2 million operating businesses in the country. By international standards this is a small number given the size of the Russian economy. For example, countries such as Mexico and South Korea have more businesses than Russia despite the total output of these countries' economies being smaller. In addition, the rate of 31 registered enterprises per one thousand of the working population is far below OECD countries such as Mexico (with a figure of 67) and the USA (with a figure of 102). Moreover, the modest contribution of SME activity in Russia is also revealed by looking at the figures for employment. In 2018 the Russian Statistical Office (Rosstat, 2019) reports that more than 5.7 million small and medium-sized enterprises (SMEs) and sole proprietorships operate in the Russian Federation, creating jobs for approximately 19 million citizens, which is about one-third of all working people or 38 per cent of permanent employees (Russian Economy in 2018, 2019).

At the same time, it is difficult to be definitive due to differences in the way in which the statistics on the SME sector are presented in Russia, which reflect the differences in the definition of what constitutes an SME (Barinova and Zemtsov, 2019). Nevertheless, based on OECD's report, Rosstat has produced estimates describing the size, structure and other features of Russian SMEs based on European Union (EU) definitions.

The slow growth of the SME sector in Russia is reflected in the low number of people, engaged in starting or running a new business, according to the 2019 Global Entrepreneurship Monitor (GEM) report (Bosma and Kelley, 2019), just 5.6 per cent of the adult population in Russia in 2018 were engaged in trying to establish a new business (total early-stage entrepreneurial activity). This is compared to 17.9 per cent in Brazil and 10.4 per cent in China. To understand the current situation, one needs to keep in mind that just 25 years ago Russia was an economy operating under central planning. There are many facets to this, but one is that it contributes to negative perceptions of entrepreneurs in the Russian population, particularly among the older generation for whom during their lifetime entrepreneurs were seen as crooks and criminals. Subsequently, productive entrepreneurship has been seen to be an important process to encourage. As a consequence, from a policy perspective there needs to be a major push to change these perceptions, certainly if the rate of business start-up is to significantly improve over time.

The contribution of the SME sector to Russia's gross domestic product (GDP) increased by 0.5 percentage points from 2011 to 2017, and is approximately 22 per cent. It was estimated that SMEs create up to 43 per cent of business economy GDP[1] (Russian Economy in 2018, 2019), whilst the OECD average is more than 55 per cent (OECD, 2015). The share of the SME sector in employment and in GDP depends on the structure and size of the economy. Russia in this case is closer not to the EU countries but to the USA, Canada and Japan, due to the development of labour-intensive and capital-intensive industries. In Russia, it may be argued that the problem is not that SMEs are few but that the public sector occupies too large a share.

Along with other transition economies, Russia has a large informal sector which undoubtedly helps to explain the relatively low number of SMEs in the formal economy. An International Labour Organization survey (ILO, 2015) suggested that the Russian Federation may have approximately 7.78 million undeclared jobs, which is one of the contributing factors to the informal economy. At the same time, there are different methodologies for assessing the scale of the informal economy and these have measured this using an alternative approach. The Schneider measure suggests that as much as 40 per cent of economic activity in the Russian Federation could be informal in nature. Certainly, this figure is significantly higher than in most OECD countries. In addition, the official statistics shows that the informal sector has been growing, with 12.6 million people working in the sector in 2006, increasing to 14.2 million people in 2017 (Russian Economy in 2018, 2019).[2]

Another key feature of the SME sector in Russia is its uneven development, which has led some researchers to emphasise the need for a regional dimension to SME policy (Chepurenko et al., 2017; Zemtsov and Tsareva, 2018; Barinova et al., 2018). It is argued that this is essential in order to broaden the current focus on Moscow and St Petersburg as the main centres of small business and entrepreneurship in the country. According to researchers (for example, Chepurenko et al., 2017), people's motivation and readiness to open businesses differ greatly across regions. However, policy makers in Russia emphasise that regulation and institutional conditions are the same throughout the country. SME support is provided mainly through federal laws. Although regions in Russia have the right to introduce their own tax preferences and finance pro-grammes, few of them take up this opportunity because of their budget deficits (Chepurenko and Vilenski, 2016). However, according to papers by Aidis et al. (2008), Yakovlev and Zhuravskaya (2013) and Barinova et al. (2018), the dif-ferences in the institutional background of the various regions create different conditions for the implementation of laws.

The overall conclusion is that entrepreneurship is at a lower level in the Russian Federation in comparison with other countries. What is more important, the SME sector in Russia differs from those abroad: there are fewer start-ups, fewer technology-based companies and fewer innovations, and the export of SME products is lower (Russian Economy in 2018, 2019).

Several specific legal acts aimed at SME development were adopted in 2016–17, including the SME Strategy Development 2030.[3] In addition, the SME Corporation[4] was established and the basic SME support infrastructure was formed in the majority of Russian regions. The Unified SME Register was created[5] to allow public access to the monthly dynamics of basic SME development indicators in Russia. There are some positive trends in the entre-preneurial activity growth and in the role of SMEs in the economy as a whole. Nevertheless, this sector remains relatively underdeveloped in comparison with other countries.

Basic SME development indicator dynamics

Whilst commentators and officials agree that SME development in Russia is increasing, the absence of data over long time periods that use a consistent definition is a problem. However, from 2016 onwards the most accurate SME data is contained in the Unified SME Register, which is updated monthly. According to the Unified SME Register data, there were more than 6 million

SMEs in Russia in June 2019 (Table 7.1), including about 3.41 million sole proprietorships. Almost 96 per cent of all Russian SMEs are micro companies (5.9 million) with an average of one to two employees. There are 247 133 small firms in Russia (about 4 per cent of all SMEs) and 18 617 medium enterprises (0.3 per cent of all SMEs).

In general, the overall SME structure is stable and the main indicators have stayed at the same level for several years. Between 2008 and 2016, the total number of SMEs increased by 30 per cent, from 4.1 million to 5.3 million. The most rapid increase was seen between 2014 and 2016 (by 17 per cent), mainly due to changes in SME definitional criteria. They were widened in order to make them closer to international criteria (Barinova and Zemtsov, 2019). In addition, small enterprises have a special tax regime that significantly reduces the tax burden. Moreover, during this period, tools for state support and access to public procurement were significantly expanded for small enterprises.

The structure of the SME sector in Russia in 2018 is as follows (Rosstat, 2019): 39.2 per cent of all SMEs, including sole proprietorships, are wholesale and retail trade; 6.7 per cent are real estate activities; 9.3 per cent are transport and storage; 8.6 per cent are construction; 6.5 per cent are manufacturing; and 29.7 per cent are other industries. Medium-sized enterprises are prevalent in the manufacturing industry (26.0 per cent) and agriculture (14.5 per cent). These industries require a larger set of competencies. The larger the size of the enterprise, the higher the firm's capacity to implement complex activities (manufacturing), capital-intensive activities (extractive industry) and risky activities (agricultural).

The share of employees in sole proprietorships is more than 50 per cent of the total number of employees in SMEs in underdeveloped regions such as the Republic of Tuva, the Chechen Republic and the Republic of Kalmykia. Sole proprietorships have a smaller set of competencies in primitive industries; the vast majority are engaged in trade, agriculture and domestic services, and do not enter foreign markets. In underdeveloped regions markets are smaller and institutional conditions are worse, therefore businesses do not scale.

A key feature of the Russian SME sector is the low level of new technology usage. For example, the GEM Innovation Indicator (Bosma and Kelley, 2019) for Russia is 8.1 per cent (ranked 47th out of 48), which is several times lower than that of other countries within the BRICS (Brazil, Russia, India, China and South Africa) grouping and much lower than the USA. In addition, the majority of entrepreneurs in Russia are not aiming to grow their businesses, although this is not a feature confined to Russia. As a consequence, it is not surprising

Table 7.1   SME sector structure, in terms of size and organisational form, 2017–19

Indicator	Total	Enterprises		
		Micro	Small	Medium
2017				
Legal entities				
Number of enterprises, units	2 756 724	2 498 152	238 893	19 679
Share of SMEs total, %	47.024	42.613	4.075	0.336
Share of legal entities, %	100	90.620	8.666	0.714
Sole proprietorships[a]				
Number of enterprises, units	3 105 636	3 079 056	26 446	134
Share of SMEs total, %	52.976	52.522	0.451	0.002
Share of all sole proprietorships, %	100	99.144	0.852	0.004
All SMEs				
Number of enterprises, units	5 862 360	5 577 208	265 339	19 813
Share of SMEs total, %	100	95.136	4.526	0.338
2018				
Legal entities				
Number of enterprises, units	2 684 619	2 441 283	224 741	18 595
Share of SMEs total, %	44.7	40.7	3.7	0.3
Sole proprietorships				
Number of enterprises, units	3 316 472	3 288 368	27 780	324
Share of all sole proprietorships, %	100	99.15	0.838	0.00977
All SMEs				
Number of enterprises, units	6 001 091	5 729 651	252 521	18 919
Share of SMEs total, %	100	95.477	4.208	0.315

Indicator	Total	Enterprises		
		Micro	Small	Medium
2019				
Number of SMEs	6 184 204	5 918 454	247 133	18 617
Legal entities	2 774 161	2 535 614	220 245	18 302
Sole proprietorships	3 410 043	3 382 840	26 888	315

Note: [a] According to Russian law, sole proprietorships statistically are referred to as persons, not legal entities.
Source: The Unified SME Register data, https://ofd.nalog.ru/.

perhaps that the share of necessity-driven entrepreneurs in the total number of SMEs is approximately 31 per cent. The SME sector in Russia is very unevenly developed and heterogeneous, both structurally and regionally.

The business environment

The business environment in Russia has not been encouraging from an SME point of view. In terms of exports, there is a dependence upon natural resource exports, pointing to the need for diversification of the economy, which would be in the interest of SME development. Secondly, foreign direct investment (FDI) is at a relatively low level. This is potentially important from an SME point of view because in many developing countries FDI represents a potential market for local SMEs, as well as a potential source of technology and management know-how.

Moreover, there are barriers to market entry for new products that result from the role of the state. For example, there are still large numbers of state-owned enterprises in Russia, with the state sector accounting for more than 46 per cent of GDP (Abramov et al., 2018). Market interventions also include price controls. Corruption is endemic and likely to be a constraint on business operation in the case of innovative enterprises. It is also likely to push some businesses owners towards the informal economy. Another constraint is regulatory burdens, although for start-ups these burdens have been reduced significantly in recent years. For example, the number of days required to complete the administrative procedures required when starting a business fell from 43 days in 2004 to just 15 days in 2014.

The Russian Federation has a long tradition of innovation, particularly innovation that is technology based. One of the major problems with respect to the innovation system is the relatively low level of commercialisation when compared with other countries (Zemtsov et al., 2016). It is also the case that Russia has been badly affected by the out-migration of top scientists and technologists to countries like the USA. A further constraint on entrepreneurship is the weak financial markets. As a result, they do not perform the function of being the source of loans and other financial products that start-ups in other countries have access to, including many of the so-called 'transition economies' these days.

Although the combined effects of these various characteristics of the business environment for SMEs in Russia has been, and continues to be, a constraint, the Russian government has taken a number of steps in the right direction. Only time will tell how efficiently and vigorously these new developments have been implemented. Nonetheless, they include some reduction in the level of business taxation. According to the OECD (2015), the rate of corporate income tax was reduced from 24 per cent to 20 per cent in 2010. The total corporate tax rate as a percentage of business profits was reduced from 60 per cent to 51 per cent between 2006 and 2014.

Entrepreneurship and SME policy in Russia

In transition economies such as Russia, one of the roles of the state with respect to private sector development is to create a legal framework which recognises the existence of SMEs and defines what they are. In the case of Russia, whilst the legal reforms that are technically necessary for SMEs to become established were introduced, their application has been patchy. Moreover, in the early days of transition the issue was essentially to establish an institutional framework to regulate, but also to promote, private sector SMEs. As has been said previously, the role of the state in the emerging market economy requires a major transformation. In former times, the functions of the state were to act as entrepreneur, to supply finance, to control the labour market, to plan the entire production system, and to define the rules and ensure that they were actually applied.

A key question, and a recurrent one, in former socialist economies concerns the so-called 'implementation gap', where a public policy is declared but, in fact, no budget is allocated to it. As a result, typically not very much happens. It has been argued that one of the benefits that Central and East European countries gained when they joined the EU was a framework which links together strategy with budget and actions. In Russia, SME support now implies project management, which is being implemented at all levels of public administration, including regional and local. Several priority projects have been launched, including that for 'Small Business and Enterprise Support' and 'National Champions' (for medium enterprises). The regional target model 'Support of Small and Medium Enterprises' has also been introduced.

The strategy contains a number of key targets for SME development in Russia. The main targets are:

- SME turnover 2.5 times higher than in 2014 (in real terms)
- SME labour productivity twice as high as in 2014 (in real terms)
- Manufacturing turnover share in the SMEs total turnover – 20 per cent
- Share of people employed in SMEs in total employed – 35 per cent

A strategic goal for the SME sector is to provide 40 per cent of GDP by 2030. The annual growth of this share should be 1 per cent or more.

The strategy includes a number of key elements in current SME policy in Russia. None of the eight measures listed below are traditional for Russia. In fact, all are innovations in public policy for entrepreneurship in Russia. These are:

- Integration of SME support. Hitherto the SME support policy has appeared to be unstructured, with a lack of consistency in implementation creating uncertainty about what was on offer. Moreover, the level of trust in institutions was very low. However, in 2016 the Strategy 2030 for the Development of Small and Medium-Sized Entrepreneurship in the Russian Federation was adopted, making the SME support policy more consistent and coherent. New institutions were established and new programmes were launched.
- Stimulating demand for SME products. The main focus with respect to this strategic goal has been an attempt to open up public procurement contracts to enable more SMEs to participate. In 2017, the total volume of contracts for procurement from SMEs exceeded 2.1 trillion rubles in value.
- Creating conditions for SME labour productivity increase. To achieve this more investment is required in manufacturing SMEs. The integration of SME support involves a comprehensive and consistent policy providing support to SMEs at every stage of their development, from start-up to micro firm, from micro to small, from small to medium-sized enterprise.
- Ensuring the availability of financial resources for SMEs. This is facilitated by the establishment in 2015 of the Federal Corporation for SME Development (SME Corporation). Since then, the SME Corporation has

been actively involved in giving credit and guarantee support. This is reflected in the significant increase in the volume of lending to SMEs, which in the first eight months of 2017 was more than twice the volume of loans received by SMEs in 2015.

- Improving the tax policy and non-tax payments. The attempt to improve the tax environment involves focusing on a number of key measures including special tax schemes. The tax environment for SMEs in Russia is focused on two key measures. Special tax schemes have been developed for SMEs, for example the STS (simplified taxation system) for companies with an annual revenue of 150 million rubles. An STII (single tax on imputed income) is also still available, which is a simple tax scheme for SMEs (with 100 employees or less) that enables them to pay one simple tax instead of several taxes with complicated calculation schemes.

- Improving the quality of state regulation for SMEs. A state SME support programme has been implemented by the Ministry of Economic Development since 2005. It uses both direct financial and indirect support measures, such as grants to start a business, preferential lease subsidies for production modernisation, social entrepreneurs' subsidies, young entrepreneurs' subsidies – on the one hand – and creating infrastructure support objects (in the spheres of consulting, finance, property, innovation, export) on the other hand. However, the programme's funding has declined from 7.5 billion rubles in 2017 to 5 billion rubles in 2018, whilst the number of supported SMEs has also declined. Another area of current priority has been to improve the regulatory environment for SMEs. The priority programme in this regard is entitled 'The Supervisory and Audit Activities Reform', which is aimed at cutting red tape for SMEs. The administrative burden on SMEs was reduced through the introduction of a risk-based approach to control and supervise activities, the introduction of 'supervisory and audit holidays',[6] and the replacement of an administrative fine with a warning for a first-time administrative offence, which reduced the total number of business inspections by 22 per cent.

- SME development in selected territories. The Ministry of Economic Development of the Russian Federation, together with the JSC 'Delovaya Sreda',[7] developed the first national education platform of knowledge and services for SMEs. A total of 541 MSCs[8] for companies were opened in 2016, in 39 Russian regions.

- Strengthening entrepreneurial potential. A new policy measure in this regard is known as the Business Navigator. This is a free type of business support which is designed to help entrepreneurs to choose a company's specialisation; draw up a business plan; learn more about financial and guarantee support, credits and security bonds; find out about available support measures, premises, public competitive procurements and tenders; and get access to analytics. The SME Business Navigator materials cover 171 cities in Russia with a population of more than 100 000 people. Over 220 000 new companies have already been registered. Different training programmes for entrepreneurs have been launched, including those of the SME Corporation, which include 'A-B-C for Entrepreneurs' (how to start a business) and 'A School of Entrepreneurship' (how to develop a business).

In addition to state support programmes and other forms of SME support, an important policy for stimulating entrepreneurship development is the creation of favourable business conditions, including the reduction of administrative burden and cutting of red tape. The investment climate in Russian regions has also improved: the average index of the national rating of the investment climate[9] increased by 5.3 percentage points between 2016 and 2017, reflecting the increase in the share of SME public procurements, as well as the reduction in the quantity of both real estate ownership registration procedures and construction permits application procedures.

In an attempt to improve the implementation of the programme, it is now delivered through the service model; in other words, by providing services to SMEs using special support infrastructure. SME infrastructural support has been developed according to the one-stop approach, and single support standards have been introduced. At the end of 2016 there were 330 business infrastructure support objects in the Russian regions. More than 167 000 SMEs received state support in 2016, 39 509 new jobs were created and 303 800 jobs were saved. The creation of regional export centres contributed to an increase in the number of exporting firms – from 10 600 in 2014 to 30 100 in 2017. The strategy has involved some institutional change; for example, with reference to finance, the most important development institutions are the SME Bank, the Small Innovative Enterprises Assistance Fund for high-tech companies and the Ministry of Agriculture for farmers and agricultural small firms.

In May 2018, the Russian president named several priorities for the coming years, with SME development being one of them. Thus, the SME Development Strategy 2030 is to be prolonged until 2036, and a new project 'Small and Medium Entrepreneurship and the Individual Entrepreneurial Initiatives Support'[10] has been launched, with its aims to be reached in 2024. It consists of several federal projects, including business environment improvement, expanding access to financial resources for SMEs, acceleration of SMEs, rural cooperation and farm support, and the promotion of entrepreneurship.

The main SME support challenges in Russia

The 2015 OECD report (OECD, 2015) stated the main weaknesses and challenges of policy development. Most of them have already been addressed by now, but some issues are still to be discussed and improved. Thus, the report distinguishes several main directions of SME support policy improvement, such as framework conditions, policy foundations, start-up support, infrastructure support development, access to finance, and regional policy aspects.

Firstly, the SME Development Strategy 2030[11] provides clear and comprehensive policy foundations, as described above. Secondly, its structure covers most of the important issues listed in the OECD report, namely access to finance, framework conditions, infrastructure support development and regional SME development. The measures suggested by the strategy's roadmap 2016–17 also address these issues. Thirdly, the strategy indicators listed above include workforce employed, SME turnover, labour productivity and manufacturing turnover share, which helps to identify certain measures for each key performance indicator (KPI). Fourthly, a number of programmes and initiatives, including those described above, are specifically aimed at resolving these problems, making it easier for new private firms to enter the markets. This risk-oriented approach is supposed to cut red tape.[12] The training and educational programmes are aimed at providing entrepreneurs with new skills and competencies. The SME Corporation financial support programmes make it easier for entrepreneurs to obtain credits; the infrastructure support programmes stimulate companies to innovate; and the national project for high-tech companies, called 'National Champions', promotes the most promising innovative companies (Medovnikov et al., 2016).

The Agency for Strategic Initiatives[13] implements the 'SME Target Model' and other target models, which contain clear KPIs on administrative procedures' duration and simplicity (including those for getting construction permits, export and import permissions, and obtaining electricity), so they will hopefully help to create a favourable investment climate in the Russian regions. The Ministry of Economic Development of the Russian Federation is launching a programme on entrepreneurship promotion, with the aim of raising awareness and encouraging a positive attitude towards entrepreneurs.

However, there are still many challenges to creating an effective SME support policy. For example, the amount of money for SME federal support programmes has been decreasing in the last few years. Russia needs to strengthen the information and communications technology (ICT) solutions in its public sector; for example, there is no one automated system for gathering information and data processing for SMEs. Although the Unified SME Register has been created, there is still no repository of credit information on individuals and businesses listing their transactions with state-backed finance bodies. There is no register for companies that have received governmental support, so it is very difficult to access the effects of the support programmes.

Many problems with the SME support policies may be identified at the regional level. One of the most important is the mismatch between regional SME support powers and budget capabilities. That is why only a few regional SME support programmes really work. Another problem is that the current budget system provides no motives towards SME development, either at the regional level or at the local level. Whilst local authorities are the first to be interested in SMEs abroad, in Russia today's fiscal system does not contribute to their systematic interactions with the SME sector. What is more, even considering the diversity of the Russian regions, the government still provides almost no variation in stimulating regions to support SMEs. The principle for subsidising regional authorities does not help to prioritise the support between the Russian regions. There is a lack of understanding of the specifics about SMEs and differences in different territories, including the unification of legislation and the provision of support, regardless of the type of business and place of its activity. This leads to a mismatch between measures and business needs, a lack of clear support priorities, and policy inconsistency. The decision to give the regions new fiscal arrangements that could allow sub-national governments to retain more of the gains from increased business taxes is being discussed.

Another problem is the corruption perception and the lack of trust between governmental and municipal authorities and businesses. A very important issue is the unpredictability and volatility of the state support policy, which has fluctuated several times over the last 25 years. This has resulted in increased entrepreneurship risk and a higher rate of unpredictability, making it more difficult for entrepreneurs to plan long term. So despite the fact that the SME Development Strategy was adopted, it seems that some of its points are still being argued and discussed. One of the most arguable questions refers to the ways of supporting self-employed people that work unofficially in Russia. A test application that helps to legalise migrants easily has been launched in three regions to see if it is worth rolling out nationwide.

Another question is that of regional entrepreneurship policy, where many experts, politicians and economists argue about which regions should receive support for SME development – the weakest, to make economic development in Russia more evenly distributed, or the strongest, to promote economic drivers. There is also a question of whether the entrepreneurial support policy should rely on direct measures (financial, infrastructural) or create preferable conditions and a friendly environment for SMEs. This divergence shapes the governmental policy towards SMEs, tilting towards direct measures implemented by the SME Corporation. Since 2017, direct support measures (subsidies, loans, public procurement) have prevailed. An alternative approach could be local SME development through engaging a pool of professional investors, creating specialised private and non-commercial infrastructure, and providing support for networks of entrepreneurs (in collaboration with consultants, local authorities and so on). Finally, the declining role of the Ministry of Economic Development has enabled SME support to become better tuned to the needs and priorities of SMEs in different regions in Russia.

Conclusion

Clearly, the analysis of entrepreneurship in any country can benefit from international baselines, in order to put the level of entrepreneurship in the country into context. Until recently this was really difficult in Russia because of differences in the definition of what constitutes an SME compared to other countries. As seen above, the Russian Statistical Office has shown some flexibility in re-working the Russian data based on EU size definitions. This has been a useful exercise, not least because the comparison with other countries shows the SME sector in Russia to be contributing rather less to the economy and economic development than SMEs in other countries.

Despite these differences in definition, the evidence across a whole range of indicators is consistent in showing that the size of the SME sector in Russia is below that of comparable OECD countries. This clearly reflects Russia's recent past as a socialist economy based on central planning. At the same time, however, Russia has not made the same level of progress in developing its SME sector as some of the other former socialist countries have done. This would certainly apply to the Central and East European countries, and even China where the government is rather more enthusiastic about encouraging SMEs than the Russian government appears to be. Having said that, recent evidence such as Russia joining the OECD could indicate a real change in the future.

Another conclusion one might draw is that, hitherto, Russia has experienced major twists and turns in public policy over the years, with programmes being well developed in some cases but without budget allocation. This has resulted in a so-called 'implementation gap'. Only time will tell whether or not the new programme of support for SMEs is sustained. Certainly, it represents a step forward in SME policy in Russia.

It is probably fair to say that in Russia it is still 'SME policy' rather than 'entrepreneurship policy', and this is supported by the fact that the business support for new start-ups is extremely variable across the country. As pointed out previously, there is no national network of business support centres, so the support for business start-ups is fragmented and arguably not highly effective. There are business incubators, although these vary in their effectiveness. Business support in Russia is uneven in terms of the distribution across regions and would benefit from improvements in quality.

Finally, it is widely recognised in Russia that innovation needs a policy stimulus. Russia has lost some of its top scientists through so-called 'brain drain' over the last 25 years. This, together with a lack of emphasis on commercialisation within many of the research institutes, has resulted in a fairly modest development of innovation. Herein lies an opportunity to give a kick start to the more highly value-added start-ups and bring together entrepreneurship with innovation policy.

Current priorities and challenges

Looking back over the transition period, there have been a series of major changes in the emphasis and orientation of SME policy in Russia, starting with generalist attempts to support both SMEs and start-ups using a broad set of instruments. From the early 1990s onwards, the development of SME policy in Russia has lacked consistency, occurring in a series of fits and starts. Currently, in the context of a growing presence of the state in the economy in general, SME and entrepreneurship policy is becoming more centralised. Given the huge territorial extent of Russia this would seem to be problematic. As a consequence, perhaps the most urgent problem facing SME and entrepreneurship policy makers is the need for a policy which encourages the regions to attract sufficient finance to establish their own SME and entrepreneurship policies adjusted to their needs, which may not be exactly the same as the national ones. This is emphasised by Chepurenko and Vilenski (2016) in a very thorough review of Russian SME and entrepreneurship policy.

It is also a key point of emphasis in the recommendations made by the OECD (2017), following its review of the development of SMEs and entrepreneurship in Russia, and its policy approaches that have been used in that connection.

The OECD emphasised that achieving ambitious targets for national growth in SMEs and entrepreneurship is dependent upon stimulating improvements in local regulations and programmes spread across the regions of the Russian Federation. At present, many regions do not participate in key federal programmes, and the diversity of Russia's regions needs to be reflected in a flexible approach with respect to the allocation of resources from the centre. The OECD report also recommends improvements in framework conditions, but to move away from the high levels of product market regulation and state involvement in the economy, and place more emphasis on privatisation of the large state-owned enterprises that are still involved in production in Russia.

Although, as mentioned previously, the number of days required to start a business has been reduced to 15 days, at the same time there are still significant obstacles with respect to, for example, construction permits, export and import licences and obtaining electricity. Nevertheless, there are significant reforms that can be built on. In the Doing Business ranking,[14] which assesses formal conditions for doing business, Russia rose from 124th place in 2010 to 31st place in 2019 due to improved business registration procedures, easier access and reduced time to connect to infrastructure, and improved arbitration court systems.

There is evidence that people looking to start businesses in Russia and/or moving to self-employment rather overestimate the skills required to achieve this, perhaps because of a lack of inherited knowledge or experience from the past. As a consequence, the OECD recommendation is to increase the emphasis on programmes focusing on raising the capabilities of SMEs and start-ups. Linking this to the previous recommendation, it is important that these training and business support programmes for SMEs are not confined to more prosperous regions but are rolled out across the Russian Federation.

This leads on to the question of the adequacy of the existing incubators and business development service centres. Although there are business incubators in most Russian regions, especially in universities, most of them are state supported and not very efficient. In addition, there is no monitoring of their performance and some are just used as offices. As a result, the business support system in Russia is patchy. The evidence from other developing countries suggests that there is scope for more emphasis to be placed on business incubators, particularly those that are linked to universities and higher education institutions. This could contribute to raising the level of innovation in the Russian economy. Business incubators are rather thin on the ground in Russia, certainly in comparison with countries such as South Korea where the network of business development centres has been a key pillar in their approach to business support policies for SMEs.

The OECD also emphasised the need for new measures in an attempt to improve the access of SMEs and entrepreneurs to external finance. The creation of a federal credit guarantee agency in 2014 was a positive step but needs to be balanced with some actions on the demand side to improve the financial knowledge and skills of entrepreneurs and potential entrepreneurs. This should help to improve the quality of applications for finance.

The number of business start-ups in Russia is low, and the range narrow, certainly in comparison with OECD countries but also in comparison with many of the Central and East European countries who have also transitioned from socialism. That being the case, it is probably not sufficient to simply provide more training; there also needs to be a campaign to raise the level of the population's awareness of the opportunities presented by self-employment and small business ownership in terms of a future career. There are good examples in other countries, such as the eastern regions of Germany, of programmes designed to raise the profile of entrepreneurship, which includes, but is not confined to, those in schools and education institutions. This can include mobile exhibitions, sponsorship of 'Dragon's Den' type programmes in the media and supporting the links to a wider pattern of support for entrepreneurship.

Notes

1. Therefore, for a correct comparison with other countries, it is necessary to exclude the share of the state (46 per cent) and financial sectors (4.3 per cent) from the structure of Russia's GDP, and then divide the value added of the SME sector by the remaining part of the GDP.
2. It includes officially registered sole proprietorships, or individual entrepreneurs (5.6 million people).
3. http://economy.gov.ru/minec/main.
4. The SME Corporation was created in 2015, supported by the Decree of the President of the Russian Federation 'On SMEs further development measures' and the Federal Law 'On changes to certain laws of the Russian Federation', that deal with SMEs development in Russia.
5. https://ofd.nalog.ru/.
6. The preplanned supervisory and audit procedures were temporarily stopped for SMEs, from 1 January 2016 to 31 December 2018, excluding firms operating in healthcare, education, the social sphere, and energy and heat supply. Later, the 'holiday' period was extended to 31 December 2020.

7. Joint stock company 'Delovaya Sreda' (the name is translated as 'Business Environment') is a 100 per cent subsidiary of Sberbank, engaged in the development of small and micro business in Russia.
8. MSC stands for a multifunctional service centre, which provides state and municipal services for people and companies (separately).
9. National rating of the investment climate, 2017. https://asi.ru/eng/investclimate/rating/
10. http://government.ru/info/35563/.
11. http://economy.gov.ru/wps/wcm/connect/24360a6c-432a-49b5-b10e-69484af2f 1a1/%D0%A1%D1%82%D1%80%D0%B0%D1%82%D0%B5%D0%B3%D0%B8 %D1%8F_%D0%9C%D0%A1%D0%9F.pdf?MOD=AJPERES&CACHEID=2436 0a6c-432a-49b5-b10e-.
12. Red tape refers to the effects of regulations and laws on business. It is a term used by entrepreneurs and their representatives to describe the negative effect of government policies and actions.
13. http://asi.ru/eng/investclimate/.
14. http://www.doingbusiness.org/en/data/exploreeconomies/russia#DB_ec.

References

Abramov, A., I. Aksenov, A. Radygin and M. Chernova Mode (2018), 'Modern approaches to measuring the state sector: Methodology and empirics', *Ekonomic heskaya Politika*, **13** (1), 36–69.

Aidis, R., S. Estrin and T. Mickiewicz (2008), 'Institutions and entrepreneurship development in Russia: A comparative perspective', *Journal of Business Venturing*, **23** (6), 656–72.

Barinova, V. and S. Zemtsov (2019), 'International comparative of the role of small and medium-sized enterprises in the national economy: A statistical study', *Voprosy Statistiki*, **26** (6), 55–71. (In Russian.)

Barinova, V. A., S. P. Zemtsov and Y. V. Tsareva (2018), 'Entrepreneurship and institutions: Does the relationship exist at the regional level in Russia?', *Voprosy Ekonomiki*, **6**, 92–116.

Bosma, N. and D. Kelley (2019), *Global Entrepreneurship Monitor: 2018/2019 Global Report*, Global Entrepreneurship Research Association, London Business School.

Chepurenko, A., E. Popovskaya and O. Obraztsova (2017), 'Cross-regional variations in the motivation of early-stage entrepreneurial activity in Russia: Determining factors', in A. Sauka and A. Chepurenko (eds), *Entrepreneurship in Transition Economies*, Cham: Springer, pp. 315–42.

Chepurenko, A. and A. Vilenski (2016), 'SME policy of the Russian state (1990–2015): From a "generalist" to a "paternalist" approach', HSE Working Paper WP1/2016/02, Moscow: National Research University Higher School of Economics.

ILO (2015), *Transition from the Informal to the Formal Economy Recommendation 2015 (No. 204)*, Geneva: International Labour Organization.

Medovnikov, D., T. Oganesyan and S. Rozmirovich (2016), 'Candidates for the championship: Medium-sized high growth companies and state-run programs for their support', *Voprosy Ekonomiki*, **9**, 50–66. (In Russian.)

OECD (2015), *Russian Federation: Key Issues and Policies*, OECD Studies on SMEs and Entrepreneurship, Paris: OECD Publishing.

OECD (2017), *Entrepreneurship at a Glance 2017*, Paris: OECD Publishing.

Rosstat (2019), *SMEs in Russia 2018*, Moscow: Rosstat.

Russian Economy in 2017 (2018), *Trends and Outlooks*, Moscow: Gaidar Institute Publishers.

Russian Economy in 2018 (2019), *Trends and Outlooks*, Moscow: Gaidar Institute Publishers.

Yakovlev, E. and E. Zhuravskaya (2013), 'The unequal enforcement of liberalization: Evidence from Russia's reform of business regulation', *Journal of the European Economic Association*, **11** (4), 808–38.

Zemtsov, S., A. Muradov, I. Wade and V. Barinova (2016), 'Determinants of regional innovation in Russia: Are people or capital more important?', *Foresight and STI Governance*, **10** (2), 29–42.

Zemtsov, S.P. and Y.V. Tsareva (2018), 'Entrepreneurial activity in the Russian regions: How spatial and temporal effects determine the development of small business', *Zhournal Novoi Ekonomicheskoi Associacii*, **1** (37), 145–65.

8 Entrepreneurship and the middle-income trap: the case of Poland

Anna Rogut and Bogdan Piasecki

Introduction

According to official ratings, Poland has joined the high-income club (World Bank Group, 2017) and is an aspiring economic growth leader (Forgó and Jevčák, 2015; Raiser et al., 2016; World Bank Group, 2016). Nevertheless, Poland's development compared to the European Union (EU) average, as measured by GDP per capita, still amounts to dozens of percentage points. Poland has been in the process of transition from an effectiveness-driven economy to an innovation-driven one for quite some time (Schwab, 2017). What is more, it appears to suffer from the 'ailments' characteristic of economies stuck in the middle-income trap (Garrett, 2004; Gill and Kharas, 2007; UNDP et al., 2013). Even though the existence of the middle-income trap as an economic phenomenon is debatable (Aiyar et al., 2013; Bulman et al., 2017; Han and Wei, 2015; Ye and Robertson, 2013, 2016), the fact is that Poland has been losing its cost advantages without balancing them out with a technological edge (European Commission, 2016; Rada Ministrów, 2017). Moreover, labour productivity, which acts as a countervailing factor to the middle-income trap (Agenor et al., 2012; Canuto and Giugale, 2010; Gönenç, 2017; OECD, 2014), remains at a relatively low level in Poland (Adamczyk-Łojewska, 2017; European Commission, 2018a; Ministerstwo Przedsiębiorczości i Technologii, 2018). Thus, the latest OECD report (2018) recommended that the country should reorient its development strategy towards productivity by enhancing technology adoption and boosting its own innovation capacity.

In this respect, a major role is played by entrepreneurship (Aghion and Bircan, 2017; Wang, 2016), understood as 'the mindset and process to create and

develop economic activity by blending risk-taking, creativity and/or innovation with sound management, within a new or an existing organization'
(European Commission, 2003, p. 6).[1]

Indeed, for many years now Poland has been stimulating entrepreneurship,
thus construed, with the help of substantial transfers from EU Structural
Funds. A sizeable proportion of that money is dedicated to innovative
capacity, translating into the ability to implement more or less disruptive
technological changes (GFCC, 2012; López-Claros and Mata, 2010; Mahroum
et al., 2008; Stern et al., 2000; US Department of Commerce, 2012) and, especially, strengthening technological competitiveness (Acemoglu et al., 2006;
Landesmann, 2003; Rodrik, 2003).

In the current programme period 2014–20, Poland is the largest beneficiary
of European Structural and Investment Funds and may receive a total of up to
€86 billion by 2020. More than 20 per cent of this amount is to be dedicated
to increasing innovative capacity, which is three times as much as in the years
2007–13. However, the first evaluation reports (EGO, 2018a) revealed problems with the potential to absorb these funds. Thus, the objective of the present
chapter is to assess the effects of previous EU funding on the innovative capacity of Polish businesses (and especially small and medium-sized enterprises,
SMEs), as well as to outline lines of action conducive to greater absorption
of those funds over the coming years, which could then serve as a basis for
designing a longer-term entrepreneurship policy for Poland.

The chapter is based on a literature review focused on evaluation studies, with
additional insights gained from a case study of the Łódź region.

European funds and entrepreneurship policy: from modernising enterprises to boosting innovation

Integration with the European Union constituted a twofold challenge for
the Polish economy, which had to accomplish a significant structural transformation and, at the same time, bridge the technological gap (Rogut and
Piasecki, 2011). While at the beginning of EU membership (2004–06) Poland's
entrepreneurship policy was focused on meeting the modernisation needs of
SMEs, over time it has shifted towards innovative capacity.[2] Thus, in the years
2007–13 the priority was to stimulate innovation-driven entrepreneurship
by direct investment, advisory and training assistance (both repayable and
non-repayable) aimed at developing existing businesses and creating new

ones within the three national programmes (Innovative Economy Operational Programme, Human Capital Operational Programme, Development of Eastern Poland Operational Programme) and 16 regional programmes (Ministerstwo Rozwoju Regionalnego, 2007). Additional aid was designated to improve infrastructure and create a friendly institutional, capital and legal environment.

During that time span, a total of approximately 17 per cent of all available Structural Funds were spent on measures designed to boost innovation and the competitiveness of the economy, with half of the money expended in the form of direct grants to businesses, and in particular SMEs. A substantial amount was also used to enhance public research and development (R&D) infrastructure, to finance research conducted by public entities, and to stimulate a broadly defined business environment (Imapp, 2017).

While the aforementioned funding programmes did boost the competitiveness of numerous enterprises, they failed to materially affect the competitive position of the economy as a whole (Narodowy Bank Polski, 2016; Najwyższa Izba Kontroli, 2018). Poland still lagged far behind the leading economies in terms of the availability of cutting-edge technologies (Schwab, 2017).

Similar conclusions were presented in a number of evaluation reports (Fundacja WiseEuropa, 2017; Fundacja WiseEuropa and OPI PIB, 2017; Imapp, 2017; Kapil et al., 2012; Millward Brown and OPI, 2014; Najwyższa Izba Kontroli, 2018). These reports noted that due to the narrow group of direct beneficiaries (less than 1.7 per cent of all businesses) and the relatively low allocation level (on average 1.5–2 per cent of GDP), the macroeconomic effects of entrepreneurship policy in the years 2007–13 were not impressive, especially in terms of innovation improvement, which fell short of expectations. The assistance provided to businesses mostly expanded the scale of their activity (higher revenues, new products, investment and so on) rather than innovation levels or the utilisation of the latest technologies. Even though some enterprises became more innovative, the overall innovativeness of the economy did not grow significantly (Hollanders and Es-Sadki, 2013, 2015; Ministerstwo Przedsiębiorczości i Technologii, 2018). Importantly, most aid was given to enterprises in the low- and medium-technology sectors, rather than those in the high-technology ones.

This is corroborated by a report from the European Commission (2018a), which showed that despite the country's efforts to stimulate an innovative economy, Poland still ranks low on most indicators of the European Innovation Scoreboard, with spending on research and innovation failing to translate into substantial outcomes. Although in the years 2007–16 expenditures on R&D rose by 0.41 per cent of GDP (to 0.97 per cent of GDP), that amount corresponded to only half of the EU average (2.03 per cent of GDP), despite public assistance (with 60 per cent of funding derived from the European Structural and Investment Funds). As a result, companies' spending on R&D, which increased from 0.22 per cent of GDP in 2011 to 0.63 per cent in 2016, still remained below the EU average (1.3 per cent of GDP), leading to slower overall productivity growth.

Therefore, the innovativeness and competitiveness of individual businesses, and the economy as a whole, remained principal priorities of Poland's entrepreneurship policy in the years 2014–20 (Box 8.1); especially as, according to a report by Najwyższa Izba Kontroli (2018), previous assistance programmes did not identify innovation types and scales that would be preferable with a view to overall economic development. As a result, funding was often granted to projects that amounted to little more than intra-company innovation far from the global scale promised in the application documents. Consequently, the programmes fell short of launching innovative products or technologies that could be showcased as flagship achievements of the Polish economy, advancing its competitive position.

Box 8.1   Priorities of the Polish entrepreneurship policy for the years 2014–20

Entrepreneurship policy is a significant component of the Strategy for Responsible Development until 2020, and especially its part dedicated to sustainable knowledge-based economic growth. The fundamental pillars of that policy include:

- Reindustrialisation, with the object of raising the ability of companies to compete in an open and global economy by developing and implementing innovations. Here the measures are targeted at selected sectors with a stable market position and a large or growing share in manufacturing and exports, which exhibit competitive potential in global markets.
- Development of innovative companies, with the object of boosting enterprise competitiveness in domestic and international markets, and especially enhancing the technological quality of products; stimulating new technological and organisational solutions based on the company's own resources; and enhancing the competitive advantages of internationally offered products by improving quality and innovativeness to a greater extent than before.
- Small and medium-sized enterprises, with the object of increasing the

    number of SMEs equipped with the resources necessary for growth;
    implementing cutting-edge organisational, marketing and technolog-
    ical innovations; and developing state-of-the-art support mechanisms
    (whether financial, organisational or advisory in nature).

- Capital for development, with the object of mobilising different sources
  of financing to markedly increase overall investment in the economy.
- International expansion, with the object of maintaining a relatively high
  rate of export growth while improving its degree of innovativeness, as
  well as stimulating Polish foreign direct investment.

Source: Based on the Rada Ministrów (2017).

A significant source of financing for this policy consists of the EU Structural
Funds offered within national and regional operational programmes, with the
first and third thematic objectives dedicated to support for entrepreneurship
with a focus on innovative capacity (Box 8.2). In the years 2014–20, more than
20 per cent of the overall amount of Structural Funds will be allocated to those
objectives (Ministerstwo Przedsiębiorczości i Technologii, 2018).

Box 8.2   Structural Funds orientations supporting entrepreneurship and developing innovative capacity

First thematic objective: strengthening research, technological development
and innovation, including:

- Knowledge, innovation and R&D transfer to the economy, and in particular growth in (i) the number of enterprises conducting R&D; (ii) the
  number of R&D projects conducted involving collaboration between
  enterprises and academia; (iii) the number of R&D results and innovative solutions ready for implementation in the economy; and (iv) the
  scale of utilisation of R&D services.
- Improvement of the technology and knowledge transfer system, including companies' R&D potential, for example by closer cooperation
  of SMEs with other enterprises and organisations; development of
  cutting-edge research infrastructure; integration and consolidation of
  the R&D potential; wider availability of high-quality services supporting research, development and innovation (R&D&I); and greater accessibility of capital for financing the commercialisation of R&D outcomes
  in companies.
- Increased capacity for creating excellence in the field of research and
  innovation with a focus on (i) the concentration of R&D efforts on ar-

eas with the greatest economic potential for Poland and its regions (for example, strategic research programmes, regional R&D agendas); (ii) an increase in the quantity and quality of R&D conducted in collaboration with international research units or companies; and (iii) the development of human resources for the R&D sector.

Third thematic objective: enhancing the competitiveness of SMEs, including:

- An increase in growth-oriented investments by companies, including greater utilisation of R&D&I results; higher labour productivity and production effectiveness; and a more extensive use of digital technologies and digital enterprise management models.
- Development of an effective investing, infrastructural, financial, advisory and training environment.
- Diversification and development of new business models.

Source: Based on the Ministerstwo Infrastruktury i Rozwoju (2017).

The key Polish programme supporting the R&D&I sphere is the Smart Growth Operational Programme 2014–20 (SGOP) addressed to enterprises (especially SMEs), academic institutions, business–academic consortia and business support organisations. The programme has a budget of €8.6 billion designated for (i) supporting R&D conducted by enterprises; (ii) supporting the entrepreneurial potential and environment to stimulate R&D&I; (iii) supporting innovation in enterprises; and (iv) increasing R&D potential. At the regional level, R&D&I is to be stimulated by regional operational programmes (ROPs).

From the point of view of innovative capacity development, of special importance is support for R&D and implementation work conducted by companies and academic institutions, with more than PLN 10 billion spent for that purpose by April 2018 (a substantial portion of that funding went to enterprises). A similar, if not greater, amount[3] should be contracted by the end of 2020. However, the latest estimates indicate that the potential for absorbing those funds may be limited (in terms of the number of potential beneficiaries and the amount of funding) on the part of both business and academia (EGO, 2018a, 2018b).

At the national level, this limitation is mostly attributable to (i) a lack of possibility to finance the apparatus necessary for R&D activity (although its depreciation qualifies as an eligible cost); (ii) a lack of support (with small exceptions) for projects with budgets of less than PLN 1 million; and (iii) legal and administrative barriers to obtaining, implementing and financial clearing of grants. This last barrier often arises from the inflexibility of the financing institutions.

At the regional level, an additional problem is the strong competition between SGOP and ROP financing of innovative capacity objectives, especially with respect to assistance, beneficiaries and amount of funding (Box 8.3).

Box 8.3   Internal competition between the various instruments supporting innovative capacity financed by the EU Structural Funds at the national and regional levels

- *The subject matter of assistance:* both types of programmes (the SGOP and ROPs) support industrial research[4] and development work.[5] In principle, R&D funding does not cover the acquisition of research apparatus (although depreciation of such equipment constitutes an eligible cost). Therefore, projects which fall under the first and fourth SGOP axes may also be co-financed by ROPs. Interestingly, two regions (Warmińsko-Mazurskie and Wielkopolskie) offer broader assistance, additionally covering the implementation of R&D results and investments in research infrastructure.
- *Beneficiaries:* in both types of programmes the financing dedicated to innovative capacity development is mostly addressed to enterprises and their consortia, or consortia between businesses and academia. Furthermore, while both types of programmes offer assistance to SMEs and large companies, the difference is that within the SGOP the latter have a separate pool of funds, and within the ROPs they have to directly compete with SMEs for financing. Given the above, it should be noted that the SGOP and ROPs overlap in terms of their potential beneficiaries.
- *Amount of funding:* both types of programmes accept applications for R&D projects with budgets ranging from PLN 1 million to 5 million. However, in contrast to the SGOP, ROPs also offer funding for projects of less than PLN 1 million, and that is the only area in which the SGOP and ROPs do not compete with one another in terms of the assistance offered.

Source: Based on EGO (2018a).

Other factors limiting the Structural Funds absorption potential at the regional level include (i) lengthy application assessment procedures; (ii) low frequency of competitions; (iii) difficult application procedures, and in particular complicated forms with numerous annexes and a multiplicity of assessment criteria; which lead to (iv) lower attractiveness of the Structural Funds available at the ROP level (EGO, 2018a).

Bottlenecks in the use of European funds: the case of the Łódź region

The limited Structural Funds absorption potential may have particularly harmful consequences for regions with relatively low outlays on R&D activity and modest R&D results (as compared to the national and EU average), as those regions may not be able to use all the funding available for enhancing their innovative capacity. One of these is the Łódź region, which is in 11th place (out of the 16 Polish provinces) in terms of the percentage of innovatively active industrial companies,[6] and 14th place in terms of the percentage of industrial companies implementing innovations (GUS, 2017a). Also, overall spending on R&D in the region is rather low (8th place), with the proportion of companies' own resources in overall outlays on R&D being even lower, putting the region in 11th place (GUS, 2017b). As a result, the region has been classified in the moderate innovator group of the Regional Innovation Scoreboard (Hollanders and Es-Sadki, 2017).

The relatively low R&D intensity was also reflected in a questionnaire study (Box 8.4), which showed that regional companies have a rather low opinion of the role of their own R&D activity as a source of innovation (only 1.9 out of 5).[7] In contrast, these companies tended to attach much greater importance to their own ideas (3.6) and acquisitions of cutting-edge machinery, production lines and other manufacturing equipment (2.6).

Box 8.4   Characteristics of the questionnaire study

The 2017–18 study was commissioned by the Spatial Planning Office of the Łódź Region in order to develop tools for monitoring the region's innovativeness, using the entrepreneurial discovery process for the purpose of updating the Regional Innovation Strategy LORIS 2030. The questionnaire was sent to 1056 innovative enterprises in the Łódź region to assess, among other things, (i) the system of improving knowledge, competence and skills; (ii) the effectiveness of the sources of innovation processes in enterprises; (iii) the correspondence between the R&D sphere and the market needs of enterprises; (iv) the relational capital of enterprises in the context of the effectiveness of internal and external communication and exchange of information; (v) the degree of enterprise internationalisation; and (vi) the accessibility of information about new technologies. Other efforts aimed at developing tools for the monitoring of the region's innovation included desk research and critical analysis, statistical analyses based on economic structure specialisation indicators and benchmarking, in-depth individual interviews, focus groups, smart labs, innovation maps, expert discussions and brainstorming.

Source: Based on Rogut et al. (2018).

Even though the Łódź region designated approximately 30 per cent of the overall amount of its ROP for 2014–20 to entrepreneurship and innovative capacity stimulation, that is, the first and third thematic objectives (Urząd Marszałkowski Województwa Łódzkiego, 2018), according to estimates only a little more than 20 per cent of that pool had been used by April 2018 (EGO, 2018a).

The underlying causes of this state of affairs were elucidated by the aforementioned studies (Rogut et al., 2018). According to them, significant barriers to R&D activity include the limited resources of companies (not only SMEs) and especially human resources, as well as the distant prospects for the expected results. While R&D takes time, many companies would prefer immediate outcomes. Additional barriers include difficulties in cooperation with other enterprises, regional R&D units and business support organisations.

On the side of enterprises, these obstacles tend to arise from a competitive, rather than cooperative, approach and from concerns that business secrets may be appropriated by third parties; this breeds mistrust and a belief that enterprises should keep a low profile and act alone. An additional adverse factor is the absence of leaders (individuals, entities or institutions) who would have a clear concept of cooperation as well as the knowledge and skills necessary to reconcile the disparate interests of various stakeholders. Of significance are also insufficient human resources, which make it difficult to conduct in-house R&D activity and collaborate with external R&D units. This is particularly visible in the strongly 'dispersed' sectors dominated by micro and small enterprises. Another major obstacle results from the divergent objectives pursued by enterprises and R&D units; while the former are keen on maximising profits in the short term, the latter aim at maximising their scientific output and research publications.

A further barrier to enterprises arises from the costs and time needed to reach desirable outcomes. While R&D units operate within two- to three-year-long projects, entrepreneurs need results 'here and now'; thus, they prefer purchasing an existing solution over getting involved in R&D efforts, whether on their own or in collaboration with third parties. The former strategy is less risky, where solutions have been tried and tested elsewhere and are ready for implementation, and less costly, with the adaptation of an existing solution being cheaper than the generation of a new one from scratch. Last but not least, the R&D&I needs of enterprises are not in line with the services provided by business support organisations and R&D units. Even though the latter should constitute an actual R&D base for the industry, unfortunately they often fail to follow the latest technological trends and do not keep 'a step ahead' of the enterprises' needs.

In turn, on the R&D side, barriers to effective cooperation with enterprises are attributable mainly to the lack of possibility for scientists to publish the research results over an extended period of time, as companies demand confidentiality in relation to the development of new technologies or chemical compounds. Thus, the researchers cannot get credit for their scientific work, which would otherwise contribute to their academic ratings as well as those of their faculties. An additional obstacle is the substantial burden placed on R&D units arising from their statutory functions, which in the case of insufficient staffing may discourage the utilisation of external resources, including the Structural Funds. Of significance are also difficulties in obtaining funds for R&D activity and subsequent financial clearance (complicated procedures and low accessibility).

This situation is exacerbated by additional barriers to cooperation indicated by sectoral organisations, trade and vocational chambers, and employers' associations, which include the absence of a commonality of interests, mistrust (and thus excessive caution in financing joint projects), companies' reluctance to enter cooperative arrangements or subscribe to a set of predetermined rules, relatively low activity of trade chambers, and the low profile of trade organisations.

The relatively weak effectiveness of efforts to strengthen the innovative capacity of enterprises is also attributable to both burdensome procedures linked to fund acquisition (complicated applications and a lengthy approval process) and the subsequent financial clearance. This is particularly important given the misalignment between R&D&I support instruments and the potential, expectations and needs of the stakeholders, as indicated by enterprises.

In an attempt to meet the expectations of enterprises, and especially the smaller ones, the Łódź region has recently combined two previously competing funding streams (the SGOP and ROP) in addition to public–private partnership. These efforts have given rise to a joint initiative between the Łódź region and the National Centre for Research and Development (NCRD) called 'The Łódź Region in Good Health' (Box 8.5).

Box 8.5   Joint initiative

The joint initiative is a mechanism of financing R&D carried out by the NCRD in collaboration with a third party. Its objective is to guide the activity of research units towards R&D work on technological solutions arising from the needs of individual enterprises and other public institutions. The scope of the joint initiative encompasses the development of:

- Solutions for effective prevention, diagnosis and treatment of conditions particularly relevant to active and healthy aging (including solutions enabling broader accessibility of health-care services);
- Medications and medical products increasing opportunities for active and healthy aging (for example, through the development of new medications, supplements, foods for special purposes, medication packaging promoting patient compliance, better therapeutic outcomes and so on);
- IT tools (especially those involving Big Data) supporting prevention, diagnosis, treatment and rehabilitation for active and healthy aging (ICT tools for remote health monitoring, increased patient compliance with therapeutic regimens, better diagnosis, treatment and/or rehabilitation and so on);
- Health-related solutions catering to the aging population and enabling an active and healthy aging process (solutions enhancing fitness, tools involving telemedicine and Internet of Things to improve the quality of life, and so on).

Source: Based on Florczyk (2018).

The main goal of the joint initiative is the implementation of innovative solutions aimed at stopping or reversing the negative trends concerning life expectancy and the incidence of lifestyle and metabolic diseases in the Łódź region by 2027. The NCRD and the Łódź region have committed PLN 50 million each to the budget of the initiative. Eligible R&D projects may receive funds ranging from PLN 1 million to PLN 4 million. The NCRD's contribution is financed by the SGOP, while that of the Łódź region is financed by the ROP.

Another innovative aspect of this initiative is the way in which it is being developed, involving the triple helix concept with an important part played by the local authorities. While previously the authorities largely limited themselves to providing funds, this time they aspired to the role of a leader and integrator of a variety of academic and business communities, often with conflicting interests and goals, competing and clashing with one another. However, only through joint effort is it possible for them to develop a new cooperative and collaborative culture enabling greater absorption of the Structural Funds, and thus enhancing the innovative capacity of the region's economy.

Even though this is only the beginning of the experiment (the first competition was announced in July 2018), it is expected that the joint initiative will (i) successfully fulfil the role of a mechanism integrating academia and businesses, motivating those communities to apply for funds dedicated to innovation development; (ii) strengthen the position of the Łódź region, improving the social, demographic and health situation of its inhabitants over the coming years; and, importantly, (iii) give rise to a more partnership-oriented model of entrepreneurship policy making in the region to overcome the aforementioned barriers to cooperation.

Conclusion

Poland's integration with the European Union was a major challenge for the economy, associated with the necessity to both implement structural changes and close the technological gap. While in the first years of membership (by 2006) the focus of entrepreneurship policy was on the modernisation needs of SMEs, in subsequent periods the priority was to use the Structural Funds for stimulating innovation-driven entrepreneurship. However, experience from 2007–13 showed that although the funds did have a beneficial effect on the competitiveness of many companies, they did not significantly improve the competitive position of the economy as a whole. While financial assistance mostly expanded the scale of activity of those entities, it failed to substantially boost their innovative capacity and technological competitiveness. Therefore, the development of innovative capacity, and in particular the stimulation of R&D as well as implementation work, remains a major priority of entrepreneurship policy for the years 2014–20, with even more funds allocated to enterprises, and especially SMEs (approximately PLN 20 billion, of which half should be contracted by the end of 2020).

Even though the effects of this strategy (especially in terms of productivity, growth rate and transition from an effectiveness-driven economy to an innovation-driven one) may need some time to materialise, the available research and evaluation results indicate the need to increase the Structural Funds absorption potential of both enterprises and research units; and by the same token to enhance the effectiveness of entrepreneurship policy measures financed by those funds and dedicated to boosting innovative capacity.

Among such measures, of note are those aimed at providing a greater variety of forms of assistance (a greater number of more readily available, repayable instruments, as well as guarantees and venture capital funds); access to more comprehensive regional research programmes focused on the technological needs arising from smart specialisations; and a wider use of pre-competition procurement for the stimulation of R&D activity.

It is also crucial to bolster measures/instruments that would be complementary with respect to R&D assistance, especially in the following areas: (i) education, training and re-training of workers for regional smart specialisations; (ii) market/consumer awareness; (iii) regional branding; (iv) regional social capital; and (v) cooperative/collaborative culture.

However, of special significance is the need to overcome the excessively rigid framework of action that offers insufficient opportunities to experiment with new instruments that would facilitate following trends and generates knowledge/technology useful to enterprises in the nearer or more distant future, and so on, with the help of not only financial assistance but also, for example, public–private partnership instead of traditional competitions.

This would make entrepreneurship policy a more effective instrument for attaining the overarching goal of the Structural Funds, namely EU cohesion policy, which in the subsequent programming period (2021–27) will continue to prioritise skills for smart specialisation, industrial transformation and entrepreneurship, as well as R&D potential, advanced technologies, and greater SME growth and competitiveness (European Commission, 2018b).

Notes

1. For more on the role of innovation and innovation capacity in entrepreneurship, see for example Dogan (2015), Hindle (2009), Tülücea and Yurtkur (2015), Zhao et al. (2019).

2. For more on supporting innovation and innovation capacity as part of entrepreneurship policy, see for example Gilbert et al. (2004), Hart (2003), UNCTAD (2012).
3. This includes only grant instruments, and additional funds will be available within capital and repayable instruments as well as within nationally funded programs.
4. Research aimed at the acquisition of new knowledge and skills for developing new products, processes or services or for bringing about a significant improvement in existing products, processes or services, which may include the construction of prototypes in a laboratory environment or in an environment with simulated interfaces to existing systems as well as pilot lines, when necessary for the industrial research and notably for generic technology validation.
5. The acquiring, combining, shaping and using of existing scientific, technological, business and other relevant knowledge and skills for the purpose of producing plans and arrangements or designs for new, altered or improved products, processes or services, and in particular (i) prototyping, demonstrating, piloting, testing and validation of new or improved products, processes or services in environments representative of real life operating conditions; (ii) the development of commercially usable prototypes or pilots.
6. That is, enterprises that have implemented at least one innovation or have conducted innovative or R&D activity even if it has been discontinued or has not been completed.
7. Rated on a scale of 0–5, with 0 meaning 'not at all' and 5 meaning 'to a very large extent'.

References

Acemoglu, D., P. Aghion and F. Zilibotti (2006), 'Distance to frontier, selection, and economic growth', *Journal of the European Economic Association*, **4** (1), 37–74.

Adamczyk-Łojewska, G. (2017), 'Produktywność pracy jako czynnik wzrostu polskiej gospodarki w latach 2004–2015', *Prace Naukowe Uniwersytetu Ekonomicznego we Wrocławiu*, **489**, 11–23.

Agenor, P., O. Canuto and M. Jelenic (2012), 'Avoiding middle-income growth traps', Economic Premise, No. 98, Washington, DC: The World Bank.

Aghion, P. and C. Bircan (2017), 'The middle income trap from a Schumpeterian perspective', ADB Economics Working Paper Series No. 521.

Aiyar, S., R. Duval, D. Puy, Y. Wu and L. Zhang (2013), 'Growth slowdowns and the middle-income trap', International Monetary Fund WP/13/71.

Bulman, D., M. Eden and H. Nguyen (2017), 'Transitioning from low-income growth to high-income growth: Is there a middle-income trap?', *Journal of the Asia Pacific Economy*, **22** (1), 5–28.

Canuto, O. and M. Giugale (2010), *The Day after Tomorrow: A Handbook on the Future of Economic Policy in the Developing World*, Washington, DC: The World Bank.

Dogan, N. (2015), 'The intersection of entrepreneurship and strategic management: Strategic entrepreneurship', *Procedia – Social and Behavioral Sciences*, **195**, 1288–94.

EGO (2018a), *Ocena skuteczności wdrażania PO IR (Moduł I, Etap I). Projekt raportu końcowego*, accessed 28 October 2018 at https://www.ncbr.gov.pl/fileadmin/

Ewaluacja/POIR/Raport_koncowy_modul_I_etap_I__komplementarnosc_i_zdoln osc_absorbcyjna.pdf.

EGO (2018b), *Ocena skuteczności wdrażania PO IR przez NCBR, sprawności obsługi projektów oraz identyfi-kacji dobrych praktyk w działaniu 1.1 PO IR. Raport końcowy. Moduł III*, accessed 21 October 2018 at https://www.ncbr.gov.pl/fileadmin/ Ewaluacja/POIR/Raport_kon__cowy_modul_III__skutecznosc_1.1.1.pdf.

European Commission (2003), *Entrepreneurship in Europe*, Green Paper, COM(2003) 27 final.

European Commission (2016), *Country Report Poland 2016.* Commission Staff Working Document, SWD(2016) 89 final.

European Commission (2018a), *Country Report Poland 2018.* Commission Staff Working Document, accompanying the document Communication from the Commission to the European Parliament, the Council, the European Central Bank and the Eurogroup 2018. European Semester: Assessment of progress on structural reforms, prevention and correction of macroeconomic imbalances, and results of in-depth reviews under Regulation (EU) No 1176/2011 {COM(2018) 120 final}, SWD(2018) 219 final.

European Commission (2018b), *Proposal for a Regulation of the European Parliament and of the Council on the European Regional Development Fund and on the Cohesion Fund*, COM/2018/372 final – 2018/0197.

Florczyk, E. (2018), *Wspólne Przedsięwzięcie Województwa Łódzkiego oraz Narodowego Centrum Badań i Rozwoju pn. Łódzkie w dobrym zdrowiu*, accessed 9 December 2018 at https://www.ictcluster.pl/doc/%C5%81%C3%B3dzkie%20w%20dobrym%20zdr owiu%20-%20Urz%C4%85d%20Marsza%C5%82kowski%20-%20Idea%20Mixer .pdf.

Forgó, B. and A. Jevčák (2015), 'Economic convergence of Central and Eastern European EU member states over the last decade (2004–2014)', European Economy Discussion Paper 001, Luxembourg: Publications Office of the European Union.

Fundacja WiseEuropa (2017), *Wpływ polityki spójności 2007–2013 na konkurencyjność przedsiębiorstw i rozwój przedsiębiorczości w Polsce. Raport końcowy*, accessed 21 October 2018 at https://www.ewaluacja.gov.pl/media/45723/RKPrzeds102017.pdf.

Fundacja WiseEuropa and OPI PIB (2017), *Analiza wybranych działań PO IG na poziomie sektorowym i makroekonomicznym za pomocą modelu przepływów między-gałęziowych. Raport końcowy*, accessed 21 October 2018 at https://www.ewaluacja .gov.pl/media/54674/przeplmdzygal_POIG_FIN.pdf.

Garrett, G. (2004), 'Globalization's missing middle', *Foreign Affairs*, **83** (6), 84–96.

GFCC (2012), *Innovation Capacity: Best Practices in Competitiveness Strategy*, Washington, DC: Global Federation of Competitiveness Councils.

Gilbert, B. A., D. B. Audretsch and P. P. McDougall (2004), 'The emergence of entrepre-neurship policy', *Small Business Economics*, **22**, 313–23.

Gill, I. and H. Kharas (2007), *An East Asian Renaissance: Ideas for Economic Growth*, Washington, DC: The International Bank for Reconstruction and Development/The World Bank.

Gönenç, R. (2017), 'The middle income plateau: Trap or springboard?', OECD Economics Department Working Papers, No. 1446, Paris: OECD Publishing, accessed 21 October 2018 at http://dx.doi.org/10.1787/9cba114b-en.

GUS (2017a), *Działalność innowacyjna przedsiębiorstw w latach 2014–2016*, Warsaw: Główny Urząd Statystyczny.

GUS (2017b), *Działalność badawcza i rozwojowa w Polsce w 2016 r.*, Warsaw: Główny Urząd Statystyczny.

Han, X. and S. Wei (2015), 'Re-examining the middle-income trap hypothesis: What to reject and what to revive?', ADB Economics Working Paper Series No. 436, accessed 18 October 2018 at https://www.adb.org/sites/default/files/publication/161890/ewp -436.pdf.

Hart, D. M. (ed.) (2003), *The Emergence of Entrepreneurship Policy: Governence, Start-Ups, and Growth in the U.S. Knowledge Economy*, Cambridge: Cambridge University Press.

Hindle, K. (2009), 'The relationship between innovation and entrepreneurship: Easy definition, hard policy', paper delivered to the refereed stream of the 6th AGSE International Entrepreneurship Research Exchange, 3–6 February, Adelaide, Australia, accessed 4 April 2019 at http://kevinhindle.com/publications/J4.2009 -AGSE-Hindle-Inn-Ent-Pol.pdf.

Hollanders, H. and N. Es-Sadki (2013), *Innovation Union Scoreboard 2013*, European Union, accessed 25 October 2018 at https://ec.europa.eu/growth/tools-databases/eip -raw-materials/en/community/document/european-commission-innovation-union -scoreboard-2013.

Hollanders, H. and N. Es-Sadki (2015), *Innovation Union Scoreboard 2015*, European Union, accessed 21 October 2018 at https://www.kowi.de/Portaldata/2/Resources/ fp/2015-Innovation-Union-Scoreboard-Report.pdf.

Hollanders, H. and N. Es-Sadki (2017), *Regional Innovation Scoreboard 2017*, accessed 8 September 2018 at http://ec.europa.eu/DocsRoom/documents/31491.

Imapp (2017), *Efekty polityki spójności 2007–2013 w Polsce*, accessed 21 October 2018 at https://www.ewaluacja.gov.pl/media/47055/raport_synteza_PL.pdf.

Kapil, N., M. Piatkowski, I. Radwan and J. J. Gutierrez (2012), *Poland Enterprise Innovation Support Review*, The World Bank, accessed 21 October 2018 at http:// documents.worldbank.org/curated/en/914151468093563494/pdf/753250WP0P096 60ATION0SUPPORT0REVIEW.pdf.

Landesmann, M. A. (2003), 'Structural features of economic integration in an enlarged Europe: Patterns of catching-up and industrial specialization', European Economy, Economic Papers No. 181, Brussels: European Communities.

López-Claros, A. and Y. N. Mata (2010), 'Policies and institutions underpinning country innovation: Results from the Innovation Capacity Index', in A. López-Claros (ed.), *Innovation for Development Report 2010–2011: Innovation as a Driver of Productivity and Economic Growth*, London: Palgrave Macmillan, pp. 3–63.

Mahroum, S., R. Huggins, N. Clayton, K. Pain and P. Taylor (2008), *Innovation by Adoption: Measuring and Mapping Absorptive Capacity in UK Nations and Regions*, London: NESTA.

Millward Brown and OPI (2014), *Raport końcowy z badania ewaluacyjnego: Ewaluacja instrumentów wsparcia B+R w ramach perspektywy finansowej 2007–2013*, accessed 15 October 2018 at https://www.poir.gov.pl/media/11384/Raport_ewaluacja_B_R _perspektywa_2007_2013_grudzien_2014.pdf.

Ministerstwo Infrastruktury i Rozwoju (2017), *Programowanie perspektywy finan- sowej 2014–2020. Umowa Partnerstwa*, accessed 21 October 2018 at http://www .funduszeeuropejskie.gov.pl/strony/o-funduszach/dokumenty/umowa-partner stwa/.

Ministerstwo Przedsiębiorczości i Technologii (2018), *Przedsiębiorczość w Polsce*, accessed 20 October 2018 at https://www.mpit.gov.pl/media/65640/Raport _Przedsiebiorczosc_w_Polsce_edycja_2018_b.pdf.

Ministerstwo Rozwoju Regionalnego (2007), *Polska. Narodowe Strategiczne Ramy Odniesienia 2007–2013 wspierające wzrost gospodarczy i zatrudnienie. Narodowa*

Strategia Spójności. Dokument zaakceptowany decyzją Komisji Europejskiej zatwi-erdzającą pewne elementy Narodowych Strategicznych Ram Odniesienia, accessed 21 July 2018 at http://www.funduszeeuropejskie.2007–2013.gov.pl/Dokumenty/Lists/Dokumenty%20programowe/Attachments/95/NSRO_maj2007.pdf.

Najwyższa Izba Kontroli (2018), *Wykorzystanie przez przedsiębiorców środków publicznych na innowacje i prace badawczo-rozwojowe*, accessed 30 July 2018 at https://www.nik.gov.pl/kontrole/P/17/016/.

Narodowy Bank Polski (2016), *Potencjał innowacyjny gospodarki: Uwarunkowania, determinanty, perspektywy*, Warsaw: Narodowy Bank Polski.

OECD (2014), *Perspectives on Global Development 2014: Boosting Productivity to Meet the Middle-Income Challenge*, Paris: OECD Publishing.

OECD (2018), *OECD Economic Surveys: Poland 2018*, Paris: OECD Publishing.

Rada Ministrów (2017), *Strategii na rzecz Odpowiedzialnego Rozwoju do roku 2020 (z perspektywą do 2030 r.)*, Monitor Polski z 2017, poz. 260.

Raiser, M., M. Wes and A. Yilmaz (2016), 'Beyond convergence: Poland and Turkey en route to high income', *Central Bank Review*, **16**, 7–17.

Rodrik, D. (2003), 'Growth strategies', Working Paper No. w10050, accessed 21 October 2018 at https://ssrn.com/abstract=461371.

Rogut, A. and B. Piasecki (2011), 'Creating a regional innovation system: The case of Lodz in Poland', in F. Welter and D. Smallbone (eds), *Handbook of Research on Entrepreneurship Policies in Central and Eastern Europe*, Cheltenham, UK and Northampton, MA, USA: Edward Elgar Publishing, pp. 120–40.

Rogut, A., B. Piasecki, I. Świeczewska, J. Trębska, K. Kubiak, M. Piasecki, K. Dudek and I. Jurczak (2018), *Raport końcowy z badań przeprowadzonych w ramach Stworzenia narzędzi do monitorowania innowacyjności regionu łódzkiego, z wykorzystaniem pro-cesu przedsiębiorczego odkrywania na potrzeby aktualizacji RSI LORIS 2030*, accessed 12 August 2019 at http://www.rot-lodzkie.pl/mescms/attachments/attach es/000/000/262/original/Raport_ko%C5%84cowy.pdf.

Schwab, K. (ed.) (2017), *The Global Competitiveness Report 2017–2018*, Geneva: World Economic Forum.

Stern, S., M. E. Porter and J. L. Furman (2000), 'The determinants of national innovative capacity', NBER Working Paper No. 7876, accessed 19 October 2018 at www .nber.org/papers/w7876.

Tülücea, N. S. and A. K. Yurtkur (2015), 'Term of strategic entrepreneurship and Schumpeter's creative destruction theory', *Procedia – Social and Behavioral Sciences*, **207**, 720–28.

UNCTAD (2012), *Entrepreneurship Policy Framework and Implementation Guidance*, accessed 9 October 2018 at https://unctad.org/en/PublicationsLibrary/diaeed2012d1 _en.pdf?user=17.

UNDP, MOFA and KIEP (2013), *Challenges of the Middle-Income Countries: Seoul Debates 2013*, Seoul: United Nations Development Programme, the Ministry of Foreign Affairs of Korea and the Korea Institute of International Economic Policy.

Urząd Marszałkowski Województwa Łódzkiego (2018), *Regionalny Program Operacyjny Województwa Łódzkiego na lata 2014–2020. Załącznik do Uchwały Nr 276/18 Zarządu Województwa Łódzkiego z dnia 2 marca 2018 r.*, accessed 12 October 2018 at https://rpo.lodzkie.pl/images/2018/124-zmiany-w-rpo/rpo-wl-2032018.pdf.

US Department of Commerce (2012), *The Competitiveness and Innovative Capacity of the United States*, accessed 28 July 2018 at https://www.commerce.gov/sites/ commerce.gov/files/migrated/reports/thecompetitivenessandinnovativecapacityof theunitedstates.pdf.

Wang, Y. (2016), 'The political economy of the middle-income trap: Implications for potential growth', *Asian Development Review*, **33** (2), 167–81.

World Bank Group (2016), *W kierunku innowacyjnej Polski: Proces przedsiębiorczego odkrywania i analiza potrzeb przedsiębiorstw w Polsce*, accessed 21 October 2018 at http://documents.worldbank.org/curated/en/805821467993730545/pdf/106148-RE PLACEMENT-POLISH-v2-REPORT-Web.pdf.

World Bank Group (2017), *World Development Indicators 2017*, Washington, DC: International Bank for Reconstruction and Development/The World Bank.

Ye, L. and P. E. Robertson (2013), 'On the existence of a middle income trap', Economics Discussion Paper 13.12, accessed 21 September 2018 at http://ssrn.com/abstract=2227776.

Ye, L. and P. E. Robertson (2016), 'Identifying prisoners of the middle-income trap', accessed 12 March 2017 at http://voxeu.org/article/identifying-prisoners-middle -income-trap.

Zhao, E. Y., M. Ishiharab and P. D. Jennings (2019), 'Strategic entrepreneurship's dynamic tensions: Converging (diverging) effects of experience and networks on market entry timing and entrant performance', *Journal of Business Venturing*, **34**, 579–88.

9 Policy issues for SMEs: practical lessons from Japan's experiences in the 2010s

Itsutomo Mitsui

Introduction

This chapter is concerned with stimulating business start-ups in Japan in order to reverse the declining trend of the SME sector. It will describe, firstly, the nature of the problem, secondly, the policies that have been used to try to promote and support entrepreneurship and, thirdly, views on the appropriateness of these policies. The chapter is not an empirical one, but rather a report based on primary sources and secondary information. The key point developed through the chapter is that it is necessary to promote a culture of enterprise in Japan, particularly in the education system, but also through wider promotion designed to change attitudes towards business ownership in the population at large.

Japan's history of modernisation over the past 150 years has been considerably supported by small and medium enterprises (SMEs), in terms of industrial developments, exporting businesses and employment opportunities. Even in its post-war and high economic growth era, and indeed afterwards, SMEs have played key roles in leading industries such as car production and electronics manufacturing, both as suppliers and as supporting players. At the same time, SMEs have been catering for domestic consumer markets as retailers, wholesalers and service providers, and above all creating the majority of employment opportunities including self-employment. The Japanese government's White Papers on SMEs, produced by the Japan Small and Medium Enterprise Agency (JSMEA), outlined the following roles played by SMEs: creating and maintaining employment; producing almost half of national income or aggregate value added; supplying a wide range of diversified products based on their specialty, professional skills and adaptability; supporting big industries as their suppliers or business service feeders; producing goods for export over many years; and catering for the domestic consumers market (JSMEA, 2002).

However, ironically, the SME sector in Japan started declining after the 1980s, and there may be several reasons for this. The country's demographic trend cannot be ignored, since it shows a low birth rate and a decline in population in the twenty-first century. Much fiercer competition in the global market, expanding imports and a stronger presence of large or foreign businesses in the domestic market may also be affecting and threatening small manufacturers and retailers. Even so, the most serious factor is the clearly declining trend in new business start-ups since the 1990s. If compared with other advanced economies, such as the US, UK and Germany, Japan's business birth rate is almost half, and it is much lower in comparison with newly growing economies like China, Brazil and Uganda. Although the exit rate of businesses in Japan is also rather low, it has exceeded the birth rate for three decades. As a result, the declining trend cannot easily be curbed and reversed. Moreover, Japan has been suffering a high unemployment rate for more than two decades, being at 4–5 per cent since the middle of the 1990s, a level which is unprecedented in the post-war era. Thanks to the government's large-scale spending and stimulus policy under Shinzō Abe's leadership, employment conditions have been improving during more recent years, but better and more stable job opportunities cannot be created without there being growth and prosperity in the SME sector, which still accounts for more than 70 per cent of total employment.

Interestingly, there is an inverse relationship between the business birth rate and the unemployment rate in Japan. During the high economic growth era in the 1960s and 1970s, the business birth rate was high and the unemployment rate was very low. However, since the 1990s the situation has almost reversed. In most economies, a higher unemployment rate sees an acceleration in new business start-ups, with individuals creating their own job opportunities and income sources. In European countries, such as the UK, this phenomenon occurred in the 1980s, when it was interpreted as suggesting that there were strong factors pushing people who were out of work into self-employment or small business ownership, essentially because of the limited alternative ways of earning a living. The Global Entrepreneurship Monitor (GEM) described this as necessity-pushed entrepreneurship. It should, however, be remembered that business development is a dynamic process, and therefore businesses that are set up in a particular form may not necessarily maintain that format during the rest of their development.

The policy response

For more than two decades the Japanese government concentrated its efforts on increasing the number of new business start-ups and revitalising the SME sector. In 1999, the government revised the Basic Law for SMEs for the first time in more than three decades, moving away from the previous idea of addressing their disadvantages and differentials and towards that of developing and growing a wide range of independent SMEs for greater economic vitality, and supporting self-help efforts for business innovation and start-ups. Promoting new start-ups became one of the core policy objectives, and the government launched a number of new measures, including the following laws: Promotion of Creative Activities of SMEs (1995), Limited Liability Investment Consortiums in SMEs (1998), Facilitating the Creation of New Business (1997) and Supporting Business Innovation of SMEs (1999). Many of these were later integrated into the SME Technological Advancement Law in 2005.

Under the short-lived new Democratic party's government between 2009 to 2012, the SME Charter of 2010 was endorsed by the Cabinet to consolidate the basic philosophy as well as fundamental policy principles and objectives, which took 'encouraging SMEs to start up new businesses' as a key issue. According to the charter, 'business start-up enables people to exercise potential and willingness without being bound by the framework of the existing organization, and creates new jobs. The Government will drastically upgrade the existing incentive programs for start-up to further revitalize the economy' (Government of Japan, 2010). In 2013 the Liberal Democratic Party's President Shinzō Abe returned to government and announced his Three Arrows 'Abenomics' Revitalisation and Recovery Plan following the 2008 global financial crisis. His third Arrow, the Japan Revitalisation Strategy, had 'constructing a system to support business start-ups in Japan's regions' as its key objective, and stipulated that the aims would be to ensure that 'the business start-up rate exceeds the business closure rate, and raise the business start-up and closure rate to the 10 per cent range, on a par with the rates in the USA and the UK (from the current rate of around 5 per cent)'. A 10 per cent business birth rate has become a clear policy target since then.

'Hard' support policy measures

Governments can exercise several different policy measures to increase the number of new business start-ups:

1. Legal, institutional frameworks, regulations and registration procedures for those newly set up.
2. Financial support policies:
   a. Financial measures, including favourable lending, subsidiaries and tax incentives to offer initial capital.
   b. A financially indirect, but very suitable, support for new business is to offer low-cost or low-rent premises, such as incubation facilities, shops or offices. Leasing private facilities or building one's own shops and offices is expensive for young entrepreneurs. Therefore, even in Japan, local governments or public bodies have been operating these incubation facilities and premises all over the country.
3. Private sector support for new businesses, including investments, dealings, partnerships or the offering of other resources and business opportunities, is important, but governments can only exercise indirect measures such as setting favourable frameworks for investment syndicates.
4. Public sectors may purchase from or give orders to new businesses, but this is difficult due to the need for impartiality. Even so, local governments and public bodies favour entrusting projects or operations to local social enterprises. In order to promote new business sales, trade fairs, business meetings or matching events sponsored by public institutions are also common measures which should be included within indirect 'soft' support.

Financial issues

As far as national 'hard' support for new entrepreneurs is concerned, the commonly accepted view in Japan is that legal frameworks and regulations are not a major barrier for start-ups. Even so, in 2002 JSMEA introduced a Law for Supporting SMEs' Challenges, which allowed new businesses with as little as ¥1 in capital to be registered as joint stock companies (before that amendment, the minimum capital amount was ¥10 million for a joint stock company). Later, this preferential measure was perpetuated. Though some surveys and data suggest this measure increased the number of new joint stock company registrations, most admit that this is not so clear; even before the amendment it was not difficult to get registered as a joint stock company, and a ¥1 company should increase its capital amount to ¥10 million or more within five years. Financial issues are still important, despite the fact that private financial institutions now face difficulties in attracting loan customers and their loan–deposit ratios are mostly less than 50 per cent.

Private financial institutions, such as high street banks, are not that popular among new entrepreneurs, due to a lack of availability of loans and the imposition of strict conditions. The most popular source of finance for business start-ups is the JFC's loan schemes. JFC is a public company owned by the government, and has been dedicated to supporting SMEs and micro or small businesses for many decades. In the 2012 financial year, JFC's Micro Unit provided loans to 42 452 businesses that had been in business for five years or less. Out of these, 19 469 obtained loans prior to or within one year of start-up. JFC's New Start-Up Loan Programme is popular, as it does not request any collateral or personal guarantees. In recent years, JFC has been concentrating its efforts on encouraging young and female entrepreneurs, as well as social entrepreneurs. Local governments also offer subsidised loans or subsidies to local entrepreneurs. Also, local, private, non-profit sector financial institutions, such as Shinkin (local financial associations) and Shinkumi (local financial cooperatives), offer loans to local businesses.

In 2013 the government launched start-up subsidies for promoting business start-ups such as businesses creating demand in the region. The upper limit for the amount of subsidy is ¥2 million ($17,000), but the number of beneficiaries is little more than a hundred. As far as new businesses are concerned, SMRJ (which is an independent administrative corporation under the government's control) is able to support fundraising in the above scheme, and mainly engages in offering 'Upgrading Loans' to SME organisations. It now jointly operates a venture investment fund. Credit guarantee corporations in each prefecture guarantee the money borrowed by those planning to start new projects, which also supports new business investment. In 2012, the government set up a new large-scale loan scheme, operated by the JFC, known as a 'Management Enhancing Loan', with an upper limit of ¥720 million ($6.4 million) for SMEs or ¥72 million ($0.64 million) for micro businesses. It is rather popular among new businesses for their second-stage growth plan.

Business incubation

Business incubation facilities and the provision of business premises are very common ways of providing business support for new and young businesses in Japan. The Law for Facilitating the Creation of New Business (1997) encouraged local governments and public bodies to build subsidised incubation buildings across Japan. Many are very successful, such as the Sagamihara Incubation Centre (SIC), which now offers workshops, offices and labs to more than a hundred businesses, reflecting the growing demand. SIC is now an independent corporation and is neither receiving subsidies nor city government support. It also offers various supports and advice for new entrepreneurs. Much smaller and cheaper facilities are also operating in many towns and cities, such as the Takadanobaba Incubation Support Centre which stands in central Tokyo and is operated by Shinjuku Ward. Its building is old and small but very convenient, and its monthly rent is upwards from ¥10 000 ($90) per month for a shared office desk. Its most popular support is its free information, advice and counselling services.

'Soft' support measures

Indirect, 'soft' support, particularly that which is long term and aiming to change attitudes towards business ownership, is indispensable for promoting entrepreneurship and business start-ups on a large scale. This support includes trade fairs, business meetings and matching events. Governments or public bodies commonly operate information desks, counselling services or consulting supports. They are mostly supportive and useful for those who might be thinking about starting a new business. Financial supports and incubation premises are commonly combined with advice and counselling services, as mentioned above. These services cannot, however, change the attitudes and choices of the masses regarding engagement in entrepreneurship. The long-term decline of the business birth rate in Japan must be understood as a cultural phenomenon which started changing decades ago.

According to the *White Paper on SMEs 2017* (JSMEA, 2017), the actual rate of starting a business in Japan is similar to other advanced economies, and the same goes for their success or survival rate. This means that a favourable environment is offered to those who would like to start their own business. In this respect, the support measures are strongly focused on actual start-ups and potential start-ups with clear intentions. At the same time, surveys continually reveal the relatively small number of people who wish to take advantage of this favourable environment. In addition, younger generations are not only less interested in entrepreneurship or starting their own businesses, but may fear it as an unpromising choice. Surveys conducted on people's attitudes to entrepreneurship and the possibility of starting a business revealed that the most common response was either 'No, I never ever thought of it', 'Starting a business seems too risky' or 'I am not suitable to be an entrepreneur'. The proportion of those who are indifferent towards entrepreneurship has clearly increased in Japan, in contrast with other advanced economies. And, according to Nomura Research Institute's (NRI) survey, the surprising fact is that positive entrepreneurial attitudes have been clearly declining year by year, and getting weaker among younger generations in Japan.

Therefore, the issue of how to reverse the declining trend of the SME sector and to stimulate entrepreneurship is not simply a matter of environmental, institutional or directly supporting policy frameworks, but of more comprehensive, social, cultural and long-term factors, including learning, educational, career development, community and human relationship issues. At the same time, the fact that Japanese people were once very entrepreneurially minded and started their own businesses in large numbers without any supporting policies must be considered. On the other hand, the majority of young people do not have access to support because the amount of support available is insufficient for the number of young people who need it. In addition, most young people have little idea about what entrepreneurship involves, which means that a case can be made for increasing the level of promotion of entrepreneurship targeted at young people.

Future policy priorities and learning opportunities

As entrepreneurial decisions and activities are clearly personal and subjective matters, no one can be obliged to start their own business and commit to it, but one has the right to choose what sort of working life and livelihood is best. Therefore, one's own mindset and decision making are critical for entrepreneurship development, but naturally they are considerably affected by one's own environment and life history, in other words, personal experiences, family relations and associations, education and working life, or even media influences. A very common idea is that role models, for example parents, relatives, friends and colleagues, have a significant impact on the decision to choose entrepreneurship. In addition, entrepreneurial values and an entrepreneurial mindset are necessary for an individual's self-realisation and satisfaction.

If asked, most young people would say they have never thought of entrepreneurship as a career option, or they do not know anyone who is an entrepreneur. It is highly unlikely they would suggest that starting their own business is 'a good choice, with freedom, challenge, satisfaction and rewards' (JSMEA, 2017). The reality is there is little aspiration for entrepreneurship among Japan's younger generation. Therefore, providing information on experiences, possibilities and achievements concerning entrepreneurship is now important in Japan, as well as sharing knowledge on, and methods for, business start-up, planning and practice. Promoting entrepreneurship demands better socio-cultural environments and learning opportunities to increase the number of potential entrepreneurs.

Entrepreneurship education

The reality of entrepreneurship education in Japan should be seriously examined, as school education is a key starting point for the younger generation not only to learn academic subjects and practical skills, but also to be informed of opportunities in the working world. Most schools and universities have their own career guidance services for students. However, surprisingly, this career guidance is mostly dedicated to the preparation for higher education institutions and company recruitment opportunities. For a long time, no schools or universities offered any programs on entrepreneurship within their curriculum. But now, many universities are promoting 'entrepreneurship education' and offering related subjects such as business planning and fundraising, lectures presented by successful entrepreneurs, and internship or practical off-campus business projects with local SMEs. Business plan contests are rather popular, including JFC's high school student contests, which attract nearly 3000 applications every year. At the same time, many academics are highly critical of entrepreneurship education that overly focuses on business planning.

However, not only is there the problem that entrepreneurship education is not combined with career guidance, but it is rarely integrated into official curriculum subjects and courses. Without enough knowledge and shared experience, only a small minority of students are in a position to consider entrepreneurship as a possible career choice. Therefore, the aim should be to expand the number of people targeted for entrepreneurship education; to integrate entrepreneurship education into the education curriculum whilst also prioritising collaboration with business people and senior entrepreneurs as well as career guidance services.

As far as older generations are concerned, their aspiration for entrepreneurship is more concrete, and for them it is not so difficult to find information and learning points; there are local Chambers of Commerce and Industries (CCI), incubation offices and independent organisations that are promoting and supporting new start-ups.

Promoting social entrepreneurs

Despite the fact that fewer people are entrepreneurially minded, more are interested in starting social enterprises, or getting involved in them. For instance, the number of NPOs (non-profit organisations, a legal entity) now exceeds 50 000 since its legislation in 1998. Their objectives and activities are very wide-ranging and, although some are not successful, NPOs and other organisations dedicated to social issues are attractive for potential entrepreneurs and can be successful through having clear objectives and strong support from local communities. Social entrepreneurship is more popular among middle-aged people and female entrepreneurs. JFC recently started offering loans to NPOs and social welfare corporations, and local governments mostly favour entrusting public service projects or community activities aimed at improving local people's quality of life to NPOs. However, the most basic problem for social enterprises is securing revenue and keeping a balance between their mission and their earning sources. Even so, socially oriented motivation may be key to revitalising basic entrepreneurial mindsets and working-life motivation in Japanese society.

New legal frameworks for entrepreneurs?

Those who argue for legal frameworks for entrepreneurs are essentially suggesting that because some people who come into this category are freelancers, current frameworks are not appropriate for them. In other words, 'fukugyo' or so-called 'hybrid' or 'part-time' entrepreneurs should be given more encouragement. If so, this will certainly reduce barriers to start-ups, above all minimising the danger of losing income sources. JSMEA and some government departments are now considering new frameworks which may boost the number of new start-ups and enterprises. 'Freelance' professionals are classified as those who are independent and engaged in qualified work or specialist engagements. In fact, nearly one million people can be classified as independent professionals, accounting for 20 per cent of self-employed or MDs. An expansion in the number of freelancers may encourage more people to become independent by realising their own specified skills and talents. Part-time can also mean that a gradual, heuristic and therefore stable approach to start-up is taken. This can provide more flexibility and make it easier to correct strategy as the business is being established. According to a survey by Japan Finance Corporation Research Institute (JFCRI) in 2016, more than a quarter of existing entrepreneurs answered that their start-ups were 'fukugyo' type and that was useful for their business development. They are more likely to be females and of a younger generation.

The approach of the Japanese government to some extent borrows from the French experience, which allows individuals that are out of work to register as self-employed. This has enabled these individuals to benefit from tax exemptions, and support is available for them as independent business owners whilst they are unemployed. The experience in some countries that have adopted this approach that boosts self-employment is that allowing individuals to combine working for themselves with being registered as unemployed sees an increase in the size of the shadow economy.

However, in Japan, the shadow economy is smaller than in many other countries. At the same time, a key question is whether employers will allow those who are essentially part-time employees to also work independently on a self-employed basis. On the other hand, part-time self-employment in Japan (or 'fukugyo' entrepreneurship) may expand new business opportunities with an official legal status, offer more stability, and minimise financial or psychological barriers to becoming self-employed, reducing in particular the stress often associated with a new business start-up. Even if side-line jobs are not officially banned, most employers clearly dislike them. As a result, how to boost entrepreneurship and new start-ups remains a cultural and social issue.

Problems for the working poor and entrepreneurship for better employment

In contrast, what is less attractive to government bodies and other institutions is the contribution of entrepreneurship to job opportunities for the unemployed or underemployed. In Western countries a number of policy schemes were implemented to give unemployed people, or those in less favourable working conditions, the chance of independent entrepreneurship and more income. In the UK, for example, EAS (Enterprise Allowance Scheme) benefit was given to unemployed people in exchange for other unemployment benefits for one year, which considerably boosted the number of new entrepreneurs and ignited new growth in self-employment and SME formation in the 1980s and 1990s. Self-employed status is another form of employment. Those who choose entrepreneurship as an alternative to hired employment are often called 'necessity entrepreneurs', and are criticised as having less motivation and commitment towards achieving entrepreneurial success. However, this is not necessarily the case: many successful entrepreneurs started their career under difficult and unstable circumstances, seeking a better work life, and this has led to great opportunities and success.

Under pressure from the growing unemployment rate, the Japanese Ministry of Labour and Welfare launched a New Start-Up Supporting Subsidiary

Scheme in 2002. The scheme operated for 11 years and supported nearly 14 000 unemployed people. The survival rate was high (at 90 per cent), and under the scheme an estimated 2.1 additional jobs were created by each new start-up. However, there was a basic inconsistency inherent in the scheme in that it was based on the national unemployment insurance fund, which enabled benefits to be given to those who were out of work and seeking new employment opportunities, but funding could only be provided to those who had paid their unemployment insurance premium. Other groups which needed help, such as casual workers and freelancers, were not eligible but could access the guidance and placement advice of job centres. Becoming an independent entrepreneur was not a choice at the beginning, although this was subsequently allowed. One of the problems was that job centres (and offices of the Ministry of Labour and Welfare) knew nothing about how to start a business, and had little or no knowledge on entrepreneurship.

There has been little discussion in Japan about how to encourage unemployed people to find their way to becoming successful entrepreneurs. Surprisingly perhaps, in the *White Paper on SMEs 2017* (JSMEA, 2017), young people were shown to be less entrepreneurially minded than other age groups, although there was an inverse relationship between entrepreneurial orientation and income. Among those who replied with no intention of starting a business, the largest group (almost half) were on the lowest income, at less than ¥2 million ($17 000) per year. And the most common answer when asked the reason for not intending to start a business was 'It is too risky'.

To reverse the declining number of SMEs and to encourage more start-ups, the issue of 'necessity entrepreneurship' has to be more seriously discussed and taken into account by policy makers and researchers in Japan. This issue is not far removed from the promotion of 'fukugyo', that is hybrid entrepreneurship.

A future policy agenda

As well as promoting more business start-ups, it is also important to reduce the number of business closures among existing SMEs, in order to reverse the ongoing declining trend. Some business closures may be inevitable, but there is a group of SMEs with stable performance that are obliged to close simply because there are no successors. Such cases are far from rare, and it is estimated that nearly 50 per cent of existing micro enterprises may disappear in the near future for this reason.

As a result, JSMEA and government bodies are committed to solving the problem through financial and tax incentives. This is because soaring land and asset values make inheritance or transfer tax too expensive for successors to bear. The government, therefore, has offered some measures to address these issues, including deferring payments or allowing payment by instalment. Financial institutions have also given support to new owner-managers in these situations. It is possible that the long periods of depression in the twenty-first century may release many SMEs from the burden of soaring asset values, thus lessening the 'succession problem'. Since succession is not necessarily the best choice in family businesses, its propensity is decreasing. Succession by third parties or non-family members is encouraged, but may involve more serious financial problems. In fact, in most common cases, third-party successors are employees who have been in managerial positions, shown competence and have earned the trust of many parties, such as the owner family, employees, business partners and banks. Even so, business succession inevitably involves many difficulties and complications, and the government offers a number of 'soft' support measures, including local business succession counselling centres. Entrepreneurship or management education is, again, very important in order to increase the number of competent SME successors and to make successions trouble-free and innovative. This subject should be studied further and discussed in detail.

Conclusion

The declining trend in the SME sector in Japan is a rather complicated, long-term and socio-cultural issue, and it is not easy to reverse. Nevertheless, without making SMEs the engine of economic development and innovation, as well as a key source of employment and leaders of local economies, the future will not be a bright one, least of all for younger generations. Although the Japanese government and public bodies have been implementing a variety of policy measures, it will not be easy to change the socio-economic system from the bottom up. The unpopularity of entrepreneurship is strongly rooted within Japanese society's institutions and culture as well as people's mindsets. Nevertheless, academic researchers, educators, policy makers and business practitioners must cooperate to make changes and revive the long tradition of Japanese entrepreneurship in the twenty-first century. Japan is not the only country where entrepreneurship and SME development are recognised as a challenge. In this context, there is clearly a future research priority with respect to the question of how to address the ongoing decline in the number of SMEs. In this regard, the experience of other countries may be drawn upon whilst also incorporating a strong cultural dimension, on the basis that culture may well affect the success of particular types of policy approach.

References

Government of Japan (2010), *SME Charter.*
JSMEA (2002), *White Paper on SMEs 2002.*
JSMEA (2017), *White Paper on SMEs 2017.*

10 The role of mobile technologies and inclusive innovation policies in SME development in Sub Saharan Africa

Bitange Ndemo

Introduction

If there is anything that has been primarily responsible for changing the 'Africa Rising' narrative, it is the advent of mobile technologies. These technologies have expanded relentlessly across the African continent, giving rise to greater inclusivity and necessitating the development of small and medium enterprises (SMEs) (Ndemo and Weiss, 2017). This development was made possible by the consciously enabling innovation policies that some African countries adopted as strategies to leverage information and communication technologies (ICTs) in employment creation (Ndemo, 2015). Mobile technology, therefore, has become an essential tool for development. Asongu et al. (2016) established that mobile phone penetration in the Sub Saharan Africa (SSA) market is pivotal to sustainable and inclusive human development, irrespective of a country's level of income, legal origins, religious orientation or the state of the nation.

Policy makers across the world are increasingly recognising the transformative potential of mobile technology. In the GSMA (2017) report, for example, mobile technology is identified as a 'key opportunity for accelerating the scale and reach of inclusive, digital identities that can empower citizens, protect privacy and stimulate economic and social development' (p. 43). In this context Kenya is viewed as a trailblazer, having created an enabling policy environment for mobile technologies to thrive. Moreover, in the GSMA/Deloitte Report (2015) the Democratic Republic of Congo, with its huge infrastructure gap, was identified as a country where mobile technology could provide an opportunity to connect people and financial providers at a fraction of the cost of more conventional methods. Specifically, mobile technology has enabled financial providers to take their services to remote parts of the country. Policy makers in the Congo are in the process of developing appropriate policies to promote the adoption of these technologies.

On a personal level, several factors have contributed to the author's interest in examining the nexus between inclusive innovation policies, SME development and mobile technologies in SSA. First is the increasing concern among young people about the scale of unemployment and poverty. Second, there is a fear that SSA may not achieve its sustainable development goals (SDGs) unless the continent encourages wealth creation through SME development. Third, there is the question as to whether policy interventions are enabling inclusive innovation solutions that contribute to expanding scalable SMEs. Such a development can create employment and wealth, and mitigate poverty in SSA.

SMEs are considered by most governments to be an avenue towards realising employment opportunities, which are necessary if a future crisis is to be avoided. Although some reports paint Africa in a positive light, the ballooning population presents a major challenge. As the World Bank (2016) has emphasised, 'Africa's rate of extreme poverty fell from 56 per cent in 1990 to 43 per cent in 2012. Because of population increase, however, an estimated 63 million people live in extreme poverty in Africa today than in 1990' (p. 5).

As technology changes, new concepts emerge which necessitate new methods of study and present policy makers with new challenges. In addition, the context for these changes in technology needs to be recognised. Ndemo and Weiss (2017) acknowledge that the remarkable adoption rates suggest that digital technologies are making their way into every facet of life in African societies. That is why, in this chapter, three research questions are considered:

- Given the fact that new and innovative technologies continue to emerge, what role do policy makers play in facilitating new technologies?
- What policy measures are taken to sustain the diffusion of mobile innovation technology and its application to the development of SMEs in Africa?
- In an evolving technology landscape, what are the inclusive policy interventions that governments should adopt as strategies to support the development of SMEs?

Operational definitions of key concepts

Mobile technologies

Mobile technology refers to portable devices that can offer instantaneous access to information (Coates et al., 2009). The technology includes feature phones, smartphones, Personal Digital Assistants (PDAs), tablets and e-book readers (Adeeb and Hussain, 2009). PDAs and smartphones are mobile devices that are mainly used for communication in real time (Chang et al., 2012). Due to their flexibility, simplicity and portability, they are increasingly used by individuals, as well as SMEs, as their tools of trade. As far back as 2006, an SME survey of 14 African countries carried out by Research ICT Africa (RIA) established that ICTs are productive input factors contributing to increased labour productivity for informal, as well as formal, SMEs (RIA, 2006). In an article that followed, Esselaar et al. (2007) argued that there was still 'demand for fixed-line phones among SMEs but that mobile phones have become the default communications tool because fixed lines are either too expensive or not available' (p. 87).

Inclusive innovation policies

Planes-Satorra and Paunov (2017) define 'inclusive innovation poli-cies' as innovation policies that aim to remove barriers to participation by under-represented individuals, social groups, firms, sectors and regions in innovation, research and entrepreneurship activities. The aim is to ensure that all segments of society have an equal chance to participate in, and benefit from, innovation. These policies are meant specifically to contribute to social, industrial and territorial inclusiveness. For example, Kenya, which gave rise to mobile money, has in the recent past changed regulations to enable broad access to mobile money by allowing interoperability (referring to the ability of systems or softwares to exchange and make use of information) within the tele-communications industry. This enables SMEs to leverage mobile lending from all network operators (Ndemo, 2018). However, much more needs to be done to create policy frameworks that facilitate innovation; in other words, policies that allow risk-taking to achieve the desired goal of inclusivity (Ndemo, 2018).

SME development

Although there is no common definition for 'SMEs' across Africa, it is gener-ally accepted that these are enterprises employing between 10 and 250 persons.

They account for 90 to 95 per cent of all businesses in SSA, employ in excess of 80 per cent of the workforce, and contribute more than 30 per cent to GDP in virtually all of SSA (Fjose et al., 2010; Government of Kenya, 2016). However, not all SMEs in Africa enjoy the freedom to use technology in their businesses, because coverage is not universal. Several parts of Africa, even with Smart Africa initiatives, still lack connectivity.

In some parts of Africa, SMEs seeking to exploit the growing e-commerce markets have had to wait longer for regulatory approvals to launch their new business models utilising digital platforms. For example, Apulu and Ige (2011) studied the use of ICTs in Nigerian SMEs, reporting that electricity and infrastructural inadequacies are the most prevalent factors for non-utilisation of ICT among SMEs in the region. The increasing number of technology hubs across the African continent are churning out new ideas that, with the right digital policies, could lead to greater productivity through successful SMEs and stimulate economic development.

Sub Saharan Africa (SSA)

The area south of the Sahara is a major region that excludes Arab Africa. It is the fastest growing market in the world (GSMA, 2017). In the GSMA report, *The Mobile Economy – Sub-Saharan Africa 2017*, it was estimated that up to 2020 the region will continue to grow faster than any market in the world. In 2017, a World Bank report, *Global Economic Prospects*, indicated that of the top five fastest growing economies in the world, two were from Africa (World Bank, 2017). On average, most African economies are growing faster than other regions in the world, with growth largely coming from SMEs backed by ICTs. Ndemo (2017) argued that 'across the continent, new start up digital enterprises are emerging, while existing small and medium enterprises (SMEs) are increasingly leveraging ICTs to expand. Intensified use of ICTs presents Africa's SMEs with opportunities in virtually every sector as well as room to create jobs' (p. 42).

Theoretical underpinning and the related literature

This chapter looks at the nexus between inclusive innovation policies and SME development in relation to mobile technologies and sustainable economic development, through the prism of Rogers and Cartano's (1962) Diffusion of Innovation Theory.

Diffusion of Innovation Theory

This theory popularised by Rogers and Cartano (1962) seeks to explain how, why, and at what rate new ideas and technology spread. The three waves depicted in Figure 10.1 demonstrate how ICTs have spread in SSA since the early 1990s when the Internet emerged. The first wave was the Internet, or the World Wide Web, now simply known as the Web; this was followed by the advent of mobile telephony, referred to as Mobility; and last and the most recent wave has been the emergence of Blockchain. The Web, characterised by search engines such as Google, has enabled the creation of new enterprises and precipitated productivity improvement in SMEs. Mobility intensified the improvement of SME productivity by enabling even smaller SMEs to leverage its disruptiveness. Even in its formative stages, Blockchain has shown promise when it comes to intensifying SME productivity further, as discussed later in the chapter.

Early adopters of these technologies were countries that had the necessary infrastructure and enabling policies. SSA, however, did not have the infrastructure, and telecommunication companies were mostly state-owned monopoly enterprises. Internet adoption was delayed until the infrastructure and policy issues were dealt with in 2012 (Ndemo, 2015). Since 2012, the problem of ICT infrastructure has been addressed and many countries, notably Kenya, South Africa, Ghana and Nigeria, have been hot spots for innovation (Osiakwan, 2016).

Using Rogers and Cartano's (1962) Diffusion of Innovation Theory, Figure 10.1 explains major technology innovation adoption waves. The Internet gave rise to search engines like Google, Yahoo, Baidu and so on; Mobility brought thousands of mobile platforms; and Blockchain has brought hundreds of cryptocurrencies despite its infancy. Studies (Kendall et al., 2011) show that Mobility played a key role in enabling the emergence of mobile money that was first adopted in Kenya and rapidly grew to other countries across the world.

The adoption of the Mobility wave overlapped with the Internet. This meant that even after new policies were introduced, for example in Kenya (Ndemo, 2015), it took some time before their impact could be felt. The Mobility wave enabled the advent of small start-ups, which grew to become mega platforms across the world. These included Facebook, Twitter, Amazon and Alibaba, and the list continues to grow.

The 2018 *Global Competitiveness Report* by the World Economic Forum introduced a new Global Competitiveness Index referred to as Industry 4.0

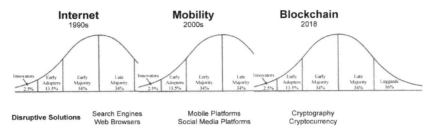

Figure 10.1   Major innovation adoption waves

(World Economic Forum, 2018a). This new index introduced a set of drivers of productivity that underpinned the emerging Fourth Industrial Revolution (World Economic Forum, 2018b). The report provided greater clarity for policy makers in shaping economic strategies and monitoring them. It was also the basis for proposing the third wave mentioned in this chapter. Besides Blockchain, Artificial Intelligence (AI), Internet of Things (IoT), Machine Learning and Big Data are among the emerging technologies that will underpin the Fourth Industrial Revolution.

To exploit the full potential of technological progress, there must be dynamic policy development, since each wave comes with unique features that require new policies. The Internet requires policies around accessible and affordable resources. This means that governments would give the necessary incentives for the development of infrastructure, as well as develop policies to create a competitive environment as a strategy to create affordability. Although many countries have enabling telecommunication policies, some countries still have telecom monopolies that have hindered the widespread use of ICTs in the development of SMEs.

The evolution of mobile technologies

Over the past two decades, mobile technology innovations have been at the centre of addressing inequalities such as lack of financial inclusion (Ndemo, 2016a). This has enabled SME growth across all sectors by improving productivity and catalysing development in emerging economies (Donner and Escobari, 2010). This initially started as a simple innovation to solve the problem of financial transfer in emerging economies, where the majority of the population did not use banks (Ndemo, 2017). This led to more complex uses of multiple technologies on the mobile platform to solve lending problems at the bottom of the pyramid (Ndemo, 2018). Many of those that receive credit as a result of using these mobile technologies leveraging Big Data, AI and Blockchain had never received any form of credit before these mobile technologies made it possible (Ndemo, 2018).

This phenomenal progress in SSA was largely policy driven. The incumbent telecommunication companies were government owned, and if policy makers had not agreed to disrupt themselves through the then emerging mobile technology, the sector's growth would still be stunted today. The author participated in the process of decoupling existing policies that allowed the incumbent telecommunication companies to double as industry regulators. It was unthinkable to create independent regulators since these companies were considered to be security installations, and wielded power within government circles. Incentives from the World Bank and strong leadership eventually created independent regulatory bodies. There are still a number of these companies in some African countries that have not been decoupled.

Governments in SSA, especially Kenya, made several deliberate policy interventions to facilitate the much-needed infrastructure, an example being the government-led development of undersea fibre-optic cables. Without this infrastructure, access and affordability of broadband would still be a major challenge. Other policy interventions that fuelled the innovative environment include the creation of open data portals to access huge data sets belonging to the government; subsidising broadband for universities and colleges through national research networks; removal of taxation from ICT devices; and providing subsidies to college students to enable them to purchase computing devices. Indeed, new innovations emerged after the governments adopted such policies and started to collaborate with the private sector.

In Kenya, for example, M-Pesa (the mobile money app) would never have taken off without close collaboration between the government and the private sector. The government allowed the app to operate without a clear policy mechanism in place, with some civil servants, including the author, taking the risk of having to accept responsibility in the case of failure (Ndemo, 2015). Several other SSA countries came to learn from Kenya and eventually implemented the innovation in their respective countries. The success in Kenya gave the impetus to other SSA countries to embrace innovation. Today, virtually every country in SSA has an innovation hub (Kelly and Firestone, 2016) and is developing new apps in several sectors including agriculture, health, education, transport and financial services.

The ubiquity of mobile technology has influenced the development of mobile applications in several Tech Hubs (an open space where aspiring technology enthusiasts collaborate to realise their innovations) across Africa. New research by Disrupt Africa (2017) found that the number of African technology-based start-ups that raised funds increased from 146 in 2016 to 159 in 2017. Considering that in 2015 only 125 start-ups managed to attract any funding, this is a significant improvement and demonstrates a growing interest in African technology ventures that have begun to dot the African SME landscape.

In terms of funding, the report says that these start-ups managed to raise a total of 195 060 845 US dollars – a slightly more than 50 per cent increase over the previous year's investment into Africa. Some of these start-ups do indeed spark entrepreneurialism and help stimulate SME growth.

Ndemo and Weiss (2017) identified a number of key dimensions for unlocking Africa's future through digital transformation. Each of these dimensions is a cog in the wheel that will drive technology adoption. The three main dimensions identified are summarised in Box 10.1.

Box 10.1 Key dimensions for unlocking Africa's future

Social dimension – the relational fabric and network configurations in which mobile technology development, adoption and diffusion take place.

Economic dimension – actions that bring economic activity into the digital realm, build and expand markets and institutionalise new pathways to economic value creation. It is how government actions create and maintain a favourable political climate for creativity in the use of mobile technology to take place.

Cultural dimension – customs, attitudes and beliefs existing in a community or organisation at any one time. Organisational features involve the ability to disrupt existing organisational arrangements in favour of a new form of organisation to affect performance, operations and resources.

Mobile technologies and inclusive innovation policies

The widespread use of the mobile phone in Africa makes it an essential tool for those at the bottom of the pyramid (Heeks et al., 2014). In their quest to understand the definition, nature and dynamics of inclusive innovation through mobile case studies in Kenya, Heeks et al. established that 'inclusive innovation needs to be understood and developed in the context of a holistic conception of the innovation cycle, the distinction between process and product innovation and the roles played by the poor as both producers and consumer' (p. 175).

In their recent study, Asongu and Nwachukwu (2016) established that inclusive human development is persistently tied to the use of mobile phones in knowledge diffusion. They argue that countries with 'low levels of inclusive human development are catching up with their counterparts with higher development' (p. 133). Their recommendation is that policy development should lay emphasis on using these findings to promote inclusive development.

Foster and Heeks (2016) make the case for inclusive innovation policy, highlighting a number of considerations. These include broadening the scope of innovation to encompass more marginalised groups, and ensuring that innovations focus on new goods and services that are required to address economic and social development for those in the lowest income brackets (Juma and Yee-Cheong, 2005). In spite of the poor fit between innovations and low-income groups, there is a problem in the sense that inclusive innovations do not scale up, and even when these innovations are diffused, they may not lead to a significant impact.

Inclusive innovation takes a different approach from traditional innovation, by focusing on the marginalised groups (Foster and Heeks, 2016). During the time the author of this chapter spent in the Kenyan government, policy making focused on creating an enabling environment without going into the intricacies of inclusive innovation policy. This was important because, in the thinking of policy makers, inclusive innovation policies were a stopgap meant to satisfy the mission before generalised innovation policies were developed. Policy making at the time could be considered dynamic, as eyes were focused on building sustainable enterprises.

Mobile technologies and SME development

While acknowledging that the concept of inclusive innovation policy had not been fully understood, Ndemo (2016b) highlighted the intricate relationship between the growth of mobile technologies and SME development leading to greater productivity, more access to finance and new business models by early adopter countries like South Africa, Kenya, Ghana, Nigeria, Senegal, Uganda and Rwanda. In the recent past, more countries in SSA have begun to stimulate SME development through the intensified use of ICTs. These countries include Tanzania, Ethiopia, Zambia, Mozambique and Ivory Coast.

Movimbela and Dube (2016) posit that the relationship between mobile technologies and SME development is well acknowledged across Africa. In their studies in South Africa, they revealed that in terms of technology, SMEs only use what is readily available and never utilise the full potential of what technology can offer, even when it is well established that technology indeed offers many potential benefits to SMEs. It was argued that in order to help SMEs utilise the full potential of technology, there needs to be a clear framework and set of rules which the government must take responsibility for providing. This is because the high costs of access and lack of infrastructure act as barriers to SME development.

Besides the accessibility and affordability of the technologies, there are other challenges that act as constraints on the growth of mobile innovation technologies and in turn slow down SME growth in countries that experience some of these challenges. Several countries need to leverage policy interventions like the removal of taxes from enabling devices, and encourage investment in technology intermediaries to help with capacity building in technology use. A 2017 report by the Alliance for Affordable Internet showed that many countries in SSA have been slow in using policy intervention to stimulate the access to technology of millions of people (Alliance for Affordable Internet, 2017). In their study of technology use in Ghana and Botswana, Asare et al. (2012) found that the most commonly reported barriers to a higher level of technology use include frequent power disruptions and a lack of technical know-how.

In Kenya, however, the government dealt with the problem through policy interventions, which encouraged the private sector to build critical infrastructure, thereby subsidising access to broadband. These measures were meant to increase the uptake of broadband, which was facilitated by public–private partnerships and an extension of the subsidy to include undersea cabling to bring power into the region (Ndemo, 2015). The subsidy was extended to both public and private universities and enabled students to acquire laptops to increase the consumption of broadband (Ndemo, 2016b). The outcome was phenomenal, with virtually every SME taking advantage, leading to new business models.

Review methodology

A systematic literature review was undertaken to identify the extent to which the three research questions outlined earlier in this chapter had been previously researched. More specifically, the aim was to identify, evaluate and integrate, highlighting the following themes (Cooper, 2003; Baumeister and Leary, 1997; Bem, 1995):

- The extent to which mobile technology has been used to stimulate economic development, as an example of open innovation policy;
- The extent to which existing research has offered specific guidance on how to reach particular targets in this regard;
- To identify any gaps, contradictions and inconsistencies which need to be clarified;
- To contribute to the ongoing conceptualisation and implications for theory development, suggesting new generalised statements or conceptualisation;
- To suggest the implications of previous research for policy makers and practitioners.

The search for peer-reviewed journals on 'mobile technologies', 'inclusive innovation policies' and 'SME development' included papers focused on different combinations of these concepts. Based on the combined variables with a focus on SSA, 60 articles were identified for further analysis.

In virtually all the papers, the benefits and challenges of mobile technologies, inclusive innovation policies and SME development were similar. Key potential benefits typically included improved communication and a higher level of productivity. Key challenges typically emphasised a lack of effectiveness in policy design and delivery, together with a lack of technological know-how. It was also clear from the literature that the concept of inclusive innovation policies has rarely been well understood.

Phases of policy change and mobile technology adoption in SSA

Until the late 1980s, when the Internet was at the early adoption stage, most of SSA had telecommunication monopolies. These monopolies also served as regulators in an industry in which they were players. In many countries they also held the mandate of postal services. As a result, only a few people had telephone services. In 1989, governments caved into pressure, mainly from Bretton Woods institutions that introduced new policies to break up the monopolies.

Liberalisation policies were followed by new South African-led initiatives to build an Africa-wide ICT infrastructure, through the New Partnership for Africa's Development (NEPAD). Since some countries did not have the capacity to develop their own policy framework, NEPAD developed the Protocol for Policy and Regulatory Framework for NEPAD ICT Broadband Infrastructure Network for Africa, in which the author of this chapter was a key player. The intent was to ensure each country had access to affordable broadband and that landlocked countries would not be treated any differently.

It was easy to deal with infrastructure policies, but when it came to applications, individual country policy frameworks were needed due to the varying risk tolerance, and levels in leveraging technology. As Osiakwan (2016) noted, there are five African nations that dominate the innovation space. So, a common SSA policy framework as proposed by the NEPAD may be counterproductive.

Already, a collaboration between IBM and Twiga Foods in Kenya has marked the first case of intensified use of technology by a medium enterprise in SSA (Ndemo, 2018). The collaboration leveraging Blockchain, Big Data, IoT and AI has changed the business models of multiple other enterprises. One significant outcome has been that the problems SMEs face in accessing finance have been effectively solved. More than 400 micro enterprises now receive credit without any collateral, which has helped them to better manage their supplies, reduce waste and become more sustainable enterprises.

Outcome of the research questions

The first research question sought to establish the role of policy makers in facilitating new technologies. The progress made so far would never have happened without policy intervention, especially on infrastructure development and ensuring accessibility and affordability. Governments, however, are hesitant when it comes to some of the applications of technology, not least because of the risk involved.

The second question sought to establish the policy measures taken to sustain the diffusion of mobile innovation technology and its application to SME development in Africa. For this to happen, policy makers must consider additional enabling policies that are necessary if the potential of these technologies is to be realised. Kenya, for example, is considering the creation of legal sandboxes or the Brazilian model of mission-oriented policies to facilitate the adoption of innovative solutions, which will have a great impact on the social and economic development of the country.

The third and last question sought to establish which inclusive policy measures governments should use to support the development of SMEs in an evolving technology landscape. As the previous example of IBM/Twiga Foods demonstrates, more incentive policies are necessary to create opportunities at the bottom of the pyramid. Financial inclusion policies can have a huge economic impact, because the absence of unsecured loans has been a major constraint. In this context, technology has made it possible to provide credit without collateral and enabled micro enterprises that significantly contribute to the growth rate of the economy to scale up their enterprises.

Policy implications

Barriers to sustaining mobile innovation technology

The review of the literature shows that there are less than a dozen SSA countries that have made progress in the use of technology in SME development. Many of the countries are still bogged down by different challenges. The barriers to greater ICT utilisation by SMEs can be categorised into: i) inadequate infrastructure; ii) insufficient technological know-how; and iii) ineffective policy interventions. Some countries, for example Botswana and Ghana, have infrastructure, but its persistent breakdown makes it unreliable. Sustainable SME development could be realised if SSA nations were to focus their attention on providing both reliable and affordable services, including services for technology capacity building. There is a need for peer learning from the countries that have dealt with such barriers.

Inclusive innovation policies supporting SME development

Although it is clear from the literature that the concept of inclusive innovation policy is not well understood, there are now several countries that have taken the risk of introducing new and innovative ideas into the area of fast-evolving mobile technologies, which the laggard countries can emulate. Inclusive innovation policies may be transient, but it must be understood that Africa has unique problems to solve before embracing the globally generalised policy frameworks. In Kenya, for example, the policy to facilitate mobile money could not have come from anywhere else, considering the fact that most developed countries already have branchless banking to send money in whatever form.

It is, however, important to understand that to sustain SMEs beyond inclusive policies, SSA must look to Schumpeter's (1934) innovation theory to build globally competitive SMEs. Prior to mobile money, virtually all SMEs in SSA suffered from lack of finance, but that is changing, as shown in the IBM/Twiga Foods case study discussed in this chapter. Policy, especially on emerging technologies, may never be similar to other countries in the formative stages. It will require some tweaking and extreme risk-taking until the mission is accomplished.

Following the positive outcomes of the IBM/Twiga Foods collaboration, the Kenyan government has appointed the author of this chapter to lead a task-force on another initiative leveraging emerging technologies to enhance inclusivity at the bottom of the pyramid, as the country studies what kind of policies will help regulate the sector if the positive outcomes outweigh the negatives. This taskforce, with a mandate to draw up a roadmap for exploiting opportunities from these emerging technologies, has made recommendations for the creation of legal sandboxes or another emerging concept of mission-oriented policy (Mazzucato, 2017). With such policy provision, policy makers can take risks with emerging technologies at the early adoption stage, as discussed in Rogers and Cartano's Diffusion of Innovation Theory, and reap the benefits before developing a comprehensive policy framework.

Recommendations

The problem of access and affordability of technology infrastructure can be solved through many existing models, including infrastructure sharing to lower the cost of capital expenditure and enable many more people and businesses to use technology. These can be done through policy interventions, either by giving incentives to share infrastructure or through tax incentives. Removal of tax from technology devices is key to enabling more people and SMEs to afford technology. Lack of technological know-how could be dealt with by working with technology intermediaries to offer e-readiness capacity building across nations.

Development of enabling policy in Africa is tricky as many countries look up to their colonial powers to provide guidance. Yet policy in Africa should never mimic developed countries, considering the fact that Africa has unique problems to deal with. For example, SSA has more marginalised communities, therefore no one policy can be generalised as in the developed nations.

Conclusion

Empirical evidence on the role of mobile technologies, reflections by the author and inclusive innovation policies on SME development in Africa highlight positive outcomes for sustainable SME development, but there are still challenges. Only a few SSA countries have leveraged the potential of these relationships. Many countries still have the problem of a lack of, or poor quality, infrastructure, policy gaps and lack of technological know-how. Although the concept of inclusive innovation policy is not well understood, there is a glimmer of hope that inclusivity is being accepted through imitation of trailblazing countries. The initiative, especially in Kenya, to draw up a roadmap for adopting emerging technologies is encouraging. That is, if the outcomes lead to the development of legal sandboxes/mission-oriented policy to allow for the testing of new, unregulated technologies that can bring about inclusivity and growth of enterprises, then SSA will have to acknowledge the fact that policy making (due to the region's unique problems) must be different from that in other parts of the world.

References

Adeeb, M. A. and I. Hussain (2009), 'Role of mobile technology in promoting campus-wide learning environment', *Turkish Online Journal of Educational Technology*, **8** (3), 48–57.

Alliance for Affordable Internet (2017), *2017 Affordability Report*. Retrieved from http://a4ai.org/affordability-report/report/2017/.

Apulu, I. and E. Ige (2011), 'Are Nigeria SMEs effectively utilizing ICT?', *International Journal of Business and Management*, **6** (6), 207–14.

Asare, S. D., B. Gopolang and O. Mogotlhwane (2012), 'Challenges facing SMEs in the adoption of ICT in B2B and B2C e-commerce: A comparative case study of Botswana and Ghana', *International Journal of Commerce and Management*, **22** (4), 272–85.

Asongu, S., A. Boateng and R. Akamavi (2016), 'Mobile phone innovation and inclusive human development: Evidence from Sub-Saharan Africa', African Governance Development Institute, Working Paper WP/16/027. Retrieved from https://mpra.ub.uni-muenchen.de/75046/ 1/MPRA_paper_ 75046.pdf.

Asongu, S. A. and J. C. Nwachukwu (2016), 'Mobile phones in the diffusion of knowledge and persistence in inclusive human development in Sub-Saharan Africa', *World Development*, **86**, Elsevier Ltd: pp. 133–147.

Baumeister, R. F. and M. R. Leary (1997), 'Writing narrative literature reviews', *Review of General Psychology*, **3**, 311–20.

Bem, D. J. (1995), 'Writing a review article for Psychological Bulletin', *Psychological Bulletin*, **118**, 172–77.

Chang, C., J. Tseng and C. Yan (2012), 'Perceived convenience in an extended technology acceptance model: Mobile technology and English learning for college students', *Australasian Journal of Educational Technology*, **28** (5), 809–26.

Coates, C., C. Dearnley, M. Dransfield, J. Fairhall, J. Haigh, S. Hennessy, M. Parks, K. Riley and J. Taylor (2009), 'Using mobile technologies for assessment and learning in practice settings: Outcomes of five case studies', *International Journal on E-Learning*, **8** (2), 193–207.

Cooper, H. M. (2003), 'Psychological Bulletin: Editorial', *Psychological Bulletin*, **129**, 3–9.

Disrupt Africa (2017), *Funding Report*, Disrupt Africa. Retrieved from http://disrupt-africa.com/funding-report/.

Donner, J. and M. Escobari (2010), 'A review of evidence on mobile use by micro and small enterprises in developing countries', *Journal of International Development*, **22**, 641–58.

Esselaar, S., C. Stork, A. Ndiwalana and M. Deen-Swarray (2007), 'ICT usage and its impact on profitability of SMEs in 13 African countries', *Information Technologies and International Development*, **4** (1), 87–100.

Fjose, S., L. A. Grünfeld and C. Green (2010), 'SMEs and growth in Sub-Saharan Africa: Identifying SME roles and obstacles to SME growth', MENON Publication No. 14/2010, MENON Business Economics, Oslo, Norway.

Foster, C. and R. Heeks (2016), 'Drivers of inclusive innovation in developing country markets: A policy perspective', in N. Agola and A. Hunter (eds), *Inclusive Innovation for Sustainable Development: Theory and Practice*, London: Palgrave Macmillan, pp. 57–74.

Government of Kenya (2016), *SME Survey*, Government of Kenya.

GSMA (2017), *The Mobile Economy – Sub-Saharan Africa 2017*, GSMA.

GSMA/Deloitte (2015), *Digital Inclusion and Mobile Sector Taxation in the Democratic Republic of the Congo*, GSMA.

Heeks, R., C. Foster and Y. Nugroho (2014), 'New models of inclusive innovation for development', *Innovation and Development*, **4** (2), 175–85.

Juma, C. and L. Yee-Cheong (2005), *Innovation: Applying Knowledge in Development*, UN Millennium Project, Task Force on Science, Technology and Innovation, London: Earthscan.

Kelly, T. J. C. and R. S. Firestone (2016), 'How Tech Hubs are helping to drive economic growth in Africa', World Development Report background papers, Washington, DC: World Bank Group.

Kendall, J., P. Machoka, C. Veniard and B. Maurer (2011), 'An emerging platform: From money transfer system to mobile money ecosystem', *Innovations: Technology, Governance, Globalization*, **6** (4), 49–64.

Mazzucato, M. (2017), 'Mission-oriented innovation policy: Challenges and opportunities', UCL Institute for Innovation and Public Purpose, Working Paper, IIPP WP 2017-01. Retrieved from https://www.ucl.ac.uk/bartlett/public-purpose/sites/public-purpose/files/moip-challenges-and-opportunities-working-paper-2017-1.pdf.

Movimbela, R. and E. Dube (2016), 'Can an internet adoption framework be developed for SMEs in South Africa', *Journal of Entrepreneurship and Innovation in Emerging Economies*, **2** (2), 120–35.

Ndemo, B. (2015), 'Political entrepreneurialism: Reflections of a civil servant on the role of political institutions in technology innovation and diffusion in Kenya', *Stability: International Journal of Security and Development*, **4** (1), 1–14.

Ndemo, B. (2016a), 'Enabling an inclusive innovation ecosystem and SME development in Kenya: The role of ICTs', in N. Agola and A. Hunter (eds), *Inclusive Innovation for Sustainable Development: Theory and Practice*, London: Palgrave Macmillan, pp. 39–56.

Ndemo, B. (2016b), 'Inside a policymaker's mind: An entrepreneurial approach to policy development and implementation', in B. Ndemo and T. Weiss (eds), *Digital Kenya: An Entrepreneurial Revolution in the Making*, London: Palgrave Macmillan, pp. 339–62.

Ndemo, B. (2017), 'Foresight Africa viewpoint: Growth of African SMEs and jobs will depend on technology uptake', Brookings Institute. Retrieved from https://www.brookings.edu/author/bitange-ndemo/.

Ndemo, B. (2018), 'How Blockchain can grow small businesses', *Business Daily*, 18 April.

Ndemo, B. and T. Weiss (2017), 'Making sense of Africa's emerging digital transformation and its many futures', *Africa Journal of Management*, **3** (3–4), 328–47.

Osiakwan, E. M. K. (2016), 'The KINGS of Africa's digital economy', in B. Ndemo and T. Weiss (eds), *Digital Kenya: An Entrepreneurial Revolution in the Making*, London: Palgrave Macmillan, pp. 55–84.

Planes-Satorra, S. and C. Paunov (2017), 'Inclusive innovation policies: Lessons from international case studies', OECD Science, Technology and Industry Working Papers, No. 2017/02, Paris: OECD Publishing.

RIA (2006), *Towards an African e-Index: SME e-ACCESS AND USAGE across 14 African Countries*. Retrieved from https://researchictafrica.net/publications/Research_ICT_Africa_e-Index_Series/SME%20e-Access%20and%20Usage%20in%2014%20African%20Countries.pdf.

Rogers, E. M. and D. G. Cartano (1962), 'Methods of measuring opinion leadership', *Public Opinion Quarterly*, **26** (3), 435–41.

Schumpeter, J. A. (1934), *The Theory of Economic Development: An Inquiry into Profits, Capital, Credits, Interest, and the Business Cycle*, Piscataway: Transaction Publishers.

World Bank (2016), *Poverty in a Rising Africa: Africa Poverty Report*, Washington, DC: World Bank.

World Bank (2017), *Global Economic Prospects: A Fragile Recovery*, Washington, DC: World Bank.

World Economic Forum (2018a), *Global Competitiveness Report*, World Economic Forum. Retrieved from https://www.weforum.org/reports/the-global-competitveness-report-2018.

World Economic Forum (2018b), *The Fourth Industrial Revolution: What It Means, How to Respond*, World Economic Forum. Retrieved from https://www.weforum.org/agenda/2016/01/the-fourth-industrial-revolution-what-it-means-and-how-to-respond/.

11 Stimulating entrepreneurship in South Africa's townships

Thami Mazwai[1]

Introduction

Late in 2019 the South African government announced a 'Township and Rural Economies Revitalisation Strategy' to stimulate entrepreneurship and small business development in areas where the majority black population lives. This initiative follows the groundbreaking Township Economy Revitalisation (TER) effort launched in 2014 by the Gauteng Provincial Government.

The country is thus reviewing competition, empowerment and procurement policies which, it hopes, will lead to more effective programmes in enhancing entrepreneurship, small business development and enhanced economic activity in townships (defined below), informal settlements and rural areas, where the bulk of the black community lives.

It was hoped that the end of Apartheid – statutory racial discrimination – in 1994 would also end the economic exclusion of blacks. Regretfully, 26 years into the new democracy economic marginalisation is still the order of the day. The impact of the Covid-19 virus and two credit rating downgrades by Moody's and Fitch have worsened the situation.

Unfortunately, Turok (2008, p. 12) argues that the transition to democracy was based on the conservative orthodoxy in the global environment as South Africa wanted to avoid massive retaliation by international and domestic capital. This meant that a specific policy path was followed, which, regretfully, has led to the country now being faced with a rebelling black community.

Hence, government is reviewing policies, and, in addition, the nine provinces are also coming in with more direct interventions. The Gauteng Provincial

Government, which has jurisdiction over the larger black settlements including Soweto, took the lead when it introduced the TER strategy to stimulate and escalate economic activity in its townships. Initial progress shows that this strategy could be extended to the whole country.

A township in the South African sense is a settlement created during the Apartheid era in which the black population were located in designated areas to solely provide labour to the white business districts. Entrepreneurship and small business development were taboo in these communes (Pernegger and Godehart, 2007, p. 2; Cogta, 2009, p. 6; Cities Support Programme, n.d.).

Hence, Peberdy et al. (2017) attest that despite new policies since 1994, people living in peripheral areas such as townships are still less likely to have amenities and areas set aside for commercial and industrial purposes, or any economic activity for that matter. Apartheid spatial planning and inequalities persist in the demographics of the province, Peberdy et al. (2017) stressed.

Problem statement

The basis of this chapter is the lack of effectiveness of policies in transforming the local economies of the formerly oppressed and exploited and, in the light of new approaches, the potential for ensuring that entities owned by those in the black population become critical players in wealth creation in their areas.

Policy and entrepreneurship/SME development

'Entrepreneurship' and 'small business development' are inter-related concepts, but different. Thurik and Wennekers (2004, p. 140) and Stevenson and Lundström (2002, p. 23) make the point that 'entrepreneurship' refers to the identification of opportunities, whether in big or small organisations. On the other hand, 'small business development' refers to the provision of support to small businesses. Stevenson and Lundström (2002) attest that entrepreneurship policy focuses on the individual, and Acs and Szerb (2007) postulate that it revolves around the recognition of opportunities in conjunction with the cognitive decision to commercialise such opportunities.

Smallbone (2016) concurs and adds that while entrepreneurship results from the creativity, drive and skills of individuals, government and its policies influence, positively and negatively, the external environment in which entrepreneurship takes place. Conversely, Lekhanya and Mason (2014) argue that the same external environment in which entrepreneurship takes place influences the creativity, drive and skills of individuals.

As small and medium enterprise (SME) policy is aimed at strengthening new or existing small businesses, it is entity orientated. In this regard, Dennis (2011) advocates a strategy that eliminates impediments and simultaneously offers incentives. He argues that this approach tightly controls business activity but also provides otherwise unavailable resources to allow small businesses to pursue policy-favoured activities.

Smallbone (2016) stresses the importance of the social, economic, historical and particularly institutional context. Historical background is particularly relevant to South Africa, as restrictive and pernicious racial policies create locations that are not attractive to new business development. Hence, Smallbone (2016) suggests that policies on inclusive entrepreneurship can contribute to increasing the participation of under-represented groups. This would include people in the townships.

Arshed et al. (2014) suggest six steps for effective policy formulation, and these are: (1) identification of need or interest; (2) the formulation of the brief and identification of experts; (3) the collection of the data or evidence to justify the need for the policy; (4) the analysis of the data and information; (5) the announcement or promulgation of the policy; and (6) the implementation of the White Paper or draft policy.

As stated, black South Africa is up in arms and not without reason; the next section deals with the contradictions in the economy that, arguably, justify this anger.

South African economy

South Africa is arguably the most modern economy in Africa, and it is the third biggest, second to Nigeria and Egypt. The OECD (2017a) puts South Africa's GDP at 317 billion USD. Despite the scale of the South African economy and 25 years of democracy, unemployment, poverty and inequality remain prominent in black communities, and particularly in the townships and rural villages.

This resonates with the latest diagnosis of South Africa by the World Bank (2018b), which stresses that the country's transition is incomplete. For instance, in terms of the latest figures from Stats SA (2020, p. 21), the unemployment rate has increased to 29.1 per cent in the fourth quarter of 2019. The broad unemployment rate, which includes people who have given up looking for work, is at 38.7 per cent (p. 37).

The percentage of young persons aged 15–34 years who were not in employment, education or training (NEET) stands at a crisis 40.1 per cent (p. 8), most of them being black. The broad unemployment rate for black South Africans is 43.0 per cent, for the white population 9.8 per cent, for Coloureds 30.1 per cent and for the Indian community 20.6 per cent (pp. 39–40).

Inequality is stark as, according to figures from Oxfam (2018), the top 10 per cent in South Africa shares 50 per cent of all income, while the bottom 50 per cent shares 12 per cent of all income. The World Bank (2018a) reinforces the extent of the inequality with reports that household wealth held by the top 10 per cent was 71 per cent, while the bottom 60 per cent held 7 per cent of the net wealth. In addition, Stats SA (2017) states that nearly half of the population is considered to be chronically poor. In 2015, 30.4 million people were reported as living in poverty (in other words, earning less than 70 USD or ZAR 1000 per person per month). Furthermore, Stats SA (2017) asserts that those living in extreme poverty (in other words, earning less than 35 USD or ZAR 441 per person per month) increased from 11.0 million in 2011 to 13.8 million in 2015.

Realising the challenges it faces, the national government set up the National Planning Commission (NPC) to determine a strategy for an inclusive economy. This resulted in the National Development Plan (NDP). It proposes that for South Africa to get out of the woods, the country must, by 2030, have created 11 million jobs, 90 per cent of which must come from the small business sector (NPC, 2012).

South Africa's small business community

In 2015 the Small Enterprise Development Agency (Seda), in association with the Stellenbosch University-based Bureau of Economic Research (BER), estimated that there were 2.25 million small, medium and micro enterprises (SMMEs) in South Africa, of which just 30 per cent were formal entities (Seda, 2015). The small scale of the formal economy was reinforced by the Small Business Institute (SBI), which claimed that South Africa only has a quarter of a million formal SMMEs (Business Tech, 2018).

Finmark Trust (2010) disclosed that more than 70 per cent of informal entities had a turnover of less than 6000 USD per annum, while over 30 per cent had a turnover of less than 3000 USD per annum. In terms of economic activity, SMMEs in South Africa contributed 48 per cent of GDP and accounted for 68 per cent of total employment (Mthente, 2016). This means that the scale of the formal SMME sector appears to be small by international standards. Most notably, OECD (2017b) argues that small businesses account for approximately 70 per cent of jobs globally.

While South Africa matches the OECD average, it is a concern that 30 per cent of the 68 per cent contribution of SMMEs to total national employment is by micro enterprises, which ostensibly means survivalism given the research by Finmark Trust (2010). This is confirmed by the SBI (Business Tech, 2018), whose research shows that while 98.5 per cent of the country's economy is made up of SMEs, they are only delivering 28 per cent of all jobs. This suggests that there is more potential in the SMME sector than is currently being realised.

Thus, and realistically, formal small businesses contribute to between 28 per cent and 38 per cent of employment, far below the world average. The situation in the township enterprises is very disappointing. A study by Njiro and Mazwai (2010) found that only 7 per cent of businesses in Gauteng townships, including Soweto, had turnovers of over 80 000 USD per annum and 39 per cent had turnovers of around 1000 USD also per annum. Research by Finmark Trust (2006) revealed that more than 70 per cent of black-owned small businesses in Gauteng Province, mostly in black communities, have a turnover of less than 6000 USD per annum.

Nkosi (2011) and the World Bank (2002) agree that township enterprises have low turnovers and are hand to mouth operations with a high failure rate. They cite several factors for this, including lack of essential business and management skills, lack of credit, poor infrastructure and services, lack of investment training and lack of exit planning. Shopping malls in the townships, ironically developed out of the new and open economy of the democracy era, have compounded the problem; as Ligthelm (2012) reports, of 300 businesses selected in 2007, almost three in every five (56.8 per cent) closed their doors between 2007 and 2011.

The next section traces the evolution of policy since 1994. What must be considered is whether there was a deliberate focus on previous policies.

Evolution of policy since 1994

The Nelson Mandela government, elected in 1994, introduced the first ever strategy on small business in South Africa in 1995, with the White Paper on 'National Strategy for the Development and Promotion of Small Business in South Africa'. This was followed by the Small Business Act a year later (Department of Trade and Industry, 1995; RSA, 1996).

This Act, which defines and classifies small businesses, has gone through several amendments, and went through another policy review in 2019. While it standardised the definition between government entities, the turnover threshold that it determined for micro, namely ZAR 5 to 20 million depending on the sector, is inexplicable, as only 10 per cent of black small businesses have a turnover of above ZAR 1 million; the remaining 90 per cent should have been subjected to further, narrower classifications to ensure appropriate interventions.

Mthente (2016) notes that, in general, the policies that informed small business development, the restructuring of the economy and the empowerment of blacks also included the National Strategy for the Development and Promotion of Franchising in South Africa (released in 2000), Competition Policy (1998) and the Micro-Economic Reform Strategy (released in 2002).

Specific legislation on economic empowerment for black people was the Broad-Based Black Economic Empowerment (B-BBEE) Legislation (2004). In addition, economic growth policies directly and indirectly linked to empowerment included the Accelerated and Shared Growth Initiative (released in 2006), Industrial Policy Action Plans (released in 2007), National Industrial Policy Framework (released in 2007), New Growth Path (released in 2011) and the National Development Plan (released in 2012). To this must be added the Preferential Procurement Policy Framework Act of 2000, which was designed to increase empowerment but, in practice, stressed the performance of suppliers under this programme. As a result, this initiative was criticised by black entrepreneurs, who claimed white business would always outperform black entities.

As News24 (2014) states, the government established the Department of Small Business Development (DSBD), with a brief to coordinate policy and interventions related to small business development. While the creation of a dedicated department for small business was timely, the effort has not gone far enough.

According to figures released by the Treasury (2019), the consolidated expenditure for the 2019–20 financial year amounts to ZAR 1.83 trillion. Of this ZAR 2.56 billion was allocated to the DSBD. In USD terms, the consolidated expenditure is 123.9 billion USD. The DSBD then got 173 million USD. This works out at 0.14 per cent of the economy but, as spend on small business development by other departments, the provinces and municipalities has not been factored in, the 0.14 percentage could be slightly higher.

The allocation reflects South Africa's schizophrenia, stressing small business in speeches but not putting money where the mouth is. It also reinforces assertions by Turok (2008) on the fear of breaking the mould.

As previous research has emphasised, there is a difference between policies targeted at entrepreneurs and those targeting small businesses, although the full effect of government policy on the sector needs to consider policies that can impact on small businesses, even though this is not their prime objective.

As economic empowerment has yet to reach the majority of black South Africa, the government is currently reviewing the policy portfolio with respect to small business, which includes competition policy, public procurement policy and other policies relating to empowerment. Cogta (2019) has revealed that as from August 2019, the government has introduced a district-based approach which, it argues, will ensure alignment even in small business development.

Justification for the focus on black areas

The Gauteng Government (2014) and NPC have argued that the generic problems that small businesses face are more intense in black areas. It is, therefore, not surprising that a study by the NPC (2017) also revealed that small business support services by government do not even reach the townships and rural areas, as illustrated below.

As can be seen in Table 11.1, small businesses in the townships and rural areas mainly complained of a lack of finance and ineffective local business institutions, as well as a lack of entrepreneurial and management skills and a lack of a suitable business premise for local businesses. Incidentally, the findings are supported by those from the European Union (2010), which recommended that government must improve on its strategies for local economic development, after it identified serious shortcomings in the implementation of such development by municipalities.

Table 11.1   Barriers to small business development in townships and rural areas

Dimension		SMMEs limiting success factors	Khayelitsha	Mamelodi	Uitenhage (townships)	Lehurutshe (Zeerust)	Hluhluwe	Thohoyandou	Diepsloot
Business development services	1	**Limited access to finance**	-	-	-	-	-	-	-
	2	*Lack of entrepreneurial and management skills*	-	-	-	-	-	-	
	3	Limited access to markets and procurement opportunities			-	-	-		-
	4	Limited access to information and advice	-			-		-	
	5	Limited access to appropriate technology	-		-	-	-		
	6	Lack of skilled workforce	-					-	
	7	Lack of business feasibility assessment			-			-	
	8	Lack of proper business marketing and promotion	-	-			-	-	
	9	Distance from input suppliers					-		
	10	Lack of access to input material						-	

Dimension	SMMEs limiting success factors	Khayelitsha	Mamelodi	Uitenhage (townships)	Lehurutshe (Zeerust)	Hluhluwe	Thohoyandou	Diepsloot
Local economic development	**11** **Ineffective local business development institutions**	-	-	-	-	-	-	-
	12 Lack of interventions monitoring and evaluation	-					-	
	13 Forced entrepreneurship and cooperatives				-		-	
	14 Lack of business competitiveness				-			
	15 *Impeding regulations and policies*	-	-	-			-	
	16 *Lack of regulatory enforcement and compliance*	-		-	-	-		-
	17 Buyers' late payment		-					
	18 *High level of public sector corruption*		-	-	-		-	
	19 High crime rate	-	-			-		
	20 Lack of supply chain networks	-	-					
	21 *Large and foreign-owned businesses dominance*		-	-		-	-	-
	22 Cost of doing business					-		
Social capital	23 Weak business networks			-	-		-	
	24 Local buyers not buying/supporting local businesses			-	-		-	
	25 Lack of trust (trust deficit)	-		-			-	
	26 Lack of intergenerational succession in small businesses						-	

Dimension		SMMEs limiting success factors	Khayelitsha	Mamelodi	Uitenhage (townships)	Lehurutshe (Zeerust)	Hluhluwe	Thohoyandou	Diepsloot
Infrastructure	27	Lack of access to land and land tenure				-	-	-	
	28	*Lack of suitable business premises*	-	-	-	-	-	-	
	29	Unreliable electricity and water supply			-		-		

Note: Bold refers to occurrence in all areas, italics to occurrence in almost all areas and underlined to least problematic.
Source: NPC (2017, p. 32).

The constraints described in Table 11.1 were used as a starting point for the review of policies by the national government and the initiation of strategies by provincial governments for townships or deprived communities. The next section details the policy interventions.

New policy interventions

The law on black economic empowerment has been amended (RSA, 2003) so that all multinationals, corporations and major companies must have supplier and enterprise development strategies, which include procurement from black-owned entities. If companies do not comply, they will not have access to government business and, more seriously, severe penalties are in store for defaulting companies. Secondly, a new Procurement Act (RSA, 2017) has been promulgated which stipulates that 30 per cent of all procurement from and by government and its entities must be subcontracted to black-owned small business suppliers, with an emphasis on businesses owned by the youth, women and people with disabilities.

Regarding these changes to procurement policy, Mathebula (2018) stated that the changes will allow local and provincial authorities to accept bids for tenders from designated groups such as the black population, women, the youth, the disabled and army veterans on a price preference system. This means that these groups will compete against each other within a specified price range. In addition, local and provincial authorities can determine that while bids will be accepted from designated groups, they must also be from entrepreneurs in specific localities such as the local township or settlement.

Thirdly, amendments to competition policy (RSA, 2018) eliminate price discrimination or excessive pricing by dominant firms; after all, these make it hard for SMEs to compete. It is also expected that other abuses by large firms stemming from their dominance (like predatory pricing, margin squeezes and refusing to supply scarce resources) that could impede the ability of SMEs to operate will be litigated by the authorities. The Bill also has provisions which make it easier for the authorities to exempt collaboration between SMEs which enables industrial expansion, better aggregate employment and economic growth, transformation and development. Severe penalties are also in place for defaulting companies.

Regarding local strategies, in 2014 the Gauteng Government introduced its TER Strategy (GDED, 2017). This is a five-year game plan to 'revitalise and build township economies by supporting township enterprises, cooperatives and SMMEs so that they produce goods and services that meet the needs of township residents'. It wants to ensure that the township economy contributes at least 30 per cent of Gauteng's GDP by 2030 (Gauteng Government, 2014). The Gauteng Government has thus introduced programmes and aligned policy to enable local entrepreneurs to supply goods to local communities, thus creating local economic ecosystems. In the last four years the Gauteng Government (2018) has procured goods and services to the value of 4.63 billion USD from 12 041 firms owned by historically disadvantaged individuals. Needless to add, other provinces have similar strategies. For instance, the North West provincial government has a strategy (NWPG, 2017) aimed at villages, townships and small dorpies, which is dubbed the VTSD strategy, reflecting the acronym. Other provinces are also designing township and village enterprise programmes.

Justification for policy reviews

The problems faced by small businesses in South Africa currently include challenges found in other transition economies, as previous research has demonstrated (Welter and Smallbone, 2011; Calza and Goedhuys, 2017). Facilitating institutional change is a particular challenge, not least because organisations can change, staffing can change, but neither may necessarily be reflected in the behaviours of institutions. Hence, Smallbone (2016) and Lekhanya and Mason (2014) stressed the impact of the environment on policy. Likewise, the NPC (2012) also rightly argued that in transforming human settlements, policy must respond systematically to entrenched spatial patterns across all geographic scales that exacerbate social inequality and economic inefficiency.

It is also not surprising that papers presented at a summit of township and rural economies in South Africa highlighted environmental dynamics that have militated against policies to grow black-owned small businesses (Summit, 2018). For instance, despite policies on black economic empowerment, major development activities and investment were not linked to local economic development in which black entrepreneurs proliferate.

Furthermore, and of critical importance, Lekhanya and Mason (2014) pointed out that the South African economy is highly concentrated and anti-competitive behaviour is widespread. Mazwai (2013, p. 269) concurs and adds that this concentration is exacerbated by a national macro culture, too strong a labour movement, conflicting government regulations and lack of implementation. Against all logic, these high levels of concentration, which the World Bank, Organisation for Economic Co-operation and Development (OECD) and International Monetary Fund have warned against over the years, are now being transplanted into the townships and rural areas directly and through horizontal and vertical relationships.

The amendments to competition policy are, therefore, timely, as the high levels of concentration in which the incumbents protect their market share give very little hope of sustainability to the new entrants. Arguments by Dopfer et al. (2016) hold sway as these refer to downward and upward complementarities and the relationships and networks on the meso or institutional level. The complementarities and relationships Dopfer et al. (2016) referred to limit the entry of small businesses, particularly as they lack the understanding of environmental dynamics and thus do not have strategic responses to overcome these barriers (Paunescu, 2013; Gomez, 2012). Furthermore, the small entities have neither the deep pockets nor technology needed to stand on their own.

Peters and Naicker (2013) reinforce this as they state that, while the new government saw under-developed and undeveloped SMMEs as a window of opportunity to address the challenges of job creation, economic growth and equity in South Africa, it did not take into account the realities of the environment.

Gauteng interventions promise hope

It can be argued that the latest policies and actions by the Gauteng Government directly and indirectly created local economies in which production and consumption by the locals generated local economic activity. For policies to be effective there must be awareness of the important role of both entrepreneurs and potential entrepreneurs. One way of achieving this is through the development of high-profile campaigns and roadshows. In Gauteng, the objectives of any interventions were informed by a deliberate campaign from October 2015 to April 2016, which included roadshows in which officials interacted with township entrepreneurs (Gauteng Government, 2018). The campaign sought to get their buy-in and input on capacitating their entities and the creation of township economies. Databases were created, and entities were classified.

The approach has paid dividends as 6000 new jobs were created in 2018, and new targets have been set (Makhura, 2019). Between 2014 and 2017 public procurement from township enterprises by the province increased from

ZAR 600 million (40 million USD) to ZAR 17 billion (1.1 billion USD). The Gauteng administration has set new targets and fine-tuned its processes and offerings following a strategic session (Gauteng Government, 2019). It now has a specialised clearing house for township entities, which also allows it to capacitate them where gaps are identified. According to Makhura (2019), there is now an alignment of the SMMEs to specific pipelines in relevant economic sectors. This results in broader partnerships, and the SMMEs are also part of developments in a sector and the appropriate workforce. This contributes to economic development.

The administration is also using governmental spending catalytically to drive SMME and entry-level workforce development in areas with strong private sector crossover, such as facilities maintenance and construction. The government is, Makhura (2019) adds, engaging highly evolved semi-formal industries – particularly the minibus taxi industry – as partners in economic development, by targeting, for example, taxi ranks as SMME development nodes.

Finally, in line with postulations by Arshed et al. (2014), the province has a vigorous and comprehensive impact analysis strategy at both the supply and the demand level. In this way gaps are regularly addressed. The Gauteng strategy generates the classic economic cycle – that of stimulating economic activity and entrepreneurship in communities and ensuring money circulates within.

Markley et al. (2015) spoke of community entrepreneurship while the OECD (2016) talked about inclusive entrepreneurship. The two may be different, but they both provide concepts based on the principle of bringing in people historically on the fringes of the economy, and thus mainstreaming them. The Gauteng strategy also addresses the importance of social, economic, historical and particularly institutional environments, as stressed by Smallbone (2016). After all, the issues raised by Smallbone et al. (2014) and Welter and Smallbone (2011) speak directly to the South African environment.

Gaps in interventions

Public policy is only as effective as the implementation mechanisms used. Over the past 25 years the implementation of policy in South Africa has been of major concern. The civil service has consistently failed to come to the party. Instead, and in addition to ineffective delivery methods, corruption has mushroomed. These two issues – the corruption in government and the inadequacy of the civil service and its poor mechanisms – are the biggest threats to the interventions. However, these issues are not confined to South Africa, and there are undoubtedly lessons that can be learned from countries where the issues have been best addressed.

Secondly, more needs to be done on the demand side in coordination with the supply side, which hitherto has been more dominant. Government procuring from black entities – the demand element – will always be short term and a medium- to long-term strategy is required. The proposed linkages with the private sector referred to above may do the trick. At the same time, black entrepreneurs and small business owners must be more entrepreneurial, rejecting dependency despite the difficulties they may have faced in the past. The increasing development of international and global markets is resulting in the emergence of new opportunities for small businesses in developing countries to participate in global value chains, this being a new but rapidly increasing phenomenon.

However, if this is to be achieved it will require commitment on the part of local SMEs to work towards the high-quality standards required in global markets by foreign investing companies. Developing these linkages is potentially an important development tool, as examples in Singapore and Kazakhstan demonstrate (UN, 2011). This is an under-researched area but one with considerable development potential.

A shortcoming of current policies relates to the need for increased access to professional expertise to help design and implement effective local economic development strategies. While there is growing financial procurement from township entrepreneurs, there is no link with any development of a value chain that would then result in strengthening the local economy and building specific expertise in clearly demarcated areas.

Another major shortcoming of the strategy is that there is no clear policy focus that will result in informal entities being formalised, and thus fitting snugly into the general strategy by the Gauteng Government. Calza and Goedhuys (2017) specifically stated that policy interventions in developing countries should not disregard the multitude of informal and micro entities, as these hold the potential to create more robust entities.

Conclusion

Clearly, the proof of the pudding will be in the eating. However, there is optimism in South Africa that the policy interventions undertaken will contribute to levelling the playing field and give black entrepreneurs greater participation in South Africa's economy. The black–white divide continues to span the macro, meso and micro levels, and this is strongly reflected in the small business community. This divide must be eliminated in order to create a new and equitable South Africa.

It is clear that the context for entrepreneurship policy in South Africa is very specific. While the business environment in South Africa shares many features with the former socialist economies of Central or Eastern Europe that have been transitioning, in many respects the change that needs to take place, in terms of attitude and behaviour, is even more challenging than the situation faced in these economies. One aspect of this is the concentration of deprived people spatially in the townships, which themselves represent major challenges to those concerned with local economic policy.

It is also evident that the approaches to entrepreneurship policy in South Africa that have been used hitherto have in general not had much positive impact on these townships. Given the nature of the black small business community, together with the alienation of many of the population of these townships, the size and the complexity of the challenge is greater. Conceptually, the South African context represents an extreme situation with respect to social exclusion. In this regard, it is difficult to find experience from other countries which provides relevant lessons that can be taken on board. As an example, however, McInnis-Bowers et al. (2017) recount the entrepreneurial journey of the Boruca, Costa Rica, which transformed the lives of locals.

Just as people with the right kinds of skills and capacity took advantage of economic opportunities and managed rapid social changes in Northern Saskatchewan communities (Zhang and Swanson, 2014), Gauteng Province could be showing the way in getting entrepreneurship to reduce social exclusion and marginalisation in South Africa, which the renowned *Time Magazine* has now dubbed the most unequal country in the world (Pomerantz, 2019).

Note

1. My thanks go to Professor Watson Ladzani for his assistance in editing this chapter; and to Mr Jak Koseff of the Gauteng Government for his valuable insights and data on the TER strategy.

References

Acs, Z. J. and L. Szerb (2007), 'Entrepreneurship, economic growth and public policy', *Small Business Economics*, **28** (2–3), 109–22.

Arshed, N., S. Carter and C. Mason (2014), 'The ineffectiveness of entrepreneurship policy: Is policy formulation to blame?', *Small Business Economics*, **43** (3), 639–59.

Business Tech (2018), 'The alarming truth about the number of small businesses in South Africa', *Business Tech*, 25 July.

Calza, E. and M. Goedhuys (2017), 'Addressing entrepreneurial heterogeneity in developing countries: Designing policies for economic growth and inclusive development', in C. Williams and A. Gurtoo (eds), *Routledge Handbook of Entrepreneurship in Developing Countries*, London: Routledge, pp. 529–46.

Cities Support Programme (n.d.), Township Economic Series. Department of National Treasury, accessed 17 July 2019 at http://csp.treasury.gov.za.

Cogta (2009), 'Township transformation timeline', Department of Cooperative Governance and Traditional Affairs, Pretoria, South Africa.

Cogta (2019), 'New district coordination model to improve the coherence and impact of government service delivery and development August 2019', Department of Cooperative Governance and Traditional Affairs, Pretoria, South Africa.

Dennis, W. J., Jr (2011), 'Entrepreneurship, small business and public policy levers', *Journal of Small Business Management*, **49** (2), 149–62.

Department of Trade and Industry (1995), 'White Paper on national strategy for the development and promotion of small business in South Africa', Government Gazette, 28 March.

Dopfer, K., J. Potts and A. Pyka (2016), 'Upward and downward complementarity: The meso core of evolutionary growth theory', *Journal of Evolutionary Economics*, **26**, 753–63.

European Union (2010), *Review of the National Framework for Local Economic Development in South Africa (2006–2011)*, report by the European Union commissioned by the Government of South Africa.

Finmark Trust (2006), *Pilot Study: Survey Highlights including BSM Model Small Business Survey Highlights 2006*, Johannesburg: Finmark Trust.

Finmark Trust (2010), *FinScope South Africa Small Business Survey 2010*, Midrand, South Africa: Finmark Trust.

Gauteng Government (2014), *Gauteng Townships Economy Revitalisation Strategy: 2014–2019*, Johannesburg: Department of Economic Development, Gauteng Government.

Gauteng Government (2018), *Budget Speech by Treasury*, Johannesburg: Gauteng Government.

Gauteng Government (2019), *Driving Spatially-Targeted Township Economic Revitalization through Priority/Special Projects*, Johannesburg: Gauteng Government.

GDED (2017), *Strategic Plan 2014-2019*, Johannesburg: Gauteng Department of Economic Development, Gauteng Government.

Gomez, E. T. (2012), 'Targeting horizontal inequalities: Ethnicity, equity, and entrepreneurship in Malaysia', *Asian Economic Papers*, **11** (2), 31-57.

Lekhanya, L. M. and R. B. Mason (2014), 'Selected key external factors influencing the success of rural small and medium enterprises in South Africa', *Journal of Enterprising Culture*, **22** (3), 331-48.

Ligthelm, A. A. (2012), 'The viability of informal micro businesses in South Africa: A longitudinal analysis (2007-11)', *African Journal of Business Management*, **6** (46), 11416-25.

Makhura (2019), 'Gauteng leads revitalisation of township economies: Makhura', State of the Province Address, Gauteng Government, accessed 5 September 2019 at www .sabcnews.com.

Markley, D. M., T. S. Lyons and D. W. Macke (2015), 'Creating entrepreneurial communities: Building community capacity for ecosystem development', *Community Development*, **46** (5), 580-98.

Mathebula, W. (2018), 'Presentation to summit on township and rural economies', Presidential Council for Black Economic Empowerment, London, 18-20 July, accessed 15 April 2019 at www.thedti.gov.za/economic_empowerment/advisory _council.

Mazwai, E. T. (2013), 'South Africa's embedded entrepreneurial dynamics and their impact on entrepreneurship and small business development: A critical appraisal', in M. Ndletyana and D. Maimela (eds), *Essays on the Evolution of the Apartheid State: Legacies, Reforms and Prospects*, Johannesburg: Mapungubwe Institute for Strategic Reflection, pp. 269-98.

McInnis-Bowers, C., D. L. Parris and B. L. Galperin (2017), 'Which came first, the chicken or the egg? Exploring the relationship between entrepreneurship and resilience among the Boruca Indians of Costa Rica', *Journal of Enterprising Communities: People and Places in the Global Economy*, **11** (1), 39-60.

Mthente (2016), *Annual Review of Small Business and Cooperatives in South Africa*, Cape Town: Mthente Research and Consulting Services.

News24 (2014), 'New ministry for small business', accessed 5 September 2019 at www .news24.com.

Njiro, E. and T. Mazwai (2010), 'A situational analysis of small businesses and enterprises in the townships of the Gauteng Province of South Africa', presented at the First International Conference, University of Johannesburg, 20-25 January 2010.

Nkosi, E. Y. (2011), 'Skills required in the management of small businesses in the retail sector in Soweto', mini thesis, University of Johannesburg.

NPC (2012), *National Development Plan 2030: Our Future – Make It Work*, Pretoria: National Planning Commission.

NPC (2017), *Research on the Limited Success of Entrepreneurial Activity by Locals in Townships and Rural Areas: Seven Dialogue Locations: Townships, Rural and Informal Settlement*, Pretoria: National Planning Commission.

NWPG (2017), *Villages, Townships and Small Dorpies (VTSD) Development Plans*, Mahikeng: North West Provincial Government.

OECD (2016), *Inclusive Business Creation: Good Practice Compendium*, Paris: OECD Publishing.

OECD (2017a), *OECD Economic Surveys: South Africa 2017*, Paris: OECD Publishing.

OECD (2017b), *Enhancing the Contributions of SMEs in a Global and Digitalised Economy*, report of Meeting of the OECD Council, Paris.

Oxfam (2018), 'Reward work, not wealth', research report presented to the World Economic Forum, January 2018.

Paunescu, C. M. (2013), 'Challenges of entering the business market: The pre-entry knowledge and experience', *Management and Marketing Challenges for the Knowledge Society*, **8** (1), 63–78.

Peberdy, S., P. Harrison and Y. Dinath (2017), *Uneven Spaces: Core and Periphery in the Gauteng City-Region*, Johannesburg: GCRO.

Pernegger, L. and S. Godehart (2007), *Townships in the South African Geographic Landscape: Physical and Social Legacies and Challenges*, Pretoria: National Treasury.

Peters, R. and V. Naicker (2013), 'Small medium micro enterprise business goals and government support: A South African case study', *South African Journal of Business Management*, **44** (4), 13–24.

Pomerantz, K. (2019), 'The world's most unequal country', *Time Magazine*, May 2019.

RSA (1996), *National Small Business Enabling Act No. 102 of 1996*, Pretoria: Government Printers.

RSA (2003), *Broad-Based Black Economic Empowerment Act No. 53 of 2003*, Pretoria: Department of Trade and Industry, Government Gazette.

RSA (2017), *Preferential Procurement Regulations 2017*, Pretoria: Department of Finance, Government Gazette.

RSA (2018), *Competition Amendment Bill*, Pretoria: Government Gazette.

Seda (2015), *Annual Review: Seda Technology Programme*, Pretoria: Small Enterprise Development Agency.

Smallbone, D. (2016), 'Entrepreneurship policy: Issues and challenges', *Small Enterprise Research*, **23** (3), 201–18.

Smallbone, D., F. Welter and J. Ateljevic (2014), 'Entrepreneurship in emerging market economies: Contemporary issues and perspectives', *International Small Business Journal*, **32** (2), 113–16.

Stats SA (2017), *Poverty Trends in South Africa: An Examination of Absolute Poverty between 2006 and 2015*, Pretoria: Statistics South Africa.

Stats SA (2020), *Quarterly Labour Force Survey. Quarter 4: 2019*, Pretoria: Statistics South Africa.

Stevenson, L. and A. Lundström (2002), *Beyond the Rhetoric: Defining Entrepreneurship Policy and Its Best Practice Components*, Örebro: Swedish Foundation for Small Business.

Summit (2018), 'Dialogue at summit on township and rural economies', Presidential Economic Advisory Council, London, 18–20 July, accessed 15 April 2019 at www .thedti.gov.za/economic_empowerment/advisory_council.

Thurik, R. and S. Wennekers (2004), 'Entrepreneurship, small business and economic growth', *Journal of Small Business and Enterprise Development*, **11** (1), 140–49.

Treasury (2019), *Estimates of National Expenditure 2019. Abridged Version*, Pretoria: Department of Finance.

Turok, B. (2008), *From the Freedom Charter to Polokwane: The Evolution of ANC Economic Policy*, Cape Town: New Agenda.

UN (2011), *Best Practices in Investment for Development: How to Create and Benefit from FDI–SME Linkages: Lessons from Malaysia and Singapore*, New York and Geneva: United Nations.

Welter, F. and D. Smallbone (2011), 'Institutional perspectives on entrepreneurial behaviour in challenging environments', *Journal of Small Business Management*, **49** (1), 107–25.

World Bank (2002), *South Africa – Constraints to Growth in Johannesburg's Black Informal Sector: Evidence from the 1999 Informal Sector Survey*, Washington, DC: World Bank Group.

World Bank (2018a), *Overcoming Poverty and Inequality in South Africa: An Assessment of Drivers, Constraints and Opportunities*, Washington, DC: World Bank Group.

World Bank (2018b), *Republic of South Africa Systematic Country Diagnostic. An Incomplete Transition: Overcoming the Legacy of Exclusion in South Africa*, Washington, DC: World Bank Group.

Zhang, D. D. and L. A. Swanson (2014), 'Toward sustainable development in the north: Exploring models of success in community-based entrepreneurship', *Northern Review*, **38** (1), 99–118.

Index